THE SEARCH FOR SIGNIFICANCE

Book and Workbook
Revised and Expanded

Robert S. McGee

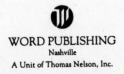

WORD PUBLISHING
Nashville
A Unit of Thomas Nelson, Inc.

WORD PUBLISHING Nashville, Tennessee

Book design by Kandi Shepherd

Library of Congress Cataloging-in-Publication Data

McGee, Robert S.
    The search for significance / by Robert S. Mcgee.
      p. cm.
    Rev. ed. of: The serach for significance book. 2nd ed. c1990.
    Includes bibliographical references.
    ISBN 0-8499-4091-5
    1. Self-esteem—Religious aspects—Christianity. 2. Christian
life. I. McGee, Robert S. Serach for significance book.
II. Title
BV4647.S43M387   1998
248.4—dc21

                           98–10096
                             CIP

ISBN 0-8499-4092-3

Printed in the United States of America
8 9 0 1 2 3 4 5 9 QBP 9 8 7 6 5

*To my wife, Marilyn, who has given of herself so that
I might minister these truths, both personally
and now by the written word.*

Contents

Acknowledgments vii

Introduction ix

   1.   The Light Comes On 1

   2.   The Origin of the Search 13

Introduction to Chapters 3–10 27

   3.   The Performance Trap 31
        I must meet certain standards to feel
        good about myself.

   4.   God's Answer: Justification 43

   5.   Approval Addict 55
        I must be approved by certain others
        to feel good about myself.

   6.   God's Answer: Reconciliation 67

   7.   The Blame Game 81
        Those who fail are unworthy of love and
        deserve to be punished.

   8.   God's Answer: Propitiation 95

   9.   Shame 103
        I am what I am. I cannot change. I am hopeless.

 10.   God's Answer: Regeneration 113

 11.   Agent of Change 123

 12.   Guilt Versus Conviction..139

 13.   The Trip In 149

The Search for Significance Workbook

Introduction 163

Section I: Background

Step 1 The Light Comes On....................................167

Step 2 The Origin of the Search 175

Section II: Satan's Lies Versus God's Truth

Step 3 The Performance Trap 193

Step 4 God's Answer: Justification 203

Step 5 Approval Addict..213

Step 6 God's Answer: Reconciliation 223

Step 7 The Blame Game 231

Step 8 God's Answer: Propitiation 241

Step 9 Shame 261

Step 10 God's Answer: Regeneration 269

Section III: Application

Step 11 Agent of Change 281

Step 12 Guilt Versus Conviction 301

Step 13 The Trip In 305

Notes 339

Services Provided by Search Resources..................................340

Resources of Interest 341

Acknowledgments

The concepts presented in this book have been utilized at our counseling centers and seminars for many years. The results have been so phenomenal that we were compelled to produce this book.

Many have contributed to *The Search for Significance*. I want to thank Larry Gillum, Rujon Morrison, LaDean Williamson, and Marland Williamson for their insights, friendship, and assistance, which have been invaluable to me in the preparation of this book. I especially want to thank my mother, Minerva McGee. Each of these have made significant contributions to *The Search for Significance*. I also express my appreciation to the many who, with great dedication, spread the message of these truths.

Introduction

When Christ told His disciples, "Ye shall know the truth, and the truth shall make you free" (John 8:32,KJV), He was referring not only to an intellectual assent to the truth but also to the application of truth in the most basic issues of life: our goals, our motives, and our sense of self-worth. Unfortunately, many of us give only lip service to the powerful truths of the Scriptures without allowing them to affect the basis of our self-esteem in a radical way. Instead, we continue to seek our security and purpose from worldly sources: personal success, status, beauty, wealth, and the approval of others. These rewards may fulfill us for a short time, but they soon lead us to a sense of urgency to succeed and the need to be approved of again.

To meet these compelling needs, we drive ourselves to achieve, doing virtually anything to make people happy with us, and we spend countless hours and dollars trying to look "just right." Often, we avoid situations and people where the risks of failure and rejection are high. It's a rat race that can't be won by simply running faster. We need to get off this hopeless treadmill and learn to apply the foundational truths that can motivate us to live for Christ rather than for the approval of other people.

Christ's death paid the penalty for our sins, and His resurrection gives us new life, new goals, and new hope. He has given us complete security and challenging purpose. These are not based on our abilities but on His grace and the power of His Spirit. Yes, Christ wants us to be zealous and ambitious, but not about our success or status. If we understand His forgiveness and acceptance, we will pursue the right things—Christ and His cause—and we will be free to enjoy His love.

The principles and insights in this book have been gleaned from years of counseling experience and from the writings of many psychologists and Bible teachers. I am indebted to their scholarship and wisdom.

This book focuses on how our thoughts affect our emotional, relational, and spiritual development. It is not a textbook for professionals. Instead, the goal of this book is to enable a wide range of people to apply the Scriptures specifically and deeply to real issues in their lives. The scope of this material does not include some factors. For instance, some emotional problems have a physiological source (schizophrenia, learning disabilities, chemical imbalances, and so forth); and some disorders have their roots in emotional and relational pain but are complicated by physiological symptoms like chronic fatigue, mood swings, weight loss or gain, and migraines. These factors, if they exist, should certainly be addressed by a competent, qualified physician or psychotherapist.

The response from those who have read the book and used the workbook has been overwhelming. It is my prayer that the Lord will use these materials to convince you of His love, forgiveness, and purposes for your life.

"For the love of Christ controls us, having concluded this, that one died for all, therefore all died; and He died for all, that they who live should no longer live for themselves, but for Him who died and rose again on their behalf" (2 Cor. 5:14–15).

1

The Light Comes On

Search me, O God, and know my heart; test me and know my anxious thoughts. See if there is any offensive way in me, and lead me in the way everlasting. (Ps. 139:23–24, NIV)

Dave was a handsome, highly successful businessman. He had always been able to live life on his own terms. To Dave, being strong meant being in control. He had a way of controlling his wife and intimidating his children to keep them from being much of a bother to him.

It wasn't that he didn't know how he affected his wife and children. It wasn't even that he didn't notice how isolated and alone he really was. He had just concluded that this was simply how he was and everyone would just have to tolerate him.

But now he wept like a small child. Life had caught up with Dave. Gone were his wife, his children, and much of everything he had worked so hard for. He just repeated over and over again how he would be different if only he could have another chance. Reality had turned on the light in Dave's dark world, and he realized that the worst part of his world was himself. He just couldn't believe that he had been so wrong for so long.

Hopefully, we won't find ourselves in Dave's situation with all its consequences. However, if we are honest with ourselves, from time to time, we find the light being turned on in our world, and we are amazed (and sometimes embarrassed) at what we see. It isn't that we don't know that certain things are not right. We just don't realize how destructive these things are until the light comes on.

Many of us are hurt emotionally, relationally, and spiritually, but because we are unaware of the extent of our wounds, we don't take steps toward healing and health. Our problem is not stupidity but a lack of objectivity. Because of this, we fail to see the reality of pain, hurt, and anger in our lives.

A college student is considered "the life of the party." She is intelligent, witty, and sociable, but when she is alone, she experiences deep loneliness and seething resentment.

A businessman who, as a child, was neglected by his ambitious father thinks, *If I can just get that promotion, then I'll be happy. Success is what really counts in life!* He gets many promotions and raises because he is driven to perform well, but happiness continues to elude him.

A housewife with three children painfully wonders, *Why don't I feel close to my husband?* Having grown up with an alcoholic father and a demanding mother, this woman has never felt lovable and therefore isn't able to receive her husband's love.

An articulate pastor speaks powerfully about the unconditional love and grace of God, yet he is plagued by guilt. He is driven to succeed in his public ministry but is passive and withdrawn around his family. He has never understood how to apply his own teaching to his life and relationships.

Why do some of us lack objectivity? Why can't we see the reality in our lives? Why are we afraid to turn on the light? There are a number of answers to these questions, and they vary for each person. Perhaps we feel that our situations are "normal," that experiencing loneliness, hurt, and anger is really all there is to life. Perhaps we want to be "good" Christians, and believing that good Christians don't have problems or feelings like ours, we deny the existence of our emotions. Perhaps our lack of objectivity is a learned response from childhood. All of us desperately want our parents to be loving and supportive. If ours aren't (or weren't), we may protect our concept of them by blaming ourselves for their lack of love, and we may deny that we have been hurt by their behavior.

We all develop elaborate defense mechanisms to block pain and gain significance. We suppress emotions; we are compulsive perfectionists; we drive ourselves to succeed, or we withdraw and become passive; we attack people who hurt us; we punish ourselves when we fail; we try to say clever things to be accepted; we help people so that we will be appreciated; and we say and do countless other things.

A sense of need usually propels us to look for an alternative. We may have the courage to examine ourselves and may desperately want to change but may be unsure of how and where to start. We may refuse to look honestly within for fear of what we'll find, or we may be afraid that even if we can discover what's wrong, nothing can help us.

It is difficult—if not impossible—to turn on the light of objectivity by ourselves. We need guidance from the Holy Spirit and usually the honesty, love, and encouragement of at least one other person who is willing to help us. Even then, we may become depressed as we begin to discover the effects of our wounds. Some of us have deep emotional and spiritual scars resulting from the neglect, abuse, and manipulation that often accompany living in a dysfunctional family (alcoholism, drug abuse, divorce, absent father or mother, excessive anger, verbal and/or physical abuse, and so on), but all of us bear the effects of our own sinful nature and the imperfections of others. Whether your hurts are deep or relatively mild, it is wise to be honest about them in the context of affirming relationships so that healing can begin.

Many of us mistakenly believe that God doesn't want us to be honest about our lives. We think that He will be upset with us if we tell Him how we really feel. But the Scriptures tell us that God does not want us to be superficial in our relationship with Him, with others, or in our own lives. David wrote, "Surely you desire truth in the inner parts; you teach me wisdom in the inmost place" (Ps. 51:6, NIV).

The Lord desires truth and honesty at the deepest level and wants us to experience His love, forgiveness, and power in all areas of our lives. Experiencing His love does not mean that all of our thoughts, emotions, and behaviors will be pleasant and pure. It means that we can be real, feeling pain and joy, love and anger, confidence and confusion. The Psalms give us tremendous insight about what it means to be honest with the Lord. David and other psalmists wrote and spoke honestly about the full range of their responses to situations. For example, David expressed his anger with the Lord because he felt abandoned by Him:

I say to God my Rock, "Why have you forgotten me? Why must I go about mourning, oppressed by the enemy?" (Ps. 42:9, NIV)

At times, David was very angry with others, and he expressed his anger to the Lord in terms that reveal the depth of his feelings:

Break the teeth in their mouths, O God; tear out, O LORD, the fangs of the lions! Let them vanish like water that flows away; when they draw the bow, let their arrows be blunted. Like a slug melting away as it moves along, like a stillborn child, may they not see the sun. Before your pots can feel the heat of the thorns—whether they be green or dry—the wicked will be swept away. (Ps. 58:6–9, NIV)

David wrote of his despair about difficult situations:

My heart is in anguish within me; the terrors of death assail me. Fear and trembling have beset me; horror has overwhelmed me. (Ps. 55:4–5, NIV)

And he communicated his despair to the Lord:

Why do you hide your face and forget our misery and oppression? We are brought down to the dust; our bodies cling to ground. (Ps. 44:24–25, NIV)

Sometimes he was confused:

How long, 0 LORD? Will you forget me forever? How long will you hide your face from me? How long must I wrestle with my thoughts and every day have sorrow in my heart? (Ps. 13:1–2, NIV)

Sometimes David communicated his love for the Lord:

As the deer pants for streams of water, so my soul pants for you, 0 God. My soul thirsts for God, for the living God. When can I go and meet with God? (Ps. 42:1–2, NIV)

At times David trusted in the Lord:

The LORD is my light and my salvation—whom shall I fear? The LORD is the stronghold of my life—of whom shall I be afraid? When evil men advance against me to devour my flesh, when my enemies and my foes attack me, they will stumble and fall. Though an army besiege me, my heart will not fear; though war break out against me, even then I will be confident. (Ps. 27:1–3, NIV)

At other times he was filled with praise for God:

I will exalt you, my God the King; I will praise your name for ever and ever. Every day I will praise you and extol your name for ever and ever. Great is the LORD and most worthy of praise; his greatness no one can fathom. (Ps. 145:1–3, NIV)

These passages demonstrate that God, who spoke of David as a man after His own heart, wants us to be open and honest with Him about all of our emotions, not just the pleasant ones.

Many read and study, go to seminars and meetings—they may even be in relationships where they are loved and encouraged—but they may not see substantive change in their lives and patterns of behavior. One reason for this spiritual and emotional inertia is a sense of hopelessness. For various reasons (family background, past experiences, poor modeling), we may have negative presumptions that determine our receptivity to love and truth. In some cases, God's light may have revealed our pain and wall of defenses, but it may not yet have penetrated to our deepest thoughts and beliefs about ourselves. These beliefs may not be clearly articulated but often reflect misperceptions such as these:

- *God doesn't really care about me.*
- *I am an unlovable, worthless person.*
- *Nobody will ever love me.*
- *I'll never be able to change.*
- *I've been a failure all my life. I guess I'll always be a failure.*
- *If people really knew me, they wouldn't like me.*

When the light of love and honesty shines on thoughts of hopelessness, it is often very painful. We begin to admit that we really do feel negatively about ourselves—and have for a long time. But God's love, expressed through His people and woven into our lives by His Spirit and His Word, can, over a period of time, bring healing even to our deepest wounds and instill within us an appropriate sense of self-worth.

The purpose of this book is to provide clear, biblical instruction about the basis of your self-worth by helping you:

1. Identify and understand the nature of man's search for significance.

2. Recognize and challenge inadequate answers.

3. Apply God's solutions to your search for significance.

This is a process that we will examine throughout the following pages. At this point, simply ask the Lord to give you the courage to be honest. Give Him permission to shine His Spirit's light on your thoughts, feelings, and actions. You may be surprised by additional pain as you realize the extent of your wounds, but our experience of healing can only be as deep as our awareness of the need for it. This takes the power of God's light. Ask Him to turn on the light.

When the light does come on in our lives, we will discover that we have tried to meet certain needs in the wrong way. It isn't that the needs are not real, it is just that we have tried to meet these needs in inappropriate ways.

How do we know if something we *want* is really something we *need?* First, the simple answer is that when we are without something we need we find ourselves uncomfortable, sometimes even miserable, perhaps even at the point of death. Without water we become very thirsty; without sleep we stay very sleepy. When we find that we perceive our lives as having no value, purpose, or significance, we become miserable. Many have even killed themselves to avoid living a life such as this. I find it amazing to discover Christians who believe (at least intellectually) that value, purpose, and significance are unimportant to life. These individuals usually have deadened themselves to their own feelings to the point that they have many relational problems they do not even recognize.

The second way we know if something is critical to our lives is to see if God gives much emphasis in His Word regarding a particular need. Reading Scripture from this perspective, we find this emphasized over and over. For instance, Jesus gives His life as a ransom for our lives. The price is too high for us to even calculate. God tells us that we are so significant to Him that He always keeps an eye on us. He manages to be so sensitive to our situation that He even keeps track of the hairs on our head. There is obviously nothing more important to God than our welfare. Even His commands to us are designed for our good. The Father says to His children, "Be careful concerning your choices. You are so precious to Me." God knows we need to know how valuable our lives are, and He spends much of His Word telling us so.

From life's outset, we find ourselves on the prowl, searching to satisfy some inner, unexplained yearning. Our hunger causes us to search for people who will love us. Our desire for acceptance pressures us to perform to gain praise from others. We strive for success, driving our minds and bodies harder and further, hoping that because of our sweat and sacrifice others will appreciate us more.

But the man or woman who lives only for the love and attention of others is never satisfied—at least, not for long. Despite our efforts, we will never find lasting, fulfilling peace if we must continually prove ourselves to others. Our desire to be loved and accepted is a symptom of a deeper need—the need that frequently governs our behavior and is the primary source of our emotional pain. Often unrecognized, this is our need for self-worth.

The case of Mark and Beth aptly demonstrates this great need. During their final semester at Cornell University, Mark and Beth fell in love. Beth's eyes sparkled, her walk had that certain lightness, and she found it difficult to concentrate on her studies. As she and Mark gazed into each other's eyes, Beth saw the special affection she had always desired. She felt that her need to feel valued and loved would be fulfilled through their relationship. Likewise, Mark was encouraged and motivated by Beth's acceptance and admiration of him. With her support, Mark thought he could boldly begin a successful career after graduation.

The summer after they graduated from Cornell, Mark and Beth married, believing their love would provide them both with a permanent sense of self-worth. Unfortunately, they were depending on each other to fill a void that could only be filled by their Creator. Each expected the other to always be loving, accepting, and forgiving no matter what the circumstances were. Soon both were disillusioned and even felt betrayed by the other. As the years passed, affirmation was replaced by sarcasm and ridicule. Each failure to provide love and acceptance was another brick in their wall of hurt and separation. Recently, Mark and Beth celebrated their tenth wedding anniversary. Sadly, although they had shared ten years together, they had experienced very little true, unconditional love. Their search for self-worth and significance ended in despair.

Another example illustrates how the promise of fulfillment through success is an empty one, often resulting in tragic consequences for ourselves and those around us: Brad and Lisa had been married for twelve years. Brad was a successful lawyer, and Lisa was a homemaker extensively involved in church activities. Their two sons, six-year-old Kyle and eight-year-old David, were well-behaved boys. Although their family appeared to be a model of perfection to those around them, Brad and Lisa were beginning to experience some real problems. True, Brad's law practice was flourishing, but at the expense of Lisa and the boys. He arrived home later and later each evening and often spent the weekend locked in his office. Brad was driven to succeed, believing that satisfaction and contentment were always just one more trial victory away. But each success gave him only temporary fulfillment. Maybe the next one . . .

Brad would not allow anything to interfere with his success, not even the needs of his family. At first, Lisa seemed to understand. She knew Brad's work was important and hated to protest when he was so busy. Not wanting to burden him, she began to feel guilty for talking to him about family problems. But as the weeks turned into months and Brad remained obsessed with his work, Lisa became resentful. She could overlook her own needs even though it was painful, but the boys needed their father. The family never had time to be together anymore, and Brad's promises sounded hollow. "When this big case is over, the pressure will be off," he'd say, but there was always another case. Brad was continually solving other people's problems but never those of his own family. Realizing that she and the boys weren't important to him, Lisa became bitter and depressed.

Brad and Lisa's problems persisted, and soon they became obvious to others. Friends began asking Lisa what was wrong. At first she found it difficult to be honest about the situation, but Lisa eventually shared her feelings. She was both hurt and surprised by the glib responses she received from well-meaning but insensitive friends. "Just trust the Lord," one said. Another close friend advised, "You shouldn't have any problems, Lisa. You're a Christian. With God's help, you can work it out."

Like falling on a jagged rock, these comments hurt deeply. Lisa began to doubt herself and wonder if she were capable of building a successful marriage and family. Feeling like a failure, she reasoned that perhaps she deserved a broken marriage; perhaps her problems with Brad were her fault and God was punishing her for her sins.

Confused and frustrated, both Brad and Lisa were searching for significance in their own ways—Brad in his success as an attorney, and Lisa in her success as a wife and mother. Their lives began to reflect that strange combination of hopelessness and compulsion. Sadly, neither Brad nor Lisa realized that their search should both begin and end with God's Word.

In the Scriptures, God supplies the essentials for discovering our true significance and worth. The first two chapters of Genesis recount man's creation, revealing man's intended purpose (to honor God) and man's value (that he is a special creation of God). John 10:10 also reminds us of how much God treasures His creation, in that Christ came so that man might experience abundant life. However, as Christians, we need to realize that this abundant life is lived in a real world filled with pain, rejection, and failure. Therefore, experiencing the abundant life God intends for us does not mean that our lives will be problem-free. On the contrary, life itself is a series of problems that often act as obstacles to our search for significance, and the abundant life is the experience of God's love, forgiveness, and power in the midst of these problems. The Scriptures warn us that we live within a warfare that can destroy our faith, lower our self-esteem, and lead us into depression. In his letter to the Ephesians, Paul instructs us to put on the armor of God so that we can be equipped for spiritual battle. However, it often seems that unsuspecting believers are the last to know this battle is occurring, and they don't know that Christ has ultimately won the war. They are surprised and confused by difficulties, thinking that the Christian life is a playground, not a battlefield.

As Christians, our fulfillment in this life depends not on our skills to avoid life's problems but on our ability to apply God's specific solutions to those problems. An accurate understanding of God's truth is the first step toward discovering our significance and worth.

Unfortunately, many of us have been exposed to inadequate teaching from both religious and secular sources concerning our self-worth. As a result, we may have a distorted self-perception and may be experiencing hopelessness rather than the rich and meaningful life God intends for us.

Christian psychologist Lawrence J. Crabb Jr. describes our need for self-esteem this way: "The basic personal need of each person is to regard himself as a worthwhile human being." And, according to William Glasser, "Everyone aspires to have a happy, successful, pleasurable belief in himself."

Some secular psychologists focus on self-worth with a goal of simply feeling good about ourselves. A biblical self-concept, however, goes far beyond that limited perspective. It is an accurate perception of ourselves, God, and others based on the truths of God's Word. An accurate, biblical self-concept contains both strength and humility, both sorrow over sin and joy about forgiveness, a deep sense of our need for God's grace and a deep sense of the reality of God's grace.

Whether labeled *self-esteem* or *self-worth,* the feeling of significance is crucial to man's emotional, spiritual, and social stability and is the driving element within the human spirit. Understanding this single need opens the door to understanding our actions and attitudes.

What a waste to attempt to change behavior without truly understanding the driving needs that cause such behavior! Yet millions of people spend a lifetime searching for love, acceptance, and success without understanding the need that compels them. We must understand that this hunger for self-worth is God-given and can only be satisfied by Him. Our value is not dependent on our ability to earn the fickle acceptance of people, but rather, its true source is the love and acceptance of God. He created us. He alone knows how to fulfill all of our needs.

In order to fully understand the provisions that God has made for our self-worth, we must look back to man's beginning, the first man and woman, and their search for significance.

2

The Origin of the Search

Has God always had the solutions for man's emotional struggles, or did He have to wait for Freud and his insights?

If He does not have the answers for our emotional needs, how can He deliver on His promise to bring joy and peace into our lives if we follow Him?

The Old Testament depicts the original incident of sin and the Fall of man:

When the woman saw that the tree was good for food, and that it was a delight to the eyes, and that the tree was desirable to make one wise, she took from its fruit and ate; and she gave also to her husband with her, and he ate. Then the eyes of both of them were opened, and they knew that they were naked; and they sewed fig leaves together and made themselves loin coverings. (Gen. 3:6–7)

To properly understand the devastating effects of this event, we need to examine the nature of man before sin caused him to lose his security and significance.

The first created man lived in unclouded, intimate fellowship with God. He was secure and free. In all of God's creation, no creature compared to him. Indeed, Adam was a magnificent creation, complete and perfect in the image of God, designed to reign over all the earth (Gen. 1:26–28). Adam's purpose was to reflect the glory of God. Through man, God wanted to demonstrate His holiness (Ps. 99:3–5); love and patience (1 Cor. 13:4); forbearance (1 Cor. 13:7); wisdom (James 3:13,17); comfort (2 Cor. 1:3–4); forgiveness (Heb. 10:17); faithfulness (Ps. 89:1, 2, 5, 8); and grace (Ps. 111:4). Through his intellect, free will, and emotions, man was to be the showcase for God's glorious character.

Adam was, therefore, a very important creation to God. To meet his needs for companionship and understanding, God created a woman for Adam and gave her to him as his wife. In keeping with their perfect character, God placed Adam and Eve in a perfect environment—a lush, beautiful garden where the Creator Himself provided for their physical needs. Adam and Eve had the challenge and responsibility of supervising this paradise of vegetation and animal life. And to satisfy their spiritual needs, God visited them and talked with them personally. Adam and Eve were perfect in body, mind, and spirit.

Like Adam and Eve, Satan also was created in perfection. At the time of his creation, his name was *Lucifer*, which means "morning star." He was an angel of the highest rank, created to glorify God. He was clothed in beauty and power, and was allowed to serve in the presence of God. Sadly, Lucifer's pride caused him to rebel against God, and he was cast from heaven with a third of the angels (Isa. 14:12–15). He appeared to Adam and Eve in the garden in the form of a serpent, more crafty than any beast of the field that the Lord God had made (Gen. 3:1).

Adam had been given authority over the earth, but if, like Lucifer, he rebelled against God, he would lose both his authority and his perfection. He would become a slave to Satan and to sin (Rom. 6:17) and a child of God's wrath (Eph. 2:3). Therefore, destroying man was Satan's way to reign on earth and, he thought, to thwart God's glorious plan for man.

To accomplish his goal, Satan began by deceiving Eve, who fell to the temptation. Eve ate from the tree of the knowledge of good and evil, believing it would make her wise and like God. Adam, however, was not deceived. He deliberately chose to forsake the love and security of God and follow Eve in sin. Paul explained this fact to Timothy:

> *And it was not Adam who was deceived, but the woman being quite deceived, fell into transgression. (1 Tim. 2:14)*

In doing this, Adam not only lost the glory God had intended for mankind but he also forfeited his close communion and fellowship with God. Adam's deliberate rebellion aided Satan's purpose, giving him power and authority on earth. From that moment on, all history led to a single hill outside of Jerusalem, where God appointed a Savior to pay the penalty for man's sin of rebellion (our attempts to find security and purpose apart from Him).Christ's death is the most overwhelming evidence of God's love for us.

Though we justly deserve the wrath of God because of that deliberate rebellion, His Son became our substitute, and He experienced the wrath our rebellion deserves. Because Christ paid the penalty for our sins, our relationship with God has been restored, and we are able to partake of His nature and character, to commune with Him, and to reflect His love to all the world.

Spread the good news! Man is not lost forever! God has not given up on us! He has bought us out of slavery to sin with the payment of Christ's death on the cross. Satan's rule can be broken, and we can reign with Christ. We can be restored to the security and significance for which we have been created—not simply in eternity but here and now as well.

We must never forget that God wants His children to bear His image and to rule with Him. Adam's sin had tragic consequences, but through God's plan of redemption, we can still have the privilege of fellowshiping with Him. God has provided the solution, but the question is this: *Will we accept Christ's death as the payment for our sins and discover the powerful implications of our salvation, or will we continue to follow Satan's lies and deceptions?*

Perhaps you are unsure of your relationship with God and need to deal conclusively with this choice now. We cannot pay for our sins; Christ has already done this for us as a gift. Paul wrote about this gift in his letter to the Ephesian Christians:

> For by grace [unmerited favor] you have been saved [rescued from spiritual death—hell] through faith [trust]; and that not of yourselves, it is the gift of God; not as a result of works, that no one should boast. (Eph. 2:8–9)

Are you trusting in your own abilities to earn acceptance with God, or are you trusting in the death of Christ to pay for your sins and in His resurrection to give you new life? Take a moment to reflect on this question: On a scale of 0 to 100 percent, how sure are you that you would spend eternity with God if you died today? An answer of less than 100 percent may indicate that you are trusting, at least in part, in yourself. You may be thinking, *Isn't it arrogant to say that I am 100 percent sure?*

Indeed, it would be arrogance if you were trusting in yourself—your abilities, your actions, and good deeds—to earn your salvation. However, if you are trusting in the all-sufficient payment of Christ, then 100 percent certainty is a response of humility and thankfulness, not arrogance.

Reflect on a second question: If you were to die today and stand before God, and He were to ask you, "Why should I let you into heaven?" what would you tell Him? Would you mention your abilities, church attendance, kindness to others, Christian service, abstinence from a particular sin, or some other good deed? Paul wrote to Titus:

> But when the kindness of God our Savior and His love for mankind appeared, He saved us, not on the basis of deeds which we have done in righteousness, but according to His mercy. (Titus 3:4–5)

We must give up our own efforts to achieve righteousness and instead believe that Christ's death and resurrection alone are sufficient to pay for our sin and separation from God.

Perhaps you have intellectually believed that Jesus Christ lived two thousand years ago, performed miracles, died on the cross, and was raised from the dead. Perhaps you have even felt close to God at times in your life. But biblical faith is more than intellectual assent or warm emotions. Consider the analogy of a wedding: An engaged couple may intellectually know they want to marry each other, and they probably feel very close to one another, but until they willfully say, "I do" to each other, they're not married. Many people are at this point in their relationship with Christ. They need to say, "I do" to Him.

If there is any question about whether you have conclusively accepted Christ's substitutionary death to pay for the wrath you deserve for your sins, take some time to think about the two questions we have examined and to reflect on His love and forgiveness. Then respond by trusting in Christ and accepting His payment for your sins. You can use this prayer to express your faith:

> *Lord Jesus, I need You. I want You to be my Savior and Lord. I accept Your death on the cross as the complete payment for my sins. Thank You for forgiving me and for giving me new life. Help me to grow in my understanding of Your love and power so that my life will bring honor to You. Amen.*

The moment you trust Christ, many wonderful things happen to you:

> *All your sins are forgiven: past, present, and future. (Col. 2:13–14)*

> *You become a child of God. (John 1:12; Rom. 8:15)*

> *You receive eternal life. (John 5:24)*

> *You are delivered from Satan's domain and transferred into the kingdom of Christ. (Col. 1:13)*

Christ comes to dwell within you. (Col. 1:27; Rev. 3:20)

You become a new creation. (2 Cor. 5:17)

You are declared righteous by God. (2 Cor. 5:21)

You enter into a love relationship with God. (1 John 4:9–11)

You are accepted by God. (Col. 1:19–22)

Think on the implications of these truths in your life. Then thank God for His wonderful grace and experience the love of Christ, which surpasses knowledge (Eph. 3:19).

The Saving Solution Versus Satan's Snare

Satan, the father of lies, twists and distorts the truth so that his deceptions appear to be more reasonable and attractive than the truth. Notice how Satan snared Eve. He told her:

For God knows that in the day you eat from it your eyes will be opened, and you will be like God, knowing good and evil. (Gen. 3:5)

Here, Satan directly questioned God's truthfulness, implying that Eve could have greater significance apart from God and that eating the forbidden fruit would reveal hidden knowledge, enabling her to know good from evil like God Himself.

Being deceived, Eve traded God's truth for the serpent's lie. She ate the forbidden fruit. Then Adam followed her in sinful rebellion against God, and he, too, ate the forbidden fruit. One of the tragic implications of this event is that man lost his secure status with God and began to struggle with feelings of arrogance, inadequacy, and despair, valuing the opinions of others more than the truth of God. This robbed man of his true self-worth and put him on a continual, but fruitless, search for significance through his success and the approval of others.

In one form or another, Satan's lie still thrives today. For example, humanism, the central philosophy of our schools and society, teaches that man is above all else, that he alone is the center of meaning. Teaching that man has meaning totally apart from God, humanism leaves morality, justice, and behavior to the discretion of "enlightened" man and encourages people to worship man and nature rather than God. Living without God's divine truth, humanity sinks lower and lower in depravity, blindly following a philosophy that intends to heighten the dignity of man but instead lowers him to the level of animals. Rather than a spiritual and emotional being, man has been classified as merely a natural phenomenon of time plus chance, no greater than rocks, animals, or clouds. The apostle Paul described this foolish and demeaning perspective of man in Romans 1:20–25:

> *For since the creation of the world His invisible attributes, His eternal power and divine nature, have been clearly seen, being understood through what has been made, so that they are without excuse. For even though they knew God, they did not honor Him as God, or give thanks; but they became futile in their speculations, and their foolish heart was darkened. Professing to be wise, they became fools, and exchanged the glory of the incorruptible God for an image in the form of corruptible man and of birds and four-footed animals and crawling creatures.*
>
> *Therefore God gave them over in the lusts of their hearts to impurity, that their bodies might be dishonored among them. For they exchanged the truth of God for a lie, and worshiped and served the creature rather than the Creator, who is blessed forever. Amen.*

In the beginning, God declared that man was created to reign with Him; however, man rejected God's truth and chose instead to believe Satan's lie. Today, man continues to reject God's truth and offer of salvation through Jesus Christ. He chooses instead to trust in his success and the opinions of others to give him a sense of self-worth, though the Scriptures clearly teach that apart from Christ, man is enslaved to sin and condemned to an eternity in hell.

Since the Fall, man has often failed to turn to God for the truth about himself. Instead, he has looked to others to meet his inescapable need for self-worth. *I am what others say I am,* he has reasoned. *I will find my value in their opinions of me.*

Isn't it amazing that we turn to others who have a perspective as limited and darkened as our own to discover our worth! Rather than relying on God's steady, uplifting reassurance of who we are, we depend on others who base our worth on our ability to meet their standards. Because our performance and ability to please others so dominates our search for significance, we have difficulty recognizing the distinction between our real identity and the way we behave, a realization crucial to understanding our true worth. Our true value is not based on our behavior or the approval of others but on what God's Word says is true of us.

Our behavior is often a reflection of our beliefs about who we are. It is usually consistent with what we think to be true about ourselves (Prov. 23:7). If we base our worth solidly on the truths of God's Word, then our behavior will often reflect His love, grace, and power. But if we base our worth on our abilities or the fickle approval of others, then our behavior will reflect the insecurity, fear, and anger that comes from such instability.

Though we usually behave in ways that are consistent with our beliefs, at times our actions may contradict them. For example, we may believe that we are generous and gracious, when we are actually very selfish. Sometimes our behavior changes what we believe about ourselves. If, for instance, we succeed in a task at which we initially believed we would fail, our confidence may begin to grow and expand to other areas of our lives. Our feelings, behavior, and beliefs all interact to shape our lives.

Our home environment plays a central role in forming our beliefs and emotions. These can have a powerful impact on our outlook and behavior. This truth is evident in the case of Scott. He grew up in a home without praise, discouraged by his parents whenever he attempted anything new and challenging. After twenty years of hearing, "You'll never be able to do anything,

Scott, so don't even try," he believed it himself. Neither Scott nor his parents could understand why he had flunked out of college and was continually shuffling from one job to another, never able to achieve success. Believing he was doing the best he could do but suspecting he would always fail, Scott consistently performed according to his self-perception.

Separated from God and His Word, people have only their abilities and the opinions of others on which to base their worth, and the circumstances around them ultimately control the way they feel about themselves.

Take the case of Stacy, a young girl who became pregnant when she was seventeen. Stacy gave her baby up for adoption, and only her family and a few close friends knew of the incident. Several years later, Stacy fell in love with a compassionate man named Ron and married him. Fearing his reaction, she didn't tell Ron about the baby. Over the years, Stacy concealed her guilt and grief until the pressure finally became so overwhelming that she admitted the entire episode to him.

Surprisingly, Ron did not respond in anger. He understood the agony his wife had carried for so many years and loved her in spite of her past. It was Stacy who could not cope at this point. Unable to accept Ron's forgiveness and knowing she had failed according to society's standards, Stacy felt unworthy of his love. She refused to forgive herself and chose to leave her husband.

In this case, Stacy fell victim to one of Satan's most effective lies: Those who fail are unworthy of love and deserve to be blamed and condemned. Because she failed in her own eyes, Stacy's perception of herself was detrimentally affected.

Each of us has probably failed badly at some point in our lives. Perhaps some particular sin or weakness has caused us to feel condemned and unworthy of love. Without the hope and healing that God can provide, our evaluation of ourselves will eventually lead to despair.

In spite of Adam and Eve's sin, God's plan is to bring man back to the destiny for which he was originally created—to bear His image. To accomplish this, God gives a new nature to all who believe in Christ. This new nature is able to reflect God's character and rule His creation. In Luke 10:19, Jesus spoke of the authority of this new nature when He said, "Behold, I have given you authority to tread upon serpents and scorpions, and over all the power of the enemy, and nothing shall injure you."

Satan, however, continues to deceive people, including many Christians, into believing that the basis of their worth is their performance and their ability to please others. The equation below reflects Satan's lie:

Self-Worth = Performance + Others' Opinions

Can we overcome Satan's deception and reject this basis of our self-worth? Can we trust God's complete acceptance of us as His sons and daughters and allow Him to free us from our dependency on success and the approval of others? Rejecting Satan's lie and accepting God's evaluation of us leads to a renewed hope, joy, and purpose in life.

We all have compelling, God-given needs for love, acceptance, and purpose, and most of us will go to virtually any lengths to meet those needs. Many of us have become masters at "playing the game" to be successful and to win the approval of others. Some of us, however, have failed and have experienced the pain of disapproval so often that we have given up and have withdrawn into a shell of hurt, numbness, or depression. In both cases, we are living by the deception that our worth is based on our performance and others' opinions—some of us are simply more adept at playing this game than others.

Our attempts to meet our needs for success and approval fall into two broad categories: compulsiveness and withdrawal. Some people expend extra effort, work extra hours, and try to say just the right thing to achieve success and please those around them. These people may have a compulsive desire to be in control of every situation. They are perfectionists. If a job isn't done perfectly, if they aren't dressed just right, if they aren't considered "the best" by their peers, then they work harder until they achieve that coveted status. And woe to the poor soul who gets in their way! Whoever doesn't contribute to their success and acclaim is a threat to their self-esteem, an unacceptable threat. They may be very personable and have a lot of friends, but the goal of these relationships may not be to give encouragement and love; it may be to manipulate others to contribute to their success. That may sound harsh, but people who are driven to succeed will often use practically everything and everybody to meet that need.

The other broad category is withdrawal. Those who manifest this behavior usually try to avoid failure and disapproval by avoiding risks. They won't volunteer for the jobs that offer much risk of failure. They gravitate toward people who are comforting and kind, skirting relationships that might demand vulnerability and, consequently, the risk of rejection. They may appear to be easygoing, but inside they are usually running from every potential situation or relationship that might not succeed.

Obviously, these are two broad categories. Most of us exhibit some combination of the two behaviors, willing to take risks and work hard in the areas where we feel sure of success but avoiding the people and situations that may bring rejection and failure.

Rob and Kathy had dated for three years. Kathy was a perfectionist. Her clothes, her hair, her work, her car, even her boyfriend, had to be perfect. Rob, a good-natured, fun-loving fellow, was not as concerned with such details. Predictably, the more intense Kathy became about having everything and everybody just right, the more passive and easygoing Rob became. This spiral of intensity and passivity continued until Rob and Kathy hit rock bottom.

After several weeks of counseling, Kathy saw that her perfectionism came from a misplaced base of security: her performance instead of Christ. But Rob said that he didn't have a problem with performance. He certainly didn't have a compelling drive to succeed, and he didn't pressure people around him to get their act together. In the midst of these explanations, I asked, "But Rob, what about your tendency to withdraw? Why do you think you do that?" It still didn't compute.

Finally, after several months, Rob understood. He based his security on his performance just as much as Kathy did, but he handled it differently. She became more compulsive to have things just right, while he withdrew to avoid failure. Both slowly began to recognize the root of their problems, and through months of encouragement and honest interaction, they started believing that their worth is secure in Christ. Today, Kathy is less intense about her performance, and Rob doesn't run from failure as much as he used to. They are learning to channel their intensity toward true significance: Christ and His kingdom.

When we base our security on success and others' opinions, we become dependent on our abilities to perform and please others. We develop a *have-to* mentality: I *have to* do well on this exam (or my security as a good student will be threatened); I *have to* make that deal (or my boss will think I am a failure); my father (or mother, spouse, or friend) *has to* appreciate me and be happy with my decisions (because I cannot cope with that person's disapproval).

Our self-esteem and view of God are usually a mirror of our parents' attitudes toward us. Those who are loved and affirmed by their parents tend to have a fairly healthy self-concept, and usually find it easy to believe that God is loving and powerful. Those whose parents have been neglectful, manipulative, or condemning usually seem to feel that they have to earn a sense of worth, and that God is aloof, demanding, and/or cruel.

Our parents are our models of the character of God. When we do not have that fundamental sense of feeling lovable and protected by them, we tend to base our self-worth on how well we perform and please others instead of on what the sovereign God of the universe, our all-wise, omniscient Savior, says of us.

We do not have to be successful or have to be pleasing to others to have a healthy sense of self-esteem and worth. That worth has freely and conclusively been given to us by God. Failure and/or the disapproval of others can't take it away! Therefore we can conclude, *It would be nice to be approved by my parents (or whomever), but if they don't approve of me, I'm still loved and accepted by God.* Do you see the difference? The *have-to* mentality is sheer slavery to performance and the opinions of others, but we are secure and free in Christ. We don't have to have success or anyone else's approval. Of course, it would be nice to have success and approval, but the point is clear that Christ is the source of our security; Christ is the basis of our worth; Christ is the only one who promises and never fails.

The transition from the slavery and compulsion of a *have-to* mentality to the freedom and strength of a *want-to* motivation is a process. Bondage to such thinking is often deeply rooted in our personalities, patterns of behavior, and ways of relating to other people. These patterns of thinking, feeling, and responding, learned over time, flow as naturally as the course of rainwater in a dry desert riverbed. Changing them requires time, the encouragement of others, the truth and application of God's Word, and the power of God's Spirit.

This book is dedicated to the process of understanding, applying, and experiencing the foundational truths of God's Word. In the remaining chapters, we will examine the process of hope and healing. We will also identify four specific false beliefs generated by Satan's deception. In addition, we will discover God's gracious, effective, and permanent solution to our search for significance.

Introduction:
Chapters 3–10

It is often helpful to see a general outline when attempting to grasp new concepts. In the next few chapters, we will examine four false beliefs resulting from Satan's deceptions with some of the consequences that accompany these beliefs. Finally, we will examine God's specific solution for our false belief system and apply this through some practical exercises.

Remember that the specific effects of false beliefs and resulting actions vary from person to person, depending on family background, personality traits, other relationships, and many other factors. Likewise, the application of biblical truths will vary according to the perception of the individual, the degree of his or her emotions, spiritual, and relational health, and the process by which the cognitive, relational, spiritual, and emotional elements are incorporated into one's life. All of this takes time, but health and hope are worth it!

The chart on the following pages provides an overview of these chapters.

Chapter	False Beliefs	Consequences
3–4 The Performance Trap	*I must meet certain standards to feel good about myself.*	The fear of failure; perfectionism; driven to succeed; manipulating others to achieve success; withdrawal from risks.
5–6 Approval Addict	*I must be approved by certain others to feel good about myself.*	The fear of rejection; attampting to please others at any cost; overly sensitive to criticism; withdrawing from others to avoid disapproval.
7–8 The Blame Game	*Those who fail (including myself) are unworthy of love and deserve to be punished.*	The fear of punishment; punishing others; blaming others for personal failure; withdrawal from God and others; driven to avoid failure.
9–10 Shame	*I am what I am. I cannot change. I am hopeless*	Feelings of shame, hopelessness, inferiority; passivity; loss of creativity; isolation; withdrawal from others.

God's Answer

Justification

Justification means that God has not only forgiven me of my sins but has also granted me the righteousness of Christ. Because of justification, I bear Christ's righteousness, and I am therefore fully pleasing to the Father (Rom. 5:1).

Reconciliation

Reconciliation means that although I was at one time hostile toward God and alienated from Him, I am now forgiven and have been brought into an intimate relationship with Him. Consequently, I am totally accepted by God (Col. 1:21–22).

Propitiation

Propitiation means that by His death on the cross Christ satisfied God's wrath; therefore, I am deeply loved by God (1 John 4:9–11).

Regeneration

Regeneration means that I am a new creation in Christ (John 3:3–6).

3

The Performance Trap

I must meet certain standards to feel good about myself.

Why do we sometimes tolerate failure in another person but cannot tolerate it in ourselves?

If we cannot tolerate failure, how many of life's opportunities will we allow to just pass us by without our even trying or without taking the challenge?

How much different would your life be if it were not for the fear of failure?

Most of us are unaware of how thoroughly Satan has deceived us. He has led us blindly down a path of destruction, making us captives of our inability to meet our standards consistently and slaves of low self-esteem. Satan has shackled us in chains that keep us from experiencing the love, freedom, and purposes of Christ.

In Colossians 2:8, Paul warns:

See to it that no one takes you captive through philosophy and empty deception, according to the tradition of men, according to the elementary principles of the world, rather than according to Christ.

Indeed, we've reached a true mark of maturity when we begin testing the deceitful thoughts of our minds against the Word of God.

We no longer have to live by our fleshly thoughts; we have the mind of Christ (1 Cor. 2:16). Through His Spirit, we can challenge the indoctrinations and traditions that have long held us in guilt and condemnation. We can then replace those deceptions with the powerful truths of the Scriptures.

A primary deception all of us tend to believe is that success will bring fulfillment and happiness. Again and again, we've tried to measure up, thinking that if we could meet certain standards we would feel good about ourselves. But again and again, we've failed and have felt miserable. Even if we succeed on a fairly regular basis, occasional failure may be so devastating that it dominates our perception of ourselves.

Consciously or unconsciously, all of us have experienced this feeling that we must meet certain arbitrary standards to attain self-worth. Failure to do so threatens our security and significance. Such a threat, real or perceived, results in a fear of failure. At that point, we are accepting the false belief: *I must meet certain standards to feel good about myself.* When we believe this about ourselves, Satan's distortion of truth is often reflected in our attitudes and behavior.

Because of our unique personalities, we each react very differently to this deception. As we saw in a previous chapter, some of us respond by becoming slaves to perfection, driving ourselves incessantly toward attaining goals.

Perfectionists can be quite vulnerable to serious mood disorders and often anticipate rejection when they believe they haven't met the standards they are trying so hard to attain. Therefore, perfectionists tend to react defensively to criticism and demand to be in control of most situations they encounter. Because they are usually more competent than most, perfectionists see nothing wrong with their compulsions. "I just like to see things done well," they claim. There is certainly nothing inherently wrong with doing things well; the problem is that perfectionists usually base their self-worth on their ability to accomplish a goal. Therefore, failure is a threat and is totally unacceptable to them.

Karen, a wife, mother, and civic leader, seemed ideal to everyone who knew her. She was a perfectionist. Her house looked perfect, her kids were spotless, and her skills as president of the ladies' auxiliary were superb. In each area of her life, Karen was always in charge and always successful. However, one step out of the pattern she had set could lead to a tremendous uproar. When others failed to comply with her every demand, her condemnation was quick and cruel.

One day, her husband decided that he couldn't stand any more of Karen's hypercritical behavior. He wanted an understanding wife to talk and share with, not an egocentric, self-driven perfectionist. Friends could not understand why he later chose to leave his seemingly perfect wife. Like Karen, many high achievers are driven beyond healthy limitations. Rarely able to relax and enjoy life, they let their families and relationships suffer as they strive to accomplish often unrealistic goals. On the other hand, the same false belief *(I must meet certain standards to feel good about myself)* that drives many to perfectionism sends others into a tailspin of despair. They rarely expect to achieve anything or to feel good about themselves. Because of their past failures, they are quick to interpret present failures as an accurate reflection of their worthlessness. Fearing more failure, they often become despondent and stop trying.

Finally, the pressure of having to meet self-imposed standards in order to feel good about ourselves can result in a rules-dominated life. Individuals caught in this trap often have a set of rules for most of life's situations, and they continually focus their attention on their performance and ability to adhere to their schedule. Brent, for example, made a daily list of what he could accomplish if everything went perfectly. He was always a little tense because he wanted to use every moment effectively to reach his goals. If things didn't go well, or if someone took too much of his time, Brent got angry. Efficient, effective use of time was his way of attaining fulfillment, but he was miserable. He was constantly driven to do more, but his best was never enough to satisfy him.

Brent believed that accomplishing goals and making efficient use of his time were what the Lord wanted him to do. Due to stress, he occasionally thought that something wasn't quite right, but his solution was to try harder, make even better use of his time, and be even more regimented in his adherence to self-imposed rules. Brent's focus was misdirected. The focus of the Christian life should be on Christ, not on self-imposed regulations. Our experience of Christ's lordship is dependent on our moment-by-moment attention to His instruction, not on our own regimented schedule.

As these cases demonstrate, the false belief *I must meet certain standards in order to feel good about myself* results in a fear of failure.

How affected are you by this belief? Take the following test to determine how strongly you fear failure.

Fear of Failure Test

Read each of the following statements; then, from the top of the test, choose the term that best describes your response. Put the number above that term in the blank beside each statement.

1	2	3	4	5	6	7
Always	Very Often	Often	Sometimes	Seldom	Very Seldom	Never

____ 1. Because of fear, I often avoid participating in certain activities.

____ 2. When I sense that I might experience failure in some important area, I become nervous and anxious.

____ 3. I worry.

____ 4. I have unexplained anxiety.

____ 5. I am a perfectionist.

____ 6. I am compelled to justify my mistakes.

____ 7. There are certain areas in which I feel I must succeed.

____ 8. I become depressed when I fail.

____ 9. I become angry with people who interfere with my attempts to succeed and, as a result, make me appear incompetent.

___ 10. I am self-critical.

___ Total (Add up the numbers you have placed in the blanks.)

If your score is:

57–70: God has apparently given you a very strong appreciation for His love and unconditional acceptance. You seem to be freed from the fear of failure that plagues most people. (Some people who score this high either are greatly deceived or have become callous to their emotions as a way to suppress pain.)

47–56: The fear of failure controls your responses rarely or only in certain situations. Again, the only major exceptions are those who are not honest with themselves.

37–46: When you experience emotional problems, they may relate to a sense of failure or to some form of criticism. Upon reflection, you will probably relate many of your previous decisions to this fear. Many of your future decisions will also be affected by the fear of failure unless you take direct action to overcome it.

27–36: The fear of failure forms a general backdrop to your life. There are probably few days that you are not affected in some way by this fear. Unfortunately, this robs you of the joy and peace your salvation is meant to bring.

0–26: Experiences of failure dominate your memory and have probably resulted in a great deal of depression. These problems will remain until some definitive action is taken. In other words, this condition will not simply disappear; time alone cannot heal your pain. You need to experience deep healing in your self-concept, in your relationship with God, and in your relationships with others.

Effects of the Fear of Failure

The fear of failure can affect our lives in many ways. The following list is not an exhaustive discussion of its resulting problems, nor are these problems explained completely by the fear of failure. However, recognizing and confronting the fear of failure in each of these experiences could result in dramatic changes.

Perfectionism

Again, one of the most common symptoms of the fear of failure is perfectionism, an unwillingness to fail. This tendency suffocates joy and creativity. Because any failure is perceived as a threat to our self-esteem, we develop a propensity to focus our attention on the one area in which we failed rather than those in which we did well. Areas where we often tend to be perfectionists include work, punctuality, housecleaning, our appearance, hobbies, and skills— practically anything and everything! Perfectionists often appear to be highly motivated, but their motivations usually come from a desperate attempt to avoid the low self-esteem they experience when they fail.

Perfectionists are often appreciated because they can be counted on to do a thorough job and are sometimes taken advantage of because of this characteristic.

Avoiding Risks

Another very common result of the fear of failure is a willingness to be involved in only those activities that can be done well. New, challenging activities are avoided because the risk of failure is too great. Avoiding risks may seem comfortable, but it severely limits the scope of our creativity, self-expression, and service to God.

It was Don's senior year in high school, and he was at the state track meet finals. Don had never run faster in his entire life and was not supposed to be in the finals! But there he was. What a great opportunity. Close to the finish line in one race, Don was near the front runners. All of a sudden, he came up lame. Now, many years later, Don is still not sure whether it was really an injury or whether he used the pain as an excuse for not trying at the very end of the race. He questioned whether he gave away an opportunity to be successful for fear of trying and then failing.

More serious than a track meet is the experience of many parents who have pleaded with a child to try harder, not realizing that the child cannot risk trying harder because he or she would then have no excuse if he or she failed. In Rapha's (a national mental healthcare service) adolescent treatment programs, we saw a remarkable change with many of our patients. Many of the adolescents who came to the treatment program experienced a stable environment and were challenged to achieve academically (they would go to school in the facility). It was the first time in years they recognized they still could be successful in school.

We have so much potential we've never recognized because we want to avoid the risk of failure. A dear friend of mine from childhood took a job well below his capabilities, and I always wondered why until I understood this risk-avoidance concept.

In many areas of our lives and in many ways we avoid even trying to achieve success because we do not want to experience the pain of failure should we not succeed.

Anger, Resentment

When we fail, when others contribute to our failure, or when we are injured or insulted in some way, anger is a normal response. What is the common first thing we do when we realize we have failed? We look for someone to blame. Believing ourselves to be diminished because of failure, we try to shift that responsibility to someone else. Of course, then the anger and resentment begin. Ask yourself a simple question: "Of the people you have anger toward, how many of those individuals are associated with some failure about which you feel bad?"

Anxiety and fear of failure are often the source of self-condemnation and the disapproval of others, both of which are severe blows to a self-worth based on personal success and approval. If failure is great enough or occurs often enough, it can harden into a negative self-concept in which we will expect to fail at virtually every endeavor. This negative self-concept perpetuates itself and leads to a downward spiral of anxiety about our performance and fear of disapproval from others.

For many of us, life is like walking through a very dark house with no lights for illumination. You may not know when you're going to trip over the next object, but reason tells you it may be very soon. The same is true with failure. There is no way to escape the experience of failure. If that experience reduces your sense of value, then with the failure will come pain. The next time you experience anxiety ask yourself what failure you sense may be about to occur.

Pride

When we base our self-worth on our performance and are successful, we often develop an inflated view of ourselves that leads to pride. Some of us may persist in this self-exaltation through any and all circumstances; for most of us, however, this sense of self-esteem lasts only until our next failure (or risk of failure). The self-confidence that most of us try to portray is only a facade to hide our fear of failure and insecurity.

Depression

Depression is generally a result of anger turned inward and/or a deep sense of loss. Experiencing failure and fearing subsequent failure can lead to deep depression. Once depressed, many become emotionally numb and passive in their actions, believing there is no hope for change. Occasionally, depressed people may also exhibit outbursts of anger resulting from failure. Generally, depression is the body's way of blocking psychological pain by numbing physical and emotional functions.

Low Motivation

Much of what is known as low motivation or laziness is better understood as hopelessness. If people believe they will fail, they have no reason to exert any effort. The pain they endure for their passivity seems relatively minor and acceptable compared to the agony of genuinely trying and failing.

Sexual Dysfunction

The emotional trauma caused by failure can cause disturbances in sexual activity. Then, rather than experience the pain of failing sexually, many tend to avoid sex altogether.

Chemical Dependency

Many people attempt to ease their pain and fear of failure by using drugs or alcohol. Those who abuse alcohol often do so with the false notion that it will increase their level of performance, thus enhancing their attempts at being successful. Alcohol, however, is a depressant and actually decreases the user's performance ability. Stimulants also are often used to increase productivity. Users of these drugs are likely to consume larger doses on an increasingly regular basis until they are addicted. This is because natural physiological processes deplete bodily resources during drug binges, so that when users come down from the chemical's high effect, they crash and are unable to rise to any occasion without it.

Taking a drink, like playing tennis, jogging, seeing a movie, or reading a book, can be a refreshing means of temporary escape. The problem is that chemical substances are addictive and often easily abused. What may have begun as a pleasurable means of temporary escape or an effort to remove pressures to perform ends with the despair of realizing an inability to cope without the substance. For those who find themselves trapped by chemical dependency, this pain-pleasure cycle continues, slowly draining life from its victim.

Because of their euphoric effect, alcohol or drugs may give us an illusion that we are on top of the world. But success, or the idea of success, regardless of how it is achieved, cannot dictate our sense of self-esteem.

In the case of chemical substances, cocaine users provide a clear example of this truth. A major reason for cocaine's popularity is its ability to produce feelings of greater self-esteem. However, it is interesting to note that a number of highly successful people use this drug. If success truly provided a greater sense of self-esteem, these people would probably not be in the market for the drug in the first place.

Addicted to Success

When J. Paul Getty was asked how much money one needs, he simply replied, "Only a little bit more." Only a little bit more is the motto of many people driven to succeed. Success can be a wonderful experience unless you are driven to it. Today's success never lasts much past midnight. Tomorrow you'll have to do it all over again. There is the next rung on the ladder to achieve. My friend Curt Dodd left pastoring a large church in Houston, Texas, to begin a church in Pueblo, Colorado. I can remember relating his story to many of my friends in the ministry and elsewhere. They were sure that no one would go from pastoring a large church to starting a church, especially in Pueblo, unless something was wrong at the previous church. I assured them over and over that he was doing this because God had directed him to do so. This lack of understanding says volumes about our general preoccupation with success: that it is being measured not by being obedient to God but through some external means.

Identity Entangled with Success

What good is success if other people do not know about it? There are two extremes when it comes to success. Some people make sure everyone knows about their success by the things and the lifestyle they possess. Others make sure they never enjoy the fruits of their success and believe that anyone who does is simply wrong.

Several years ago during the early years of Rapha I needed to see three individuals at three different locations in Los Angeles. If I left Houston at 5:00 A.M.., I might be able to see all of them, catch the last flight out, and be back home by 1:00 A.M. the next morning. Doing it this way, I could take my children to school the next morning. The only way to accomplish this was to use a car service that provided us an available limo, although I had not requested a limo. I just needed transportation.

Everything was fine until we pulled up in front of one of the largest ministries in existence then or now. It just so happened that the president of that ministry was looking out the window while we were getting out of the limo. He was certain that we were extravagant, and after that he would never have anything to do with Rapha. This holds true even today, though at our expense, Rapha has provided more churches with resources to help hurting people through small-group and support-group training than all the other ministries combined.

You can be preoccupied by success either in showing it or by taking pride in what you do not show.

Sense of Hopelessness

After several failures you can easily began to doubt your ability to make a good decision. However, there are few who have ever succeeded at anything who have not had to deal with the reality of their own failures and mistakes. When you determine not to make a mistake, it will paralyze you.

Anger at Ourselves and God

There is nothing quite as miserable as being angry at yourself, at having self-hatred. Unfortunately, your anger is not limited to yourself but will also be directed toward God. This does nothing more than alienate, isolate, and destroy the potential hope that you could receive something from God. It is not that He is not prepared to help you. It is that your anger will keep you from receiving that help.

As long as we operate according to Satan's lies, we are susceptible to the fear of failure. Our personal experience of this fear is determined by the difference between our performance standards and our ability to meet those standards.

Although we all will continue to experience the fear of failure to some degree, we must realize that as Christians, we have the power provided by the Holy Spirit to lay aside deceptive ways of thinking and be renewed in our minds by the truth of God's Word (Rom. 12:2, Eph. 4:21–25). For our benefit, God often allows us to experience circumstances that will enable us to recognize our blind adherence to Satan's deceptions. Many times these circumstances seem very negative, but through them, we can learn valuable, life-changing truths. In Psalm 107:33–36, we see a poetic example of this:

> *He changes rivers into a wilderness, and springs of water into a thirsty ground; a fruitful land into a salt waste, because of the wickedness of those who dwell in it. He changes a wilderness into a pool of water, and a dry land into springs of water; and there He makes the hungry to dwell, so that they may establish an inhabited city.*

Has your fruitful land become a salt waste? Maybe God is trying to get your attention to teach you a tremendously important lesson: that success or failure is not the basis of your self-worth. Maybe the only way you can learn this lesson is by experiencing the pain of failure. In His great love, God leads us through experiences that are difficult but essential to our growth and development

The more sensitive you become to the fear of failure and the problems it may cause, the more you will understand your own behavior as well as that of others.

4

God's Answer: Justification

When God considers you, does He deceive Himself in some way or does He know who you truly are?

If He knows who we truly are, then why do we preface His understanding of us with phrases such as "in God's eyes we are righteous" or "forgiven" or "loved" or "pleasing" and so on? Are we trying to say that God is not living in reality? That He is somehow involved in self-deception? Is He just some old grandparent type who wants to overlook the faults of His grandchildren? Either He really knows who you are or He doesn't. Playing with words this way keeps us from experiencing the reality of who we are. It also dishonors who God is.

The second question is, If you think of yourself differently than God thinks of you, who is mistaken, you or God? How often do we allow our minds to overrule what God says is true? Keep in mind, you were made by and for God. He has placed within you needs that only He can meet. If we try to have these needs met by another person or persons, we will end up frustrated, angry, and unfulfilled.

Consider this: Who do you talk to the most? Yourself, of course. What do you talk to yourself about the most? Yourself, of course. What is the main topic of the conversation you are having with yourself about yourself? Much of the time you think about how well you're doing based on your performance and others' opinions of you. How many times in your life have you used the formula:

Self-Worth = Performance + Others' Opinions

Let me demonstrate how this has affected us. A few years ago, I passed a golf course on a Friday afternoon. Often on Friday afternoon, men who are supposed to be at work are trying to get a head start on the weekend. Therefore, often the golf courses are fairly crowded. However, as I passed the course I saw something very unusual. It was a foursome (which I later learned was playing sub-par golf). The group was made up of two purple cows and two bright green elephants.

Now I can just imagine what has gone off in your head. There is a part of your thinking that said *Don't believe what you just read.* You have a belief of what animals look like and their capabilities. What I just told you was beyond what you know to be true.

When you equate your self-worth with performance and others' opinions, you are judging yourself based on a satanic formula designed to enslave you in the performance trap.

Thankfully, God has canceled this equation altogether! He has given us a secure self-worth totally apart from our ability to perform. We have been justified and placed in right standing before God through Christ's death on the cross, which paid for our sins. But God didn't stop with our forgiveness; He also granted us the very righteousness of Christ (2 Cor. 5:21)!

Visualize two ledgers: On one is a list of all your sins; on the other, the righteousness of Christ. Now exchange your ledger for Christ's. This exemplifies justification—transferring our sin to Christ and His righteousness to us. In 2 Corinthians 5:21, Paul wrote:

He made Him [Christ] who knew no sin to be sin on our behalf, that we might become the righteousness of God in Him.

I once heard a radio preacher berate his congregation for their hidden sins. He exclaimed, "Don't you know that someday you're going to die and God is going to flash all your sins upon a giant screen in heaven for all the world to see?" How tragically this minister misunderstood God's gracious gift of justification!

Justification carries no guilt with it and has no memory of past transgressions. Christ paid for all of our sins at the cross—past, present, and future. Hebrews 10:17 says, "And their sins and their lawless deeds I will remember no more." We are completely forgiven by God!

As marvelous as it is, justification means more than forgiveness of sins. In the same act of love through which God forgave our sins, He also provided for our righteousness, the worthiness to stand in God's presence. By imputing righteousness to us, God attributes Christ's worth to us. The moment we accept Christ, God declares that we are no longer condemned sinners. Instead, we are forgiven, we receive Christ's righteousness, and we are creatures who are fully pleasing to Him. God intended that Adam and his descendants be righteous people, fully experiencing His love and eternal purposes. Sin short-circuited that relationship, but Jesus' perfect payment for sin has since satisfied the righteous wrath of God, enabling us again to have that status of righteousness and to delight in knowing and honoring the Lord.

God desires for those of us who have been redeemed to experience the realities of His redemption. We are forgiven and righteous because of Christ's sacrifice; therefore, we are pleasing to God in spite of our failures. This reality can replace our fear of failure with peace, hope, and joy. Failure need not be a millstone around our necks. Neither success nor failure is the proper basis of our self-worth. Christ alone is the source of our forgiveness, freedom, joy, and purpose.

God works by *fiat,* meaning that He can create something from nothing by simply declaring it into existence. God spoke, and the world was formed. He said, "Let there be light," and light appeared. The earth is no longer void because God sovereignly created its abundance. In the same way, we *were* condemned, but *now* we are declared righteous! Romans 5:1 refers to us as having been justified by faith, a statement in the past perfect tense. Therefore, if we have trusted in Christ for our salvation, we each can say with certainty, "I am completely forgiven and am fully pleasing to God."

Some people have difficulty thinking of themselves as being pleasing to God because they link being pleasing so strongly with performance. They tend to be displeased with anything short of perfection in themselves and suspect that God has the same standard.

The point of justification is that we can never achieve perfection on this earth; even our best efforts at self-righteousness are as filthy rags to God (Isa. 64:6). Yet He loves us so much that He appointed His Son to pay for our sins and give to us His own righteousness, His perfect status before the Father.

This doesn't mean that our actions are irrelevant and that we can sin all we want. Our sinful actions, words, and attitudes grieve the Lord, but our status as holy and beloved children remains intact. In His love, He disciplines and encourages us to live godly lives—for our good and for His honor.

The apostle Paul was so enamored with his forgiveness and righteousness in Christ that he was intensely motivated to please God by his actions and his deeds. In 1 Corinthians 6:19–20, 2 Corinthians 5:9, Philippians 3:8–11, and other passages, Paul strongly stated his desire to please, honor, and glorify the One who had made him righteous.

If we know who we are, we will not try to become someone else in order to have value and meaning in our lives. If we don't know who we are, we *will* try to become someone who someone else wants us to be!

Possible Obstacles to Receiving the Truth

As wonderful as it is to be pleasing to God, as much peace and joy this would bring to our lives, what are our internal obstacles that keep us from reaching out and grasping this reality?

Addiction to the Approval of Others

Because other people can give us such approval when we are successful and because we are addicted to obtaining that approval, we often do not want to live only on the approval based on what Christ provided for us. It is not that we should not enjoy the approval of others. The problem is when we have to have it in order to live in peace and joy. (We will cover this in the next chapter.)

Our natural strengths will always fight against our dependence on God. It will be painful to consider that we have a bit of pride about us. We may not even like to realize that we have been looking down on someone because we have outperformed them. But the fact is that there are times when we enjoy our success to the degree that we don't want to live our lives based on what God has done for us. We may even look down on those who have failed and consider ourselves above those failures. I have met many Christian women who were overcoming the tragedy of a divorce. However, the greatest struggle they had was that they had been so critical previously of other women who had gone through divorce themselves. They had considered those women such failures, and now they considered themselves in the same way. They had often told others how they felt about those divorced women.

This is an excellent example of how we will always have an opportunity to walk in the same condemnation and judgment we have issued toward others. The next time you are tempted to look down on someone, realize that you are capable of going through the very same experience.

Sense of Hopelessness
A sense of hopelessness can either drive us to depend on God or drive us into passivity. We will never know the victory that God has for us when we are passive. God's way is for us to actively cooperate with Him.

Wanting to Live Life by Some Formula
Some of us only know our faith as a series of rules or steps. In order for you to experience what Christ has provided through justification, you must receive it through your relationship with Him, not by performing some ritual.

Need to Control

Most of us have a priority system that goes something like this: air, water, food, control. We can hardly stand not to be in control. However, if we are going to base our worth on what Christ did for us, then we will sense a loss of control. This will be a greater struggle than you probably anticipate. Several years ago, I was struggling with some issues. I was angry that God had allowed these issues to come up. I told Him, "I don't want to have to trust You on another issue. Why is this happening?" The Father replied, "Who do you want to trust?" It didn't take me long to confess that I was glad that He was there to trust, for indeed, He was the only One in my life who was absolutely trustworthy. It gave me great motivation for obedience.

Again, we will never achieve perfection on this earth, yet we are justified through Christ's righteousness. Some people may read statements about justification and become uneasy, believing that I am discounting the gravity of sin. As you will see, I am not minimizing the destructive nature of sin but simply trying to elevate our view of the results of Christ's payment on the cross. Understanding our complete forgiveness and acceptance before God does not promote a casual attitude toward sin. On the contrary, it gives us a greater desire to live for and serve the One who died to free us from sin. Let's look at some strong reasons to obey and serve God with joy.

Reasons for Obedience

The love of God and His acceptance of us is based on grace, His unmerited favor. It is not based on our ability to impress God through our good deeds. But if we are accepted on the basis of His grace and not our deeds, why should we obey God? Here are six compelling reasons to obey Him:

1. *Christ's Love*

Understanding God's grace compels us to action because love motivates us to please the One who has so freely loved us. When we experience love, we usually respond by seeking to express our love in return. Our obedience to God is an expression of our love for Him (John 14:15, 21), which comes from an understanding of what Christ has accomplished for us on the cross (2 Cor. 5:14–15). We love because He first loved us and clearly demonstrated His love for us at the cross (1 John 4:16–19). Understanding this will highly motivate us.

This great motivating factor is missing in many of our lives because we don't really believe that God loves us unconditionally. We expect His love to be conditional, based on our ability to earn it. Our experience of God's love is based on our perception. If we believe that He is demanding or aloof, we will not be able to receive His love and tenderness. Instead, we will either be afraid of Him or angry with Him. Faulty perceptions of God often prompt us to rebel against Him. Our image of God is the foundation for all of our motivations. As we grow in our understanding of His unconditional love and acceptance, we will be better able to grasp that His discipline is prompted by care, not cruelty. We will also be increasingly able to perceive the contrast between the joys of living for Christ and the destructive nature of sin. We will be motivated to experience eternal rewards where neither moth nor rust destroys (Matt. 6:20). And we will want our lives to bring honor to the One who loves us so much.

2. Sin Is Destructive

Satan has effectively blinded man to the painful, damaging consequences of sin. The effects of sin are all around us, yet many continue to indulge in the sex, status- and pleasure-seeking, and rampant self-centeredness that cause so much anguish and pain. Satan contradicted God in the Garden when he said, "You surely shall not die!" (Gen. 3:4). Sin is pleasant but only for a season. Sooner or later, sin will result in some form of destruction.

Sin is destructive in many ways. Emotionally, we may experience the pain of guilt and shame and the fear of failure and punishment. Mentally, we may experience the anguish of flashbacks. We may also expend enormous amounts of time and energy thinking about our sins and rationalizing our guilt. Physically, we may suffer from psychosomatic illnesses or experience pain through physical abuse. Sin may also result in the loss of property or even the loss of life. Relationally, we can alienate ourselves from others. Spiritually, we grieve the Holy Spirit, lose our testimony, and break our fellowship with God. The painful and destructive effects of sin are so profound that why we don't have an aversion to it is a mystery!

3. The Father's Discipline

Our loving Father has given us the Holy Spirit to convict us of sin. Conviction is a form of God's discipline and serves as proof that we have become children of God (Heb. 12:5–11). It warns us against making choices without regard to either God's truth or sin's consequences. If we choose to be unresponsive to the Holy Spirit, our heavenly Father will discipline us in love. Many people do not understand the difference between discipline and punishment. The following chart shows their profound contrasts:

	PUNISHMENT	DISCIPLINE
Source:	God's wrath	God's love
Purpose:	To avenge a wrong	To correct a wrong
Relational result:	Alienation	Reconciliation
Personal result:	Guilt	A righteous lifestyle
Directed toward:	Nonbelievers	His children

On the cross, Jesus bore all the punishment we deserved; therefore we no longer need to fear punishment from God for our sins. We should seek to do what is right so that our Father will not have to correct us through discipline, but when we are disciplined, we should remember that God is correcting us in love. This discipline leads us to righteous performance, a reflection of Christ's righteousness in us.

4. His Commands for Us Are Good

God's commands are given for two good purposes: to protect us from the destructiveness of sin and to direct us into a life of joy and fruitfulness. We have a wrong perspective if we only view God's commands as restrictions in our lives. Instead, we must realize that His commands are guidelines, given so that we might enjoy life to the fullest. Obedience to God's commands should never be considered as a means to gain His approval.

In today's society, we have lost the concept of doing something because it is the right thing to do. Instead, we do things in exchange for some reward or favor, or to avoid punishment. Wouldn't it be novel to do something simply because it is the right thing to do? God's commands are holy, right, and good, and the Holy Spirit gives us the wisdom and strength to keep them. Therefore, since they have value in themselves, we can choose to obey God and follow His commands.

5. Eternal Rewards

Yet another compelling reason to live for God's glory is the fact that we will be rewarded in heaven for our service to Him. Two passages clearly illustrate this fact:

> *For we must all appear before the judgment seat of Christ, that each one may be recompensed for his deeds in the body, according to what he has done, whether good or bad. (2 Cor. 5:10)*

> *Now if any man builds upon the foundation with gold, silver, precious stones, wood, hay, straw, each man's work will become evident; for the day will show it, because it is to be revealed with fire; and the fire itself will test the quality of each man's work. If any man's work which he has built upon it remains, he shall receive a reward. If any man's work is burned up, he shall suffer loss; but he himself shall be saved, yet so as through fire. (1 Cor. 3:12–15)*

Through Christ's payment for us on the cross, we have escaped eternal judgment; however, our actions will be judged at the judgment seat of Christ. There, our performance will be evaluated and rewards presented for service to God. Rewards will be given for deeds that reflect a desire to honor Christ, but deeds performed in an attempt to earn God's acceptance, earn the approval of others, or meet our own standards will be rejected by God and consumed by fire.

6. *Christ Is Worthy*

Our most noble motivation for serving Christ is simply that He is worthy of our love and obedience. The apostle John recorded his vision of the Lord and his response to His glory:

> After these things I looked, and behold, a door standing open in heaven, and the first voice which I had heard, like the sound of a trumpet speak within me, said, "Come up here, and I will show you what must take place after these things." Immediately I was in the spirit; and behold, a throne was standing in heaven, and One sitting on the throne. And He who was sitting was like a jasper stone and a sardius in appearance; and there was a rainbow around the throne, like an emerald in appearance. And around the throne were twenty-four thrones; and upon the thrones I saw twenty-four elders sitting, clothed in white garments, and golden crowns on their heads. . . . And when the living creatures give glory and honor and thanks to Him who sits on the throne, to Him who lives forever and ever, the twenty-four elders will fall down before Him who sits on the throne, and will worship Him who lives forever and ever, and will cast their crowns before the throne, saying, "Worthy art Thou, our Lord and our God, to receive glory and honor and power; for Thou didst create all things, and because of Thy will they existed, and were created." (Rev. 4:1–4, 9–11)

Christ is worthy of our affection and obedience. There is no other person, no goal, no fame or status, and no material possession that can compare with Him. The more we understand His love and majesty, the more we will praise Him and desire that He be honored at the expense of everything else. Our hearts will reflect the psalmist's perspective: "Whom have I in heaven but Thee? And besides Thee, I desire nothing on earth. . . . But as for me, the nearness of God is my good; I have made the Lord God my refuge. That I may tell of all Thy works" (Ps. 73:25, 28).

Summary

We obey God because:

1. Christ's love motivates us to live for Him.

2. Sin is destructive and should be avoided.

3. Our Father lovingly disciplines us for wrongdoing.

4. His commands for us are good.

5. We will receive eternal rewards for obedience.

6. He is worthy of our obedience.

Obeying Christ for these reasons is not a self-improvement program. The Holy Spirit gives us encouragement, wisdom, and strength as we grow in our desire to honor the Lord.

5

Approval Addict

I must be approved by certain others to feel good about myself.

How much of your life have you wasted trying to gain the approval of others?

Our self-concept is determined not only by how we view ourselves but by how we think others perceive us. Basing our self-worth on what we believe others think of us causes us to become addicted to their approval. Randy felt like a vending machine. Anyone wanting something could pull an invisible lever and get it. On the job, Randy was always doing other people's work for them. At home, his friends continually called on him to help them with odd jobs. His wife had him working weekends so that she could continue in the lifestyle to which she had grown accustomed. Even people in Randy's church took advantage of him, knowing that they could count on "good old Randy" to head a number of the programs they planned. What was the problem? Was Randy simply a self-sacrificing saint? On the surface, yes; in reality, no. Randy deeply resented those people who, by demanding so much from him, left him little time for himself. Yet he just couldn't say no. He longed for the approval of others and believed that by agreeing to their every wish he would win that approval.

Randy typifies many of us. We spend much of our time building relationships, striving to please people and win their respect. And yet, after all of our sincere, conscientious effort, it takes only one unappreciative word from someone to ruin our sense of self-worth. How quickly an insensitive word can destroy the self-assurance we've worked so hard to achieve!

The world we live in is filled with people who demand that we please them in exchange for their approval and acceptance. Such demands often lead us directly to a second false belief: *I must be approved by certain others to feel good about myself.*

We are snared by this lie in many subtle ways. Believing it causes us to bow to peer pressure in an effort to gain approval. We may join clubs and organizations, hoping to find a place of acceptance for ourselves. We often identify ourselves with social groups, believing that being with others like ourselves will assure our acceptance and their approval. Many people have admitted that their experimentation with drugs or sex is a reaction to their need to belong. However, drugs and sexual promiscuity promise something they can't fulfill, and experimentation only results in pain and, usually, a deeper need for self-worth and acceptance.

Another symptom of our fear of rejection is our inability to give and receive love. We find it difficult to open up and reveal our inner thoughts and motives because we believe that others will reject us if they know what we are really like. Therefore, our fear of rejection leads us to superficial relationships or isolation. The more we experience isolation, the more we need acceptance. Psychologist Eric Fromm once wrote, "The deep need of man is the need to overcome separateness, to leave the prison of his aloneness."

The fear of rejection is rampant, and loneliness is one of the most dangerous and widespread problems in America today. Some estimate that loneliness has already reached epidemic proportions and say that if it continues to spread, it could seriously erode the emotional strength of our country. Loneliness is not relegated only to unbelievers. Ninety-two percent of the Christians attending a recent Bible conference admitted in a survey that feelings of loneliness are a major problem in their lives. All shared a basic symptom: a sense of despair at feeling unloved and a fear of being unwanted or unaccepted. This is a tragic commentary on the people about whom Christ said: "By this all men will know that you are My disciples, if you have love for one another" (John 13:35).

For the most part, our modern society has responded inadequately to rejection and loneliness. Our response has been outer-directed, meaning that we try to copy the customs, dress, ideas, and behavioral patterns of a particular group, allowing the consensus of the group to determine what is correct for us. But conforming to a group will not fully provide the security we are so desperately seeking. Only God can provide that through His people, His Word, His Spirit, and His timing. Turning to others for what only God can provide is a direct result of our acceptance of Satan's lie: Self-Worth = Performance + Others' Opinions.

Living according to the false belief *I must be approved by certain others to feel good about myself* causes us to fear rejection, conforming virtually all of our attitudes and actions to the expectations of others. How are you affected by this belief? Take the following test to determine how strongly you fear rejection.

Fear of Rejection Test

Read each of the following statements; then, from the top of the test, choose the term that best describes your response. Put the number above that term in the blank beside each statement.

1	2	3	4	5	6	7
Always	Very Often	Often	Sometimes	Seldom	Very Seldom	Never

___ 1. I avoid certain people.

___ 2. When I sense that someone might reject me, I become nervous and anxious.

___ 3. I am uncomfortable around those who are different from me.

___ 4. It bothers me when someone is unfriendly to me.

___ 5. I am basically shy and unsocial.

___ 6. I am critical of others.

___ 7. I find myself trying to impress others.
___ 8. I become depressed when someone criticizes me.
___ 9. I always try to determine what people think of me.
___ 10. I don't understand people and what motivates them.

___   Total (Add up the numbers you have placed in the blanks.)

If your score is:

57–70: God has apparently given you a very strong appreciation for His love and unconditional acceptance. You seem to be freed from the fear of rejection that plagues most people. (Some people who score this high either are greatly deceived or have become callous to their emotions as a way to suppress pain.)

47–56: The fear of rejection controls your responses rarely or only in certain situations. Again, the only major exceptions are those who are not honest with themselves.

37–46: When you experience emotional problems, they may relate to a sense of rejection. Upon reflection, you will probably relate many of your previous decisions to this fear. Many of your future decisions will also be affected by the fear of rejection unless you take direct action to overcome it.

27–36: The fear of rejection forms a general backdrop to your life. There are probably few days that you are not affected in some way by this fear. Unfortunately, this robs you of the joy and peace your salvation is meant to bring.

0–26: Experiences of rejection dominate your memory and have probably resulted in a great deal of depression. These problems will remain until some definitive action is taken. In other words, this condition will not simply disappear; time alone cannot heal your pain. You need to experience deep healing in your self-concept, in your relationship with God, and in your relationships with others.

Effects of the Fear of Rejection

Virtually all of us fear rejection. We can fall prey to it even when we've learned to harden our defenses in anticipation of someone's disapproval. Neither being defensive nor trying to please another person's every whim is the answer to this problem. These are only coping mechanisms that prevent us from dealing with the root of our fear. Rejection is a type of communication. It conveys a message that someone else is unsatisfactory to us, that he or she doesn't measure up to a standard we've created or adopted. Sometimes, rejection is willfully used as an act of manipulation designed to control someone else. Usually, rejection is manifested by an outburst of anger, a disgusted look, an impatient answer, or a social snub. Whatever the form of behavior, it communicates disrespect, low value, and lack of appreciation. Nothing hurts quite like the message of rejection.

If this is true, why do we reject others so frequently? Again, rejection can be a very effective, though destructive, motivation. Without lifting a finger, we can send the message that our targeted individual doesn't meet our standards. We can harness this person's instinctive desire for acceptance until we have changed and adapted his or her behavior to suit our tastes and purposes. This is how rejection enables us to control the actions of another human being.

Many misguided preachers have used rejection and guilt as a forceful means of motivation. They expound upon our weaknesses, our failures, our unworthiness, and our inability to measure up to Christ's high standards. Not only is our performance declared unworthy, but we are left feeling denounced, devalued, and devastated. As a result, thousands who have been broken by this rejection have left the church without understanding Christ's accepting, unconditional love, a love that never uses condemnation to correct behavior.

However, rejection and guilt are only effective motivations as long as people are near us. This is why certain parental techniques of guilt motivation produce results only until the child matures and gains more freedom. With freedom, the child is able to remove himself or herself physically from the parents. Unrestrained, the child then can do as he or she pleases.

In this instance, both the parents and the child need to experience God's love and forgiveness. His grace and power can give understanding and strength, so that they can forgive each other, forgive themselves, and exhibit strong, loving relationships.

Another damaging result of rejection is isolation. Michael, for example, was raised in a broken home and had lived with his father since he was six years old. It wasn't that Michael's father wanted him, but his mother was too busy to care for him. Shortly after the divorce, Michael's father married another woman with three children. She began to resent spending any time or effort on Michael. She favored her own children at his expense.

It was no surprise, then, that when Michael grew up and married a beautiful girl who truly loved him, he was cautious about sharing his love with her. Michael had experienced the pain of rejection all of his life, and now, because he feared rejection, he withheld his love from someone he truly cared for. Michael was afraid of becoming too close to his wife, because if she rejected him, the pain would be too much for him to bear.

How do you react to the fear of rejection? Some of us project a cool, impervious exterior and, consequently, never develop deep, satisfying relationships. Some of us are so fearful of rejection that we withdraw and decline almost everything, while others continually say yes to everyone, hoping to gain their approval. Some of us are shy and easily manipulated; some of us are sensitive to criticism and react defensively. A deep fear of rejection may prompt hostility and promote the development of nervous disorders. Our fear of rejection will control us to the degree by which we base our self-worth on the opinions of others rather than on our relationship with God. Our dependence on others for value brings bondage, while abiding in the truths of Christ's love and acceptance brings freedom and joy. In Galatians 1:10, Paul clearly drew the line concerning our search for approval:

> *For am I now seeking the favor of men, or of God? Or am I striving to please men? If I were still trying to please men, I would not be a bond-servant of Christ.*

According to this passage, we can ultimately seek either the approval of men or the approval of God as the basis of our self-worth. We cannot seek both. God wants to be the Lord of our lives, and He is unwilling to share that rightful lordship with anyone else. Therefore, the only way we can overcome the fear of rejection is to value the constant approval of God over the conditional approval of people.

My desire for the approval of others has often been so great that I sometimes joke about having been born an "approval addict." Growing up, I had the feeling that I didn't fit in; that I was *different* from others; that there was, therefore, something inherently wrong with me. I felt inadequate and tried to win the approval of others, desperately hoping that this would compensate for the negative feelings I had about myself. But ironically, the conditional approval of others was never enough to satisfy me. Instead, being praised only reminded me of the disapproval I might encounter if I failed to maintain what I had achieved. I was thus compelled to work even harder at being successful. I occasionally find myself falling into this pattern of behavior even now, despite my improved knowledge, experience, and relationship with God.

Many people may be surprised to learn this, perhaps assuming that reading this book and completing its exercises will forever liberate them from the propensity to base their self-worth on the approval of others. I don't believe that any of us will gain complete freedom from this tendency until we see the Lord. Our God-given instinct to survive compels us to avoid pain. Knowing that rejection and disapproval bring pain, we will continue our attempts to win the esteem of others whenever possible. The good news is that because we are fully pleasing to God, a fact we will examine later in this chapter, we need not be devastated when others respond to us in a negative way.

As we grow in our relationship with God, the Holy Spirit will continue teaching us how to apply this liberating truth to different aspects of our lives at an increasingly deeper level. In fact, one evidence of His work within us is the ability to see new areas of our lives in which we are allowing the opinions of others to determine our sense of worth. With spiritual maturity, we will more often be able to identify these areas and choose to find our significance in God's unconditional love for us and complete acceptance of us. However, profound changes in our value system take honesty, objectivity, and prolonged, persistent application of God's Word.

Before we examine God's solution to our fear of failure, we must first identify and understand how this fear is manifested in our lives. Similar to the fear of failure, the fear of rejection can affect us in many ways. The explanations of the following symptoms are not exhaustive but are intended to demonstrate how rejection can trigger certain problems in our lives.

Anger, Resentment, Hostility

Anger is usually our most common response to rejection. Some of us are not honest about our anger. We may deny its existence, suppress it, and assume that it will go away. We may vent our anger in destructive explosions of wrath. Or we may use sarcasm or neglect to express anger in a more subtle way. If we don't resolve our anger through honesty and forgiveness, we can become deeply hostile and resentful. One motive for retaining anger is the desire for revenge.

How many of the people with whom you are angry or by whom you have been hurt hold an opinion of you that is less than you would hope they would? How many people would you like to somehow change their opinion of you? Why do we hold the opinions of others in such high regard that we allow their opinion of us to influence how we feel about ourselves? Why do we spend so much time thinking about those who do not hold us in high regard?

Because we value the opinions of others so much, when they do not think of us as they should, it hurts. And because it hurts we get angry, become resentful, and may even become bitter.

Being Easily Manipulated

Those who believe that their self-worth is based on the approval of others are likely to do virtually anything to please people. They truly believe that they will be well liked if they agree to every request of those who are, consciously or not, manipulating them. Many of these people despise those who are being manipulative and resent what they feel they have to do to earn their approval.

Codependency

In families affected by dependency on alcohol, drugs, work, or any other compulsion, family members often develop behavioral patterns to rescue the dependent person from the consequences of his or her behavior. This compulsive rescuing, called codependency, allows the dependent person to continue acting destructively and keeps him or her in need of being habitually rescued, so that the pattern continues.

Avoiding People

One of the most common ways people react to their fear of rejection is to avoid others, thereby avoiding the risk of rejection. Some people avoid others overtly, spending most of their time alone, but most people try to avoid the risk of rejection by having superficial relationships. They may interact with others, and they may be considered socially adept because they know how to make friends easily; but their friends never really know them because they hide behind a wall of words, smiles, and activities. These people are usually quite lonely in the midst of all their so-called friends.

Control

In an effort to avoid being hurt, some people constantly try to maintain control of others and dominate the situations they face. They have become skilled in exercising control by dispensing approval or disapproval, unwilling to let others be themselves and make their own decisions without their consent. Because such people are actually very insecure, lack of control is an unacceptable threat to them.

Depression

Depression is the result of a deep sense of loss or repressed, pent-up anger. When anger is not handled properly, the body and mind respond to its intense pressure, and the emotions and sense of purpose become dulled.

Repeat Negative Messages

One of the most interesting facets of our behavior is that we often repeat the messages that hurt the most. We do this even after the person who delivered the message the first time is no longer there—perhaps even dead. We continue to repeat to ourselves the most hurtful messages we have heard. How much of the pain you experience is related to your repeating these hurtful, negative messages?

Hypersensitivity to the Opinions of Others

Are you always vigilant concerning what others might think of you? Do you find yourself trying to anticipate their thoughts? Do you worry about what even absolute strangers might be thinking of you? How much time do you spend thinking about what other people might be thinking about you?

Many times people actually project their own negative feelings about themselves on others around them. In this way, wherever they go, they feel rejected by others. They find people who reject them in the same place that others find people who are very accepting of everyone.

Hyposensitivity

Some people are so fearful of their own emotions that they do not allow themselves to be sensitive to others or to themselves. They simply approach life as though they were an actor in a play. An actor simply fulfills a role. The actor may appear to be responding to the situation. But on closer inspection, one finds that he or she is just delivering rehearsed lines and going through preordained activities. Unfortunately many of us find ourselves in such a situation.

We experience the fear of rejection and its accompanying problems because we believe Satan's lie: Self-Worth = Performance + Others' Opinions.

We crave love, fellowship, and intimacy, and we turn to others to meet those needs. The problem with basing our worth on the approval of others is that God is the only One who loves and appreciates us unconditionally. He has provided a solution to the fear of rejection.

6

God's Answer: Reconciliation

Have you given up on experiencing God's complete acceptance of you?

Can God accept a person who is unacceptable (because of sin), or does He have to make that person completely acceptable (through salvation) first?

Is Christ's payment sufficient enough to keep you acceptable to God for the rest of your life and beyond?

God's solution to the fear of rejection is based on Christ's sacrificial payment for our sins. Through this payment, we find forgiveness, reconciliation, and total acceptance through Christ. Reconciliation means that those who were enemies have become friends. Paul described our transformation from enmity to friendship with God:

And although you were formerly alienated and hostile in mind, engaged in evil deeds, yet He has now reconciled you in His fleshly body through death, in order to present you before Him holy and blameless and beyond reproach. (Col. 1:21–22)

As I talked with Pam, it became obvious that she did not understand this great truth of reconciliation. Three years after her marriage, Pam had committed adultery with a coworker. Although she had confessed her sin to God and to her husband and had been forgiven, guilt continued to plague her. She found that it was difficult for her to feel acceptable to God. Four years after the affair, she still could not forgive herself for what she had done. Sitting in my office, we explored her reluctance to accept God's forgiveness. "It sounds as though you believe that God can't forgive the sin you committed," I said. "That's right," she replied. "I don't think He ever will." "But God doesn't base His love and acceptance of us on our performance," I said. "If any sin is so filthy and vile that it makes us less acceptable to Him, then the cross is insufficient. If the cross isn't sufficient for all sin, then the Bible is in error when it says that He forgave all your sins [Col. 2:13–15]. God took our sins and canceled them by nailing them to Christ's cross. In this way, God also took away Satan's power to condemn us for sin. So you see, nothing you will ever do can nullify your reconciliation and make you unacceptable to God."

Our unconditional acceptance in Christ is a profound, life-changing truth. Salvation is not simply a ticket to heaven. It is the beginning of a dynamic new relationship with God. *Justification* is the doctrine that explains the judicial facts of our forgiveness and righteousness in Christ. *Reconciliation* explains the relational aspect of our salvation. The moment we receive Christ by faith, we enter into a personal relationship with Him. We are united with God in an eternal and inseparable bond (Rom. 8:38–39). We are bound in an indissoluble union with Him, as fellow heirs with Christ. The Holy Spirit has sealed us in that relationship, and we are absolutely secure in Christ.

Ephesians 1:13–14 states:

> *Having also believed, you were sealed in Him with the Holy Spirit of promise, who is given as a pledge of our inheritance, with a view to the redemption of God's own possession, to the praise of His glory.*

Recently, in a group prayer meeting, someone prayed, "Thank you, God, for accepting me when I am so unacceptable." This person understood that we cannot earn God's acceptance by our own merit, but this person also seemed to have forgotten that we are unconditionally accepted in Christ. We are no longer unacceptable. The point of the cross is that through Christ's death and resurrection, we have become acceptable to God. This did not occur because God decided He could overlook our sin. It occurred because Christ forgave all of our sins so that He could present us to the Father, holy, blameless, and beyond reproach.

There is no greater theme in Scripture than the reconciliation of man to God. Study the following passages then answer the question after each one. Allow God to speak to you as you read His Word. Doing this provides a critical foundation for this entire book.

As far as the east is from the west, so far has He removed our transgressions from us. (Ps. 103:12)

What happens to our transgressions?

For this is My blood of the covenant, which is to be shed on behalf of many for forgiveness of sins. (Matt. 26:28)

Why was Christ's blood shed?

For God so loved the world, that He gave His only begotten Son, that whoever believes in Him should not perish, but have eternal life. (John 3:16)

What is God's promise?

Truly, truly, I say to you, he who hears My word, and believes Him who sent Me, has eternal life, and does not come into judgment, but has passed out of death into life. (John 5:24)

What is the promise to the person who knows and believes?

My sheep hear My voice, and I know them, and they follow Me; and I give eternal life to them, and they shall never perish; and no one shall snatch them out of My hand. (John 10:27–29)

What do His sheep have? Will they perish?

Of Him all the prophets bear witness that through His name every one who believes in Him receives forgiveness of sins. (Acts 10:43)

Of what did the prophets bear witness?

And through Him everyone who believes is freed from all things, from which you could not be freed through the Law of Moses. (Acts 13:39)

What does belief do?

For all have sinned and fall short of the glory of God, being justified as a gift by His grace through the redemption which is in Christ Jesus (Rom. 3:23–24)

By what are we justified?

Blessed are those whose lawless deeds have been forgiven, and whose sins have been covered. (Rom. 4:7)

Who is blessed?

For if while we were enemies, we were reconciled to God through the death of His Son, much more, having been reconciled, we shall be saved by His life. (Rom. 5:10)

Through what are we reconciled?

For you have not received a spirit of slavery leading to fear again, but you have received a spirit of adoption as sons by which we cry out, "Abba! Father!" (Rom. 8:15–17)

Describe the nature of our relationship with God.

Who will bring a charge against God's elect? God is the one who justifies. (Rom. 8:33)

Who shall accuse us?

For I am convinced that neither death, nor life, nor angels, nor principalities, nor things present, nor things to come, nor powers, nor height, nor depth, nor any other created thing, shall be able to separate us from the love of God, which is in Christ Jesus our Lord. (Rom. 8:38–39)

Of what is Paul convinced?

Therefore if any man is in Christ, he is a new creature; the old things passed away; behold, new things have come. . . . namely, that God was in Christ reconciling the world to Himself not counting their trespasses against them, and He has committed to us the word of reconciliation. . . . He made Him who knew no sin to be sin on our behalf, that we might become the righteousness of God in Him. (2 Cor. 5:17,19,21)

Describe what we are in Christ.

Nevertheless knowing that a man is not justified by the works of the Law but through faith in Christ Jesus, even we have believed in Christ Jesus, that we may be justified by faith in Christ, and not by the works of the Law; since by the works of the Law shall no flesh be justified. (Gal. 2:16)

On what basis are we justified? What part do works play in justification?

Even so Abraham believed God, and it was reckoned to him as righteousness. (Gal. 3:6)

On what basis did Abraham receive righteousness?

In Him we have redemption through His blood, the forgiveness of our trespasses, according to the riches of His grace. (Eph. 1:7)

According to what do we receive forgiveness?

For by grace you have been saved through faith; and that not of yourselves, it is the gift of God; not as a result of works, that no one should boast. (Eph. 2:8–9)

On what basis can we boast?

And according to the Law, one may almost say, all things are cleansed with blood, and without shedding of blood there is no forgiveness. (Heb. 9:22)

What would you have to do in order to receive forgiveness?

Now where there is forgiveness of these things, there is no longer any offering for sin. (Heb. 10:18)

After forgiveness, what is to be our offering for sin?

Fixing our eyes on Jesus, the author and perfecter of faith, who for the joy set before Him endured the cross, despising the

*shame, and has sat down at the right hand of the throne of God.
(Heb. 12:2)*

Who is the perfecter of our faith?

*Blessed be the God and Father of our Lord Jesus Christ, who
according to His great mercy has caused us to be born again to a
living hope through the resurrection of Jesus Christ from the dead,
to obtain an inheritance which is imperishable and undefiled and
will not fade away, reserved in heaven for you. (1 Pet. 1:3–4)*

Of what is Peter convinced?

Because of reconciliation, we are completely acceptable *to* and *by*
God. As these passages illustrate, we enjoy a full and complete relationship with Him, and in this relationship, His determination of our
value is not based on our performance. However, we may question
what this relationship means as we attempt to apply it in our day-to-
day experience. Let's analyze this issue: When we are born again as
spiritual beings in right standing with God, we are still tilted
toward the world's way of thinking. Because we have been conditioned by the world's perspective and values, we find it hard to
break away. Indeed, when Paul wrote the Christians at Corinth, he
called them men of flesh. Though born of the Spirit and equipped
with all provisions in Christ, these individuals had yet to develop
into the complete, mature believers God intended them to be (see
1 Cor. 3:1–4).

Many of us are like the Christians at Corinth. We still try to
obtain our significance the world's way, through success and
approval. Often, we look only to other believers rather than to
Christ Himself. We learn to use the right Christian words, claim
divine power and guidance, and organize programs, and yet so
often, our spiritual facade lacks depth and substance. Our spiritual
activities become human efforts lacking the real touch of the
Master. In effect, we live a lie.

The desire for success and approval constitutes the basis of an addictive, worldly self-worth. Certainly, withdrawal from this dependency may cause us some pain as we change the basis of our self-worth, yet we will begin to discover true freedom and maturity in Christ only when we understand that our lives mean much more than what success or the approval of others can bring.

We can do nothing to contribute to Christ's free gift of salvation; furthermore, if we base our self-worth on the approval of others, then we are actually saying that our ability to please others is of greater value than Christ's payment. We are the sinners, the depraved, the wretched, and the helpless. He is the loving Father, the seeking, searching, patient Savior who has made atonement for the lost and has extended to us His grace and sonship. We add nothing to our salvation. It is God who seeks us out, convicts us of sin, and reveals Himself to us. It is God who gives us the very faith with which to accept Him. Our faith is simply our response to what He has done for us.

So then, our worth lies in the fact that Christ's blood has paid for our sins; therefore, we are reconciled to God. We are accepted on that basis alone, but does this great truth indicate that we don't need other people in our lives? On the contrary. God very often uses other believers to demonstrate His love and acceptance of us. The strength, comfort, encouragement, and love of Christians toward one another are visible expressions of God's love. However, our acceptance and worth are not dependent on others' acceptance of us, even if they are fellow believers! Whether they accept us or not, we are still deeply loved, completely forgiven, fully pleasing, totally accepted, and complete in Christ. He alone is the final authority on our worth and acceptance.

Potential Obstacles to Receiving This Truth

The Role of Relationships
For many of us, the unconditional love, forgiveness, and acceptance of Christ seems abstract, and is difficult to comprehend. We

may understand the premise of these character traits but may still be unable to incorporate them into our personal experience. Often, we can trace this difficulty to our parental relationships.

God intends for parents to model His character to their children. According to Scripture, parents are to give their children affection, compassion, protection, provision, and loving discipline. When parents provide this kind of environment in their home, children are usually able to transfer these perceptions to the character of God and believe that He is loving, compassionate, protective, gracious, and a loving disciplinarian. In turn, they are often able to model these characteristics to their own children.

Many of us, however, have not received this parental model of God's character. On an extremely wide spectrum, some of us have had relatively healthy relationships with our parents while others have experienced various forms of neglect, condemnation, and manipulation. Still others have suffered the deeper wounds of sexual abuse, physical abuse, or abandonment. The greater the degree of dysfunction (or poor modeling) in a family, the greater the potential for emotional, spiritual, and relational wounds. Put another way, the poorer the parental modeling of God's love, forgiveness, and power, the greater our difficulty in experiencing and applying these characteristics in our lives.

Instead of being refreshed by the truth of God's love, if we have been deeply wounded, we may recoil from it, believing that we are unlovable. We may be fearful of reaching out and being hurt again. Whatever the cause, the result is withdrawal from the very idea of being loved and accepted.

Those who have received poor parental modeling need new models—loving Christian friends to experience the love and grace of God. Through His body of believers, God often provides us with models of His love, so that our perception of His character can be slowly reshaped into one that is more accurate, resulting in a healthier relationship with Him. Then our deep emotional, spiritual, and relational wounds can begin to heal, and we can more fully experience God's unconditional love. Some of us are already involved in strong relationships with people who are understanding and patient with us; some of us haven't yet been able to cultivate relationships like these, and we are still looking. If this is your situation, you may need to find a pastor or counselor who can help you get started, possibly by directing you to one or more believers who can minister to you. A small fellowship group or Bible study is often an excellent resource for intimate sharing, comfort, and encouragement. If you have tried to cultivate healthy relationships but haven't found any yet, don't give up! The Lord wants all of us to be in an environment where we can experience more of His love through our relationships with other believers.

If you ask God for guidance and are willing to continue putting forth the effort, He will lead you to some people who can provide this kind of an environment for you in His perfect time.

Healthy Versus Unhealthy Relationships

Because many of us are so vulnerable when we begin allowing ourselves to experience the pain that usually accompanies growth, it is wise to have a basic understanding of healthy and unhealthy relationships. We must first understand that while God often demonstrates His love and affirmation for us through believers and nonbelievers alike, His desire is that our relationships with others will enable us to know Him more fully. His work through others is, in part, to serve as a channel by which we can better understand His divine love and acceptance of us. Sadly, we are all prone to miss His message and mistake His messenger(s) as the source of our fulfillment. When this misperception is carried to an extreme, we can fall into emotional dependency, "the condition resulting when the ongoing presence and/or nurturing of another is believed necessary for personal security."[1] In his book *The Four Loves,* C. S. Lewis described the difference between lovers and friends:

> *Lovers are always talking to one another about their love; Friends*
> *hardly ever talk about their Friendship. Lovers are normally face*

to face, absorbed in each other; Friends, side by side, absorbed in
some common interest. Above all, Eros (while it lasts) is necessary
between two only. But two, far from being the necessary number
for Friendship, is not even the best.[2]

This well describes the difference between healthy and unhealthy
friendship, whether sex comes into the picture or not. Healthy relationships are turned outward rather than inward. Healthy relationships encourage individuality rather than conformity and are
concerned with independence rather than emotional dependence.
Healthy relationships point one's focus to the Lord and pleasing Him
rather than toward the friendship and pleasing one another.

How do we know when we've crossed the line from a healthy
relationship to one that is emotionally dependent? When either
party in a relationship:

- experiences frequent jealousy, possessiveness, and a desire for
  exclusivity, viewing other people as a threat to the relationship.
- prefers to spend time alone with this friend and becomes
  frustrated when this does not happen.
- becomes irrationally angry or depressed when this friend
  withdraws slightly.
- loses interest in friendships other than this one.
- experiences romantic or sexual feelings leading to fantasy
  about this person.
- becomes preoccupied by the person's appearance, personality,
  problems, and interests.
- is unwilling to make short- or long-range plans that do not
  include the other person.
- is unable to see the other's faults realistically.
- becomes defensive about this relationship when asked.
- displays physical affection beyond what is appropriate for a
  friendship.
- refers frequently to the other in conversation; feels free to
  "speak for" the other.

- exhibits an intimacy and familiarity with this friend that causes others to feel uncomfortable or embarrassed in their presence.[3]

Our relationships with one another are very important to God, so much so, that He has placed unity among the brethren as a priority in our relationship with Him (see Matt. 5:23–24). This is because God has reconciled us to Himself as a body in Christ (Eph. 2:16) and therefore intends for us to interact as members of one another (Eph. 4:25). Pray that God will guide you to relationships that will encourage you to be honest, practice the truth of His Word, affirm you, and thereby help you develop an appropriate love for yourself and compel you to focus on Him as the gracious provider of your needs. Eventually, your gratitude will motivate you to practice pleasing Him rather than other people.

How do we learn to reject Satan's lie, *I must be approved by certain others to feel good about myself?* How can we begin to practically apply the great truth of our reconciliation to almighty God? The following exercise will help you begin to experience the freedom and joy of reconciliation.

First Corinthians 13 describes God's unconditional love and acceptance of us. To personalize this passage, replace the word *love* with *my Father.* Then, memorize the following, and when fear comes to you, recall the love and kindness of God:

My Father is very patient and kind.
My Father is not envious, never boastful.
My Father is not arrogant.
My Father is never rude, nor is He self-seeking.
My Father is not quick to take offense.
My Father keeps no score of wrongs.
My Father does not gloat over my sins but is always glad when truth prevails.
My Father knows no limit to His endurance, no end to His trust.

My Father is always hopeful and patient.

As you memorize this passage, ask God to show you if your perception of Him is in error in any way. This will enable you to have a more accurate perception of God and will help you to experience more of His unconditional love and acceptance.

7

The Blame Game

Those who fail are unworthy of love and deserve to be punished.

Have you ever wondered how a critical, judgmental person lives with himself or herself? The answer is: not very well.

Our perception of success and failure is often our primary basis for evaluating ourselves and others. If we believe that performance reflects one's value and that failure makes one unacceptable and unworthy of love, then we will usually feel completely justified in condemning those who fail, including ourselves. Self-condemnation may include name-calling (*I'm so stupid! I can't do anything right!*), making self-deprecating jokes or statements, or simply never allowing any room for error in our performance. With others, we may be harsh (physically or verbally abusive) or relatively subtle (sarcastic or silent). But any form of condemnation is a powerfully destructive force that communicates, *I'll make you sorry for what you did.*

Matt made a serious mistake early in his life and was never able to overcome it. At age fourteen, he and several friends from school tried to slip out of a downtown department store with some cassette tapes without paying for them. They made it to the glass doors past the cashier's stand before a security guard caught them and escorted all of them into the manager's office.

Matt never heard the end of the incident. Every time he made a mistake at home, his father reminded him of what he had done.

"You're a colossal failure!" his father would scream. "You've got no values whatsoever! You're a liar and a thief, and you'll never amount to anything!"

Matt was never able to forget his humiliation. At age twenty, he sat in my office and told me very seriously that on some days he was happy until he realized that he was feeling good. Believing that he had no right to feel good about himself, he would then begin to feel depressed again. "After all," he reflected, "no one as worthless as I am should feel good about himself."

Like so many others, Matt had been brainwashed and broken by the false belief: *Those who fail are unworthy of love and deserve to be punished.*

Whether consciously or unconsciously, we all tend to point an accusing finger, assigning blame for virtually every failure. Whenever we fail to receive approval for our performance, we are likely to search for a reason, a culprit, or a scapegoat. More often than not, we can find no one but ourselves to blame, so the accusing finger points right back at us. Self-condemnation is a severe form of punishment.

If possible, we will often try to place the blame on others and fulfill the law of retribution—that people should get what they deserve. For most of our lives, we have been conditioned to make someone pay for failures or shortcomings. When a deadline is missed at work, we let everyone know it's not our fault. "I know the report was due yesterday, but Frank didn't get me the statistics until this morning." If a household chore is left undone, we quickly look to other family members to determine who is responsible. For every flaw we see around us, we usually search for someone to blame, hoping to exonerate ourselves by making sure that the one who failed is properly identified and punished.

Another reason we seek to blame others is that our success often depends on their contribution. Their failure is a threat to us. When the failure of another blocks our goal of success, we usually respond by defending ourselves and blaming them, often using condemnation to manipulate them to improve their performance.

Blaming others also helps put a safe distance between their failure and our fragile self-worth.

Whether our accusations are focused on ourselves or others, we all have a tendency to believe that someone has to take the blame. When Ellen discovered that her fifteen-year-old daughter was pregnant, she went a week without sleep, tossing and turning, trying to determine who was at fault. Was it her daughter, who had brought this reproach on the family, or was she to blame for failing as a mother? All Ellen knew was that someone had to take responsibility for the crisis.

Rather than being objective and looking for a solid, biblical solution to our problems, we often resort to either accusing someone else or berating ourselves. Sometimes we blame others to make ourselves feel better. By blaming someone else who failed, we feel superior. In fact, the higher the position of the one who failed (parent, boss, pastor, and so on) and the further they fall, the better we feel.

In other situations, however, just the opposite is true. When a parent fails, a child often accepts the blame for that failure. Even as adults, we may readily assume blame in our relationships with those in authority. We have much invested in supporting those we depend upon. This is one reason why denial is so strong in abusive families. For example, one little girl said, "I never told anybody that Daddy was molesting me because I thought that somebody would take him away from our family."

How should we respond when another fails? If the person who failed is a Christian, we need to affirm God's truth about him or her: He(or she) is deeply loved, completely forgiven, fully pleasing, totally accepted by God, and complete in Christ. This perspective can eventually change our condemning attitude to one of love and a desire to help. By believing these truths, we will gradually be able to love this person just as God loves us (1 John 4:11), forgive him or her just as God has forgiven us (Eph. 4:32), and accept him or her just as God has accepted us (Rom. 15:7). This does not mean that we will become blind to the faults or failures of others. We will continue to see them, but our response to them will change considerably over time, from condemnation to compassion. As we depend less on other people for our self-worth, their sins and mistakes will become less of a threat to us, and we will desire to help them instead of being compelled to punish them.

But what about our response to unbelievers? Although they haven't yet trusted in the cross of Christ for the removal of their condemnation before God, Jesus was very clear about how we are to treat them. In Matthew 22, He told His disciples to "love the Lord your God with all your heart, and with all your soul, and with all your mind. . . . love your neighbor [both believers and unbelievers] as yourself" (vv. 37, 39). Jesus was even more specific in Luke 6. He said, "But I say to you who hear, love your enemies, do good to those who hate you, bless those who curse you, pray for those who mistreat you" (vv. 27–28). Christ didn't come to love and die for the lovely, righteous people of the world. If He had, we would all be in trouble! Instead, He came to love and die for the unrighteous, the inconsiderate, and the selfish. As we grow in our understanding of His love for us and continue to understand that He has rescued us from the righteous condemnation we deserve because of our sins, we will gradually become more patient and kind to others when they fail. It can be very helpful if we compare the failure or sin of others with our sin that Christ died to forgive: *There is nothing that anyone can do to me that can compare with my sin of rebellion that Christ has completely forgiven.* That should give us a light of perspective!

We tend to make two major errors when we punish others for their failures. The first is that we condemn people not only for genuine sin but also for their mistakes. When people who have tried their best fail, they do not need our biting blame. They need our love and encouragement. Again, we often tend to blame others because their actions (whether they reflect overt disobedience or honest mistakes) make us look like failures, and our own failure is unacceptable to us. Husband-wife, parent-child, and employer-employee relationships are especially vulnerable to one's being threatened by the failure of another. A wife gets angry with her husband for his not-so-funny joke at an important dinner party; a parent erupts at a child for accidentally spilling milk; a manager scowls at an employee because an error in the employee's calculations has made the manager look foolish to his supervisor. People generally experience difficulty in dealing with their sins; let's not compound their problems by condemning them for their mistakes.

A second major error we often make by condemning others is believing that we are godly agents of condemnation. Unable to tolerate injustice, we seem to possess a great need to balance the scales of right and wrong. We are correct in recognizing that sin is reprehensible and deserves condemnation; yet we have not been licensed by God to punish others for their sins. Judgment is God's responsibility, not man's.

Jesus dealt specifically with this issue when several men decided to stone a woman caught in adultery. He told them that the person without sin should throw the first stone. Beginning with the eldest, all of the accusers walked away as they remembered their own sins (John 8:3–9). In light of their own sinfulness, they no longer saw fit to condemn the sins of another.

As this incident clearly illustrates, we should leave righteous condemnation and punishment in the hands of the one worthy of the responsibility. Our response should be love, affirmation, and, possibly, compassionate correction.

When others offend or insult us, should we tell them that they have made us angry or hurt our feelings? This question can be difficult to answer. Some psychologists tell us that we should vent all of our emotions because repression is unhealthy. Others tell us that our emotions will always be positive and controlled if we are truly walking with the Lord. We should avoid both of these extremes. Venting our anger uncontrollably is not a healthy solution, but neither is continued repression and denial. We need a safe environment to express our emotions: a good friend or counselor who will help us get in touch with our true feelings, which we may have suppressed for years. We can also learn to express ourselves fully to the Lord and tell Him our true feelings, fears, hopes, and dreams. (The Psalms are filled with honest expressions of anger, pain, confusion, hope, and faith.) In this safe environment, we can slowly learn how to communicate appropriately with those who have hurt us. This requires wisdom because each situation and each person often requires a different form of communication.

As we learn to relate appropriately with those who have hurt or injured us in some way, we will begin to develop a healthy sense of assertiveness—an important component shaping other people's behavior toward us. For example, if others are rude but never realize it because we passively accept their behavior in an attempt to avoid upsetting them, at least two things usually happen: We develop resentment toward them, and they never have to come to terms with their negative impact on others. They then miss an important opportunity to change, and we effectually prolong their hurtful behavior.

There are appropriate and inappropriate ways of communicating our sense of anger or resentment to others; but these feelings need to be spoken, for their benefit and for ours. We also need to remember that learning how to express our feelings appropriately is a process. We can't expect to respond perfectly to everyone. It takes time to express years of repressed pain. It also takes time to learn how to respond firmly and clearly. Be patient with yourself. We have a choice in our response to failure: We can condemn or we can learn. All of us fail, but this doesn't mean that we are *failures.* We need to understand that failing can be a step toward maturity, not a permanent blot on our self-esteem. Like children first learning to walk, we all stumble and fall. And, just like children, we can pick ourselves up and begin again. We don't have to allow failure to prevent us from being used by God.

There have been many times in my life when I felt that God was going to punish me by causing me to lose all that I had, either because I'd done something I shouldn't have or because I'd failed to do something I should have. This erroneous perception of God has driven me away from Him on many occasions when I've needed Him most, and it is completely contrary to the one whom Paul described as "the Father of mercies and God of all comfort" (2 Cor. 1:3).

If we have trusted Christ for our salvation, God has forgiven us and wants us to experience His forgiveness on a daily basis. Moses was a murderer, but God forgave him and used him to deliver Israel from Egypt. David was an adulterer and a murderer, but God forgave him and made him a great king. Peter denied the Lord, but God forgave him, and Peter became a leader in the church. God rejoices when His children learn to accept His forgiveness, pick themselves up, and walk after they have stumbled. But we must also learn to forgive ourselves. Rather than viewing our weaknesses as a threat to our self-esteem, it is God's desire that they compel us to move forward in our relationship with Him. As the author of Hebrews wrote:

> *Therefore, since we have a great high priest who has gone through the heavens, Jesus the Son of God, let us hold firmly to the faith we profess. For we do not have a high priest who is unable to sympathize with our weaknesses, but we have one who has been tempted in every way, just as we are—yet was without sin. Let us then approach the throne of grace with confidence, so that we may receive mercy and find grace to help us in our time of need. (Heb. 4:14–16, NIV)*

Some of us have a tendency to perceive Jesus as our friend and God as a harsh disciplinarian. Yet the author of Hebrews described Jesus as "the radiance of [God's] glory and the exact representation of His nature" (Heb. 1:3).

Studying passages like these and spending time with compassionate, forgiving Christians has enabled the Holy Spirit to reshape my perception of God over the years. I continue to experience remorse when I fail. But rather than hide from God, fearing His punishment, I more often approach Him with appreciation for what His love has accomplished for me. Both assuming and assigning blame for failure can have a number of detrimental consequences. Many psychologists today adhere to a theory called Rational Emotive Therapy. This very helpful theory states that blame is the core of most emotional disturbances. The answer, they insist, is for each of us to stop blaming ourselves and others and learn to accept ourselves in spite of our imperfections. How right they are! Christ's death is the complete payment for sin, and we can claim His complete forgiveness and acceptance daily.

A number of emotional problems are rooted in the false belief that we must meet certain standards to be acceptable and that the only way to deal with inadequacies is to punish ourselves and others for them. There is no way we can shoulder such a heavy burden. Our guilt will overpower us, and the weight of our failures will break us.

The false belief *Those who fail (including myself) are unworthy of love and deserve to be punished* is at the root of our fear of punishment and our propensity to punish others. How deeply are you affected by this lie? Take the following test to determine how great an influence it has in your life.

Fear of Punishment/Punishing Others Test

Read each of the following statements; then, from the top of the test, choose the term that best describes your response. Put the number above that term in the blank beside each statement.

1	2	3	4	5	6	7
Always	Very Often	Often	Sometimes	Seldom	Very Seldom	Never

___ 1. I fear what God might do to me.

___ 2. After I fail, I worry about God's response.

___ 3. When I see someone in a difficult situation, I wonder what he or she did to deserve it.

___ 4. When something goes wrong, I have a tendency to think that God must be punishing me.

___ 5. I am very hard on myself when I fail.

___ 6. I find myself wanting to blame people when they fail.

___ 7. I get angry with God when someone who is immoral or dishonest prospers.

___ 8. I am compelled to tell others when I see them doing wrong.

___ 9. I tend to focus on the faults and failures of others.

___ 10. God seems harsh to me.

___ Total (Add up the numbers you have placed in the blanks.)

If your score is:

57–70: God has apparently given you a very strong appreciation for His love and unconditional acceptance. You seem to be freed from the fear of punishment that plagues most people. (Some people who score this high either are greatly deceived or have become callous to their emotions as a way to suppress pain.)

47–56: The fear of punishment controls your responses rarely or only in certain situations. Again, the only major exceptions are those who are not honest with themselves.

37–46: When you experience emotional problems, they may relate to a fear of punishment or an inner urge to punish others. Upon reflection, you will probably relate many of your previous decisions to this fear. Many of your future decisions will also be affected by the fear of punishment unless you take direct action to overcome these tendencies.

27–36: The fear of punishment forms a general backdrop to your life. There are probably few days that you are not affected in some way by this fear. Unfortunately, this robs you of the joy and peace your salvation is meant to bring.

0–26: Experiences of punishment dominate your memory and have probably resulted in a great deal of depression. These problems will remain until some definitive plan is followed. In other words, this condition will not simply disappear; time alone cannot heal your pain. You need to experience deep healing in your self-concept, in your relationship with God, and in your relationships with others.

Effects of the Fear of Punishment and the Compulsion to Punish Others

The logical result of Satan's deception, Self-Worth = Performance + Others' Opinions, is fear: the fear of failure, rejection, and punishment. When we base our security and value on how well we perform and how we want others to perceive us, failure poses a tremendous threat to us. When threatened, we will often withdraw from the source of our fear and become very controlling of ourselves and others. For example, in an attempt to avoid failure, we may adhere to a fairly rigid schedule in which we're fairly certain of success and avoid those activities that are less promising. Because we often perceive those closest to us as a reflection of ourselves and are consequently threatened by their failures, we are likely to try to control their behavior as well. If we have also determined that those who fail deserve to be punished, we will tend to victimize ourselves and/or others for virtually any wrongdoing.

Because of our insecurity, some of us are so self-protective that we are rarely able to perceive of ourselves as being in the wrong. We may be quick to pinpoint—and condemn—the weaknesses of others, but in our own self-evaluation, we may be effectually blind to faults and frailties. This attitude may prompt us to turn others (who are "more needy") to God but may prevent us from seeking Him because of our frequent inability to see our need for Him or because when we do fail, we may believe that the fault is His.

Some of us may fall on the other end of the spectrum. We may be so absorbed in our performance and so demanding of ourselves that when failure enters our circumstances, we believe that we are solely responsible. Rather than laying blame on someone else, we inflict punishment on ourselves and protect those who hurt us by explaining their deficiencies: *She didn't mean what she said; I'm sure that he loves me, he just has a hard time showing it.* If we have a tendency to punish ourselves for failures, we may believe that we must feel remorse for a certain length of time before we can experience peace and joy again. In a twisted form of self-motivation, we may think that if we condemn ourselves enough, then perhaps we won't fail again.

Somewhere in the middle of this spectrum are those of us who are so hard on ourselves that we project our self-condemning attitude onto others. Passing judgment on others may be a response to our great need for consistency and justice. If we are going to punish failure in ourselves, we reason, then we must be consistent and punish failure in others. Insisting on justice, we may also take it upon ourselves to be God's instrument of correction. We normally don't like to see others getting away with something that they should be punished for (or perhaps, that we wish we could do ourselves).

Finally, there are those of us who determine that because punishment is inevitable, we may as well "live it up" and enjoy our sin before judgment comes.

The fear of punishment and the propensity to punish others can affect our lives in many ways. The following provides a brief description of common problems that often result from this deception.

Self-Induced Punishment

Many of us operate on the theory that if we are hard enough on ourselves, then God won't have to punish us. We fail to realize that God disciplines us in love and never punishes us in anger. Because God loves us unconditionally and does not punish us, we don't need to punish ourselves.

Perhaps you have developed a system for punishing yourself. Typically, these systems revolve around determining the magnitude of the sin and then determining the length of time that you will go into self-condemnation. If it's a "small sin," and especially if no one knows you did it, then your devaluation of yourself may last only a few hours or perhaps for the rest of the day. The greater the sin the longer the self-condemnation. Some have spent their entire lives condemning themselves. This process will never lead you to a more holy life. We will cover this in more detail in chapter 12, "Guilt Versus Condemnation."

Bitterness

In essence, we are accusing God of being what the Book of Revelation describes as the accused of the brethren. This is accusing God of behaving like Satan. This ignores the fact that God tells us that there is no condemnation for those who are in Christ Jesus.

No wonder there are so many bitter, angry Christians, considering all those who are deceived in believing that Satan's activity is really God at work in their lives. Satan enjoys this greatly because it alienates God's children from Him and leaves them vulnerable to even more of Satan's activities.

Passivity

Fear of punishment is at the root of one of the most common problems in our society: passivity. Passivity is the neglect of our minds, time, gifts, or talent through inaction. God intends for us to actively cooperate with Him, but fear can have an immobilizing effect on our will. Passivity results in a dull life, avoiding risks, and missing opportunities.

Punishing Others

Our specific response to the failure of others depends on several factors: our personalities, the nature of their failure, and how their failure reflects on us ("His mistake makes me look like I'm dumb," or a bad parent, or a poor leader, or a rotten employee). Our condemnation of those who fail may take the form of verbal abuse, physical abuse, nagging criticism, withholding appreciation and affection, or ignoring them. These responses are usually designed to make them *pay for* what they did.

Fears of All Sorts

The blame game leaves us feeling all alone without experiencing the faith we need to live without fear. Fear and faith can never be co-equal. One will always dominate the other. The more you give yourself to fear, the more difficult it is to experience faith in your life.

The fear of punishment and the desire to punish others can be overcome by realizing that Christ has borne the punishment we deserve. His motives toward us are loving and kind. His discipline is designed to correct us and protect us from the destruction of sin, not to punish us.

8

God's Answer: Propitiation

Does God conduct opinion polls to determine truth?

Does your opinion affect what truth is?

If something is true about spiritual things, does that affect the nature of that truth?

Does truth matter anymore?

Does God ever change truth?

Does God accommodate man or is man meant to accommodate God?

Before describing what propitiation is, why it was needed, and how it should affect our lives, you should think carefully about the above questions. There are some who would argue that information about God and what He has said, while true, are only relatively so. This is man attempting to make God subservient to him because he does not want to be subservient to God.

I am about to describe the "hard side" of God. But it is also the reason we can depend on God and His Word. God is holy. To be true to His holiness God punishes those whose righteousness is not the same as His. (If the last statement bothers you, you might want to reread chapter 4 on justification.)

This might not seem fair to you. Many things God says about sin may seem unfair to you. We may even think, *God, You are so big, why can't You overlook some things?* But God and what He does are not up for vote. He never runs for office because He *is* the office. He believes that He has a right to determine all the rules, and He does. He won't change to be more popular.

Only if we understand the horror of coming under the wrath of a holy God for our sins will we appreciate what Christ did on the cross. Every day our minds should be overwhelmed by thankfulness for what He did on our behalf.

When Christ died on the cross, He was our substitute. He took upon Himself the righteous wrath of God that we deserved. The depth of God's love for us is revealed by the extremity of His actions for us: The holy Son of God became a man and died a horrible death in our place. Two passages state this eloquently. The first was written by Isaiah, who anticipated the coming of Christ:

> Surely our griefs He Himself bore, and our sorrows He carried; yet we ourselves esteemed Him stricken, smitten of God, and afflicted. But He was pierced through for our transgressions, He was crushed for our iniquities; the chastening for our well-being fell upon Him, and by His scourging we are healed. All of us like sheep have gone astray, each of us has turned to his own way; but the LORD has caused the iniquity of us all to fall on Him. (Isa. 53:4–6)

And from the New Testament:

> By this the love of God was manifested in us, that God has sent His only begotten Son into the world so that we might live through Him. In this is love, not that we loved God, but that He loved us and sent His Son to be the propitiation for our sins. Beloved, if God so loved us, we also ought to love one another. (1 John 4:9–11)

Propitiation means that the wrath of someone who has been unjustly wronged has been satisfied. It is an act that soothes hostility and satisfies the need for vengeance. Providing His only begotten Son as the propitiation for our sin was the greatest possible demonstration of God's love for man. To understand God's wondrous provision of propitiation, it is helpful to remember what He has endured from mankind. From Adam and Eve's sin in the Garden of Eden to the obvious depravity we see in our world today, human history is the story of greed, hatred, lust, and pride—evidence of man's wanton rebellion against the God of love and peace. If not done with a desire to glorify Him, even our good deeds are like *filthy garments* to God (Isa. 64:6).

Our sin deserves the righteous wrath of God. He is the Almighty, the rightful judge of the universe. He is absolutely holy and perfect. "God is light, and in Him there is no darkness at all" (1 John 1:5). Because of these attributes, God cannot overlook sin, nor can He compromise by accepting sinful behavior. For God to condone even one sin would defile His holiness like smearing a white satin wedding gown with black tar. Because He is holy, God's aversion to sin is manifested in righteous anger. However, God is not only righteously indignant about sin, He is also infinitely loving. In His holiness, God condemns sin, but in the most awesome example of love the world has ever seen, He ordained that His Son would die to pay for our sins. God sacrificed the sinless, perfect Savior to turn away, *to propitiate,* His great wrath.

And for whom did Christ die? Was it for the saints who honored Him? Was it for a world that appreciated His sinless life and worshiped Him? No! Christ died for us, while we were in rebellion against Him. For while we were still helpless, Christ died for the ungodly at the right time.

> For one will hardly die for a righteous man; though perhaps for the good man someone would dare even to die. But God demonstrates His own love toward us, in that while we were yet sinners, Christ died for us. Much more then, having now been justified by His blood, we shall be saved from the wrath of God through Him. For if while we were enemies, we were reconciled to God through

the death of His Son, much more, having been reconciled, we
shall be saved by His life. And not only this, but we also exult in
God through our Lord Jesus Christ, through whom we have now
received the reconciliation. (Rom. 5:7–11)

Who can measure the fathomless depth of love that sent Christ
to the cross? While we were the enemies of God, Christ averted the
wrath we deserved so that we might become the sons of God.

What can we say of our holy heavenly Father? Surely, He did
not escape seeing Christ's mistreatment at the hands of sinful men—
the scourging, the humiliation, the beatings. Surely, He who spoke
the world into being could have delivered Christ from the entire
ordeal. And yet the God of heaven peered down through time and
saw you and me. Though we were His enemies, He loved us and
longed to rescue us from our sins, designating the sinless Christ
to become our substitute. Only Christ could avert God's righteous
wrath against sin, so in love the Father kept silent as Jesus hung
from the cross. All of His anger, all of the wrath we would ever
deserve, was poured upon Christ, and Christ became sin for us (2
Cor. 5:21). Because He paid the penalty for our sins, and God's
wrath was avenged, God no longer looks upon us through the
eyes of judgment. Instead, He now lavishes His love upon us. The
Scriptures teach that absolutely nothing can separate us from
God's love (Rom. 8:38–39). He has adopted us into a tender, intimate, and powerful relationship with Him (Rom. 8:15).

Because we are His children, performance is no longer the basis
of our worth. We are unconditionally and deeply loved by God, and
we can live by faith in His grace. We were spiritually dead, but the
Lord has made us alive and has given us the high status of sonship
to the almighty God. It will take all of eternity to comprehend the
wealth of His love and grace. Paul explains this incomprehensible
gift this way:

But God, being rich in mercy, because of His great love with which
He loved us, even when we were dead in our transgressions, made

us alive together with Christ (by grace you have been saved), and raised us up with Him, and seated us with Him in the heavenly places, in Christ Jesus, in order that in the ages to come He might show the surpassing riches of His grace in kindness toward us in Christ Jesus. For by grace you have been saved through faith; and that not of yourselves, it is the gift of God; not as a result of works, that no one should boast. (Eph. 2:4–9).

Propitiation, then, means that Christ has satisfied the holy wrath of God through His payment for sin. There was only one reason for Him to do this: He loves us; infinitely, eternally, unconditionally, irrevocably, He loves us. God the Father loves us with the love of a father, reaching to snatch us from harm. God the Son loves us with the love of a brother, laying down His life for us. He alone has turned away God's wrath from us. There is nothing we can do, no amount of good deeds we can accomplish, and no religious ceremonies we can perform that can pay for our sins. Instead, Christ has conclusively paid for them so that we can escape eternal condemnation and experience His love and purposes both now and forever.

Christ not only paid for our sins at one point in time but also continues to love us and teach us day after day. We have a weapon to use against Satan as he attacks us with doubts about God's love for us. Our weapon is the fact that Christ took our punishment upon Himself at Calvary. We no longer have to fear punishment for our sins because Christ paid for them all—past, present, and future. This tremendous truth of propitiation clearly demonstrates that we are *truly and deeply loved by God.* His perfect love casts out all fear as we allow it to flood our hearts (1 John 4:18).

Potential Obstacles to Receiving This Truth

Poor Patterns of Motivation
All our lives we have experienced being made to feel bad about ourselves as a way of motivation from others. It would only be natural that we take this methodology and use it on others as well as

on ourselves. For those who think this is a reasonable method to use, look in the Dake Study Bible, which lists 1,050 commandments to the Christian in the New Testament alone. Try putting that list on your refrigerator and condemning yourself every time you violate any one of the 1,050 commandments. This would be a sure way to lose any sense of joy that God wants you to experience. In a later chapter, we will demonstrate that the Bible warns us that accepting condemnation will actually increase sin in our lives.

Holding on to Unforgiveness

We maintain unforgiveness for several reasons including attempting to keep from being hurt again by those who have offended us. Here are a few of the reasons why we hold on to the unforgiveness:

- The offense was too great.
- He (she) won't accept responsibility for the offense.
- He (she) isn't truly sorry.
- He (she) never asked to be forgiven.
- He (she) will do it again.
- He (she) did it again.
- I don't like him (her).
- He (she) did it deliberately.
- If I forgive, I'll have to treat the offender well.
- Someone has to punish him (her).
- Something keeps me from forgiving.
- I'll be a hypocrite if I forgive because I don't feel like forgiving.
- I'll forgive, but I won't ever forget.
- I'll forgive because I have found an excuse for the offense.

As I point out in my book *The Search for Peace,* if we hold on to unforgiveness, we cannot accept our *own* forgiveness. In fact, the only way we escape the torment of having unforgiveness is to begin to contemplate our own forgiveness until it has so impacted our lives that we are able to forgive from our heart.

How do we begin to experience freedom from Satan's lie: *Those who fail are unworthy of love and deserve to be punished?* We will be increasingly freed as we understand and apply the truth of propitiation in the context of loving and supportive relationships, where we can express ourselves honestly and receive both the warmth of affirmation and the challenge of God's Word.

The Scriptures indicate that Satan accuses believers of being unworthy of God's grace. It is his desire that we cower under the fear of punishment. Consider this passage from Revelation 12:10–11:

> *And I heard a loud voice in heaven, saying, "Now the salvation, and the power, and the kingdom of our God and the authority of His Christ have come, for the accuser of our brethren has been thrown down, who accuses them before our God day and night. And they overcame him because of the blood of the Lamb and because of the word of their testimony, and they did not love their life even to death."*

How are we to overcome Satan, the accuser, and experience our acceptance in Christ? According to this passage of Scripture, there is only one way: by the sacrificial blood of Christ on the cross, the blood of the Lamb. To do this, we must first stop trying to overcome our feelings of condemnation and failure by penitent actions. Defending ourselves or trying to pay for our sins by our actions leads only to a guilt-and-penance spiral because we can never do enough on our own to justify our sins.

There have been times when I thought that I couldn't feel forgiven until I had experienced remorse about my sin for a certain period of time. These occasions led to depression because I could hardly complete my penance for one sin before I had sinned again. Then, I would have to feel bad about that for a period of time, only to sin again . . . and again . . . and again . . . and . . . well, you get the picture.

Eventually, I began to realize that I had one of three options: I could continue trying to make up for my sin by mourning over it for however long it seemed necessary (although that wasn't getting me very far); I could try to deny that I had sinned (even though I knew that I had); or I could give up on the idea of using my guilt as a form of penance and trust in Christ's forgiveness. Initially, of course, these options were not as clear as they've become with time and reflection.

No matter how much we do to make up for our sin, we will continue to feel guilty and believe that we need to do more unless we resist Satan, the accuser of the brethren. This can only be accomplished because Christ's blood has completely paid for our sins and delivered us from guilt. Secondly, we need to verbalize what the blood of Christ has done for us: We are deeply loved, completely forgiven, fully pleasing, totally accepted, and complete in Christ.

As the Bible says in Revelation 12:11, we should not love our lives (the excitement, comfort, prestige, and status) to the point of spiritual deadness. Love for the world and its pleasures renders us spiritually impotent. We must decide that our minds are no longer the source of truth and instead gain our knowledge, wisdom, and direction from the Scriptures. There are two practical steps that will help make these truths a reality in our lives:

1. On one side of a three-by-five inch index card, write the following: "Because of Christ and His redemption, I am completely forgiven and fully pleasing to God. I am totally accepted by God."

2. On the other side of the card, write the words of Romans 5:1 and Colossians 1:21–22.

Carry this card with you for the next twenty-eight days. Every time you get something to drink or do some other routine activity, look at it and remind yourself of what Christ has done for you. This exercise will help you develop a habit of reflecting on these liberating truths. As you read and memorize these statements and passages, think about how they apply to you. Memorization and application of these truths will have a profound effect in your life as your mind is slowly transformed by God's Word.

9

Shame

I am what I am. I cannot change. I am hopeless.

Is there anything about your life (past acts, something done to you, anything about your appearance) that you believe makes it impossible for you to ever experience consistent happiness, peace, or joy?

When we base our self-worth on past failures, dissatisfaction with personal appearance, or bad habits, we often develop a fourth false belief: *I am what I am. I cannot change. I am hopeless.* This lie binds people to the hopeless pessimism associated with poor self-esteem.

"I just can't help myself," some people say. "That's the way I've always been, and that's the way I'll always be. You can't teach an old dog new tricks." We assume that others should have low expectations of us too. "You know I can't do any better than this. What do you expect?" If we excuse our failures with an attitude of hopelessness, too often our personality can become glued to the failures. Our self-image becomes no more than a reflection of our past.

When Leslie approached Janet about serving a term as president of the ladies' auxiliary, Janet's outward poise and confidence vanished. "Are you serious?" she stuttered. "You know I've never been a leader and have never even gotten along well with people. No, no, I'd simply be an embarrassment to you. No, I can't do it, don't you see?" Janet was suffering from low self-esteem. Her opinions of herself were based on her past failures, and those failures kept her from enjoying new experiences.

A young man named Jeff once questioned me when I told him that he needed to separate his past from the present, that no natural law dictated his having to remain the same individual he had always been. I told Jeff that he could change, that he could rise above his past and build a new life for himself.

"But how?" Jeff asked. "I'm more of a realist than that. I know myself. I know what I've done and who I am. I've tried to change, but it hasn't worked. I've given up."

I explained to Jeff that he needed a new perspective, not just new efforts based on his old, pessimistic attitude. He needed to develop a new self-concept based on the unconditional love and acceptance of God. Both Jeff's past failures and God's unconditional love were realities, but the question was which one Jeff would value more. If he continued to value his failures, he would continue to be absorbed in self-pity. Instead, he needed to be honest. He needed someone he could talk to openly so that he could express his feelings without the fear of being rejected. He also needed to be encouraged to study and apply the truths of God's Word. As he persisted in this process, his sense of self-worth would begin to change. In addition to a changed perception of self-worth, he would eventually experience changes in every area of his life: his goals, his relationships, and his outlook.

Too often our self-image rests solely on an evaluation of our past behavior, being measured only through a memory. Day after day, year after year, we tend to build our personalities upon the rubble of yesterday's personal disappointments.

Perhaps we find some strange kind of comfort in our personal failings. Perhaps there is some security in accepting ourselves as much less than we can become. That minimizes the risk of failure. Certainly, if we expect little from ourselves we will seldom be disappointed!

But nothing forces us to remain in the mold of the past. By the grace and power of God, we can change! We can persevere and overcome! No one forces us to keep shifting our feet in the muck of old failures. We can dare to accept the challenge of building a new life.

Dr. Paul Tournier once compared life to a man hanging from a trapeze. The trapeze bar was the man's security, his pattern of existence, his lifestyle. Then God swung another trapeze into the man's view, and he faced a perplexing dilemma. Should he relinquish his past? Should he reach for the new bar? The moment of truth came, Dr. Tournier explained, when the man realized that to grab the new bar, he must release the old one.

Our past relationships may involve the intense pain of neglect, abuse, and manipulation, but if we do not begin the process of healing, we will be unable to experience the joy, challenge, and, yes, the potential for failure in the present.

I have struggled with this process of change for the greater part of my life. It may have been that I was raised in a poor family. It may have been that while I was growing up, I often felt very awkward. It may have been that there were some inadequacies in my home life. For whatever reasons, I grew up with a sense of shame about myself and my circumstance.

As I've mentioned previously, I often felt inadequate during my childhood. I had the impression that I just didn't measure up. Others might not have thought I felt this way, but my sense of inadequacy was often intense.

Being exceptionally tall and lanky, I was uncomfortable with the way I looked and felt out of place among my peers. My feelings of inferiority prevented me from pursuing dating relationships for a number of years. The threat of potential rejection prompted me to withdraw from social gatherings, preferring instead to spend time with the few friends I felt most comfortable with.

The truth that I am deeply loved, fully pleasing, and totally accepted by the God of the universe has taken me a lifetime to comprehend. But gradually, by studying God's Word and by experiencing loving relationships with other believers who genuinely care for me and appreciate me, I have continued to gain a better understanding of the way God values me. This has improved my sense of self-worth considerably.

Many of my past memories are still painful for me, and I imagine they always will be. But through Christ, my present attitude about myself is continually changing. Knowing that I have no reason to feel ashamed has motivated me to pursue a number of challenges that I wouldn't have even considered pursuing a number of years ago. In the process, I have experienced failure and success. God has used each instance to teach me that despite my circumstances, my worth is secure in Him. We need to be honest about the pain, the anger, the disappointment, and the loneliness of our past. We need to put ourselves in relationships that will encourage us to feel what we may have suppressed for many years. This will enable us to begin (or continue) to experience hope and, eventually, healing. Change is possible, but it is a process.

Does this seem strange? Does it seem difficult? We may have difficulty relinquishing what is familiar (though painful) for what is unfamiliar because our fear of the unknown often seems stronger than the pain of a poor self-concept. It seems right to hang on. Proverbs 16:25 says, "There is a way which seems right to a man, but its end is the way of death." Any change in our behavior requires a release from our old self-concept, which is often founded in failure and the expectations of others. We need to learn how to relate to ourselves in a new way. To accomplish this, we must begin to base our self-worth on God's opinion of us and trust in His Spirit to accomplish change in our lives. Then, and only then, can we overcome Satan's deception that holds sway over our self-perception and behavior.

By believing Satan's lie *I am what I am, I cannot change, I am hopeless,* we become vulnerable to pessimism and a poor self-concept. Take the following test to determine how strongly you are affected by this false belief.

Shame Test

Read each of the following statements; then, from the top of the test, choose the term that best describes the frequency of your typical response. Put the number above that term in the blank beside each statement.

1	2	3	4	5	6	7
Always	Very Often	Often	Sometimes	Seldom	Very Seldom	Never

____ 1. I often think about past failures or experiences of rejection.

____ 2. There are certain things about my past that I cannot recall without experiencing strong, painful emotions (for example, guilt, shame, anger, fear, and so on).

____ 3. I seem to make the same mistakes over and over again.

____ 4. There are certain aspects of my character that I want to change, but I don't believe I can ever successfully do so.

____ 5. I feel inferior.

____ 6. There are aspects of my appearance that I cannot accept.

____ 7. I am generally disgusted with myself.

____ 8. I feel that certain experiences have basically ruined my life.

____ 9. I perceive myself as an immoral person.

____ 10. I feel that I have lost the opportunity to experience a complete and wonderful life.

____ Total (Add up the numbers you have placed in the blanks.)

If your score is:

57–70: God has apparently given you a very strong appreciation for His love and unconditional acceptance. You seem to be freed from the shame that plagues most people. (Some people who score this high either are greatly deceived or have become callous to their emotions as a way to suppress pain.)

47–56: Shame controls your responses rarely or only in certain situations. Again, the only major exceptions are those who are not honest with themselves.

37–46: When you experience emotional problems, they may relate to a sense of shame. Upon reflection, you will probably relate many of your previous decisions to feelings of worthlessness. Many of your future decisions will also be affected by low self-esteem unless you take direct action to overcome it.

27–36: Shame forms a general backdrop to your life. There are probably few days that you are not affected in some way by shame. Unfortunately, this robs you of the joy and peace your salvation is meant to bring.

0–26: Experiences of shame dominate your memory and have probably resulted in a great deal of depression. These problems will remain until some definitive action is taken. In other words, this condition will not simply disappear; time alone cannot heal your pain. You need to experience deep healing in your self-concept, in your relationship with God, and in your relationships with others.

Effects of Shame

Susan was the product of heartless parents. Although she was a beautiful girl with dark brown eyes and long, silky hair, Susan never seemed quite as confident or as outgoing as her brothers and sisters. One reason for this was that by her eighth birthday, Susan had been approached by her father for sexual favors. Overcome by the shame this caused her, Susan withdrew from others and looked for an escape.

By the time she was sixteen, Susan was addicted to alcohol and drugs, and she was frequently stealing as well as selling her body for money. She had accepted the belief that she was nothing more than sexual merchandise. Although she was ashamed of her lifestyle and wanted to change, she saw no way out. The only people who didn't seem to reject her were the ones who used her. She was not only ashamed but was also trapped and alone.

Unlike Susan, Diana was raised by Christian parents. She had grown up in a conservative Protestant church and was very active in its youth group. Diana was diligent in witnessing to her friends at school, and her actions were always an example to those around her. Unfortunately, Diana made a mistake one night that changed her life. Alone for the evening, she and her boyfriend went too far. Shocked and ashamed by their actions, they both agreed that they must admit the incident to their parents. Tearfully, Diana confided in her mother, looking for understanding and support. But Diana's mother lost control and bitterly told her how ashamed and disappointed she was. Diana's father couldn't believe what she had done and refused even to speak to her. Her relationship with her parents continued to worsen, and six months later, Diana left home. Heartbroken and overcome by shame, she turned to her boyfriend. Soon, they began sleeping together regularly, and both began using drugs. Believing that her parents would never accept her again, Diana sought acceptance in the only way she knew how.

Both Susan and Diana suffered from the devastating effects of shame. Shame often engulfs us when a flaw in our performance is so important, so overpowering, or so disappointing to us that it creates a permanently negative opinion about our self-worth. Others may not know of our failure, but we do. We may only imagine their rejection, but real or imagined, the pain resulting from it cripples our confidence and hope.

Shame usually results in guilt and self-depreciation, but it can also lead us to search for God and His answers. Our inner, undeniable need for personal significance was created to make us search for Him. He alone can fulfill our deep need. In Him, we find peace, acceptance, and love.

Through Him, we find the courage and power to develop into the men and women He intends us to be. Although Satan wants to convince us that we will always be prisoners of our failures and past experiences, by God's grace we can be freed from the guilt of our past and experience a renewed purpose for our lives.

Shame can have powerful effects on our self-esteem, and it can manifest itself in many ways. The following is a brief list of common problems associated with shame:

Inferiority

By definition, shame is a deep sense of inferiority. Feelings of inferiority can result from prolonged patterns of failure, or they can stem from only one or two haunting instances. Either way, they can destroy our self-worth and, as a result, adversely affect our emotions and behavior. These perceptions of ourselves aren't easily altered, but they can change through honesty, the affirmation of others, the truths of God's Word, the power and encouragement of the Holy Spirit, and time. Because of Christ's redemption, we are worthy, forgiven, loved, accepted, and complete in Him.

Habitually Destructive Behavior

We often behave in a manner that is consistent with our perception of ourselves. Therefore, seeing ourselves through the eyes of shame usually results in a pessimistic outlook on life and a lifestyle of destructive behavior.

Self-Pity

Shame often prompts us to view ourselves as victims. Consequently, whether we blame others or condemn ourselves for our actions, we sink into the depths of feeling sorry for ourselves.

Passivity

Some of us try to compensate for gnawing feelings of shame through passivity, refusing to invest any part of ourselves in relationships and responsibilities. We may be compulsive perfectionists in some areas of our lives but may avoid taking risks in relationships or circumstances. We may tend to become engrossed in peripheral activities (clipping coupons, cleaning the kitchen, filing papers, reading magazines) so that we are "too busy" to experience the reality of relationships and situations.

Isolation and Withdrawal

Isolation is often a corollary of passivity. Avoiding both the risks of rejection and failure, some of us withdraw from virtually all meaningful interaction. We develop facades so that nobody can see our hurt. We may be socially active but not allow anyone to get really close to us. We are often afraid that if people really knew us, we would again experience hurt and rejection. Our deep sense of shame leads us to withdraw from others, feel isolated, and experience the pain of loneliness.

Loss of Creativity

When we are ashamed of ourselves over a period of time, the cutting edge of our creativity atrophies. We tend to become so preoccupied with our own inferiority that we are unable to come up with new ideas. Often believing that whatever we attempt will fail, we may choose to avoid doing anything that isn't a proven success and relatively risk-free.

Codependent Relationships

In an attempt to overcome their sense of shame, many people become codependent; that is, they depend on being needed by a family member or friend who has an addictive problem or compulsion. Codependents thus develop a need to rescue and take care of others. This caretaking is the codependent's subconscious way of trying to gain personal significance. Such attempts usually backfire, however, because dependent persons often use shame to manipulate the codependent. A frequent ploy is to tell the codependent that he or she is being selfish for taking care of personal affairs rather than those of the dependent person. This locks the codependent into a hopeless pattern of rescuing to gain approval and feeling ashamed because of his or her inability to develop a sense of personal value, regardless of how hard he or she tries to do so.

Despising Our Appearance

Beauty is highly valued in our society. Television commercials and programs, magazine ads, and billboards all convey the message that beauty is to be prized. But very few of us compare to the beautiful people we see in these ads and programs, and most of us are ashamed of at least one aspect of our appearance. We spend hundreds of dollars and an inestimable amount of time and worry covering up or altering our skin, eyes, teeth, faces, noses, thighs, and scalps, refusing to believe that God, in His sovereignty and love, gave us the features He wants us to have.

Sometimes oil will wash up on a beautiful ocean beach to form a tarlike substance. When this happens the tar can easily transfer on to our feet, staining our feet to the extent that sometimes we wonder if we will ever get rid of the stain. Shame is the emotional tar of our lives. Unlike the beach tar, we can't get rid of it without an act of God.

10

God's Answer: Regeneration

Which is more powerful your sin or God's ability to overcome your sin?

Can man's sin be superior to Christ's payment for that sin?

Can God, who spoke the universe into being, make a difference in your life?

By now I hope you understand that nothing can come between what you do and God's love for you as one of His children. To overcome shame you must accept how completely God desires to make changes in your life that will free you from your past.

Perhaps we wish that during regeneration God had turned us purple or perhaps given us yellow spots. At least then we would see a difference in ourselves. However, God has gone to the trouble of communicating that He has made us brand-new inside. And now it's up to us to take Him at His Word.

Perhaps no passage in the Bible better illustrates God's regeneration than the story of Zaccheus in Luke 19:1–10. Zaccheus was a tax collector, despised by the people for overtaxing their meager earnings. There were few in the Roman world more despicable than tax collectors, who obtained their wealth at the expense of others. One day, Zaccheus learned that Jesus was visiting his town, and he climbed a sycamore tree to get a good look at the man who reportedly loved even sinners and outcasts. Jesus saw him in the tree and, to the astonishment of all, including Zaccheus, invited him to come down. Then Jesus even went to his house to eat with him!

During dinner, Zaccheus experienced the unconditional love and acceptance of Christ. As a result, he became a different person. His self-concept was radically changed from a swindling, loathsome tax collector to a person who knew he was loved by God. His actions reflected this dramatic change. He pledged to repent of his sins and repay fourfold those he had swindled. He also promised to give half of his possessions to the poor. Through Christ, Zaccheus developed a new self-concept, new values, new goals, and new behavior.

Regeneration is not a self-improvement program, nor is it a clean-up campaign for our sinful natures. Regeneration is nothing less than the impartation of new life. Paul stated in Ephesians 2:5 that we were once dead in our sins, but we have since been made alive in Christ. Paul also wrote about this incredible transformation process in his letter to the young pastor Titus:

> For we also once were foolish ourselves, disobedient, deceived, enslaved to various lusts and pleasures, spending our life in malice and envy, hateful, hating one another. But when the kindness of God our Savior and His love for mankind appeared, He saved us, not on the basis of deeds which we have done in righteousness, but according to His mercy, by the washing of regeneration and renewing by the Holy Spirit, whom He poured out upon us richly through Jesus Christ our Savior, that being justified by His grace we might be made heirs according to the hope of eternal life. (Titus 3:3–7)

Regeneration is the renewing work of the Holy Spirit that literally makes each believer a new person at the moment trust is placed in Christ as Savior.

In that wondrous, miraculous moment, we experience more than swapping one set of standards for another. We experience what

Jesus called a new birth (John 3:3–6), a Spirit-wrought renewal of the human spirit, a transforming resuscitation that takes place so that the Spirit is alive within us (Rom. 8:10).

Through the gift of God's grace, we are spiritually alive, forgiven, and complete in Him. Paul wrote the Colossian Christians: "For in Him [Christ] all the fulness of Deity dwells in bodily form, and in Him you have been made complete, and He is the head over all rule and authority" (Col. 2:9–10).

In the church at Colossae, false teachers taught that "completeness" came through a combination of philosophy, good works, other religions, *and* Christ. Paul's clear message was that we are made complete through Christ alone. To attempt to find completeness through any other source, including success, the approval of others, prestige, or appearance, is to be taken captive through philosophy and empty deception (Col. 2:8). Nothing can add to the death of Christ to pay for our sins and the resurrection of Christ to give us new life. We are complete because Christ has forgiven us and given us life and the capacity for growth and change.

According to theologian Louis Berkhof, "Regeneration consists in the implanting of the principle of the new spiritual life in man, in a radical change of the governing disposition of the soul, which, under the influence of the Holy Spirit, gives birth to a life that moves in a Godward direction. In principle this change affects the whole man: the intellect . . . the will . . . and the feelings or emotions."[1]

When we trust Christ and experience new life, forgiveness, and love, our lives will begin to change. Still, regeneration does not effect an instantaneous change in the full realm of our performance. We will continue to stumble and fall at times, but the Scriptures clearly instruct us to choose to act in ways that reflect our new lives and values in Christ. As Paul wrote the Ephesians:

> *That, in reference to your former manner of life, you lay aside the old self, which is being corrupted in accordance with the lusts of deceit, and that you be renewed in the spirit of your mind, and put*

on the new self, which in the likeness of God has been created in
righteousness and holiness of the truth. (Eph. 4:22–24)

We are to put on, or envelop ourselves in, this new self that
progressively expresses Christian character in our attitudes and
behavior. We are marvelously unique, created to reflect the character of Christ through our individual personalities and behavior.
In a different and special way, each believer has the capability to
shine forth the light of God. No two will reflect light in exactly the
same way.

The truth of regeneration can dispel the specter of the past. Our
sins have been forgiven, and we now have tremendous capabilities
for growth and change because we are new people with the Spirit
of God living in us. Yes, when we sin we will experience its
destructive effects and the Father's discipline, but our sin will
never change the truth of who we are in Christ.

When we do sin, we should follow King David's example.
When Nathan confronted David about his sin of adultery with
Bathsheba, David confessed his sin to the Lord (2 Sam. 12:1–13).
David did not run from his sin or its consequences. He married
Bathsheba, and God was merciful: He enabled Bathsheba to give
birth to Solomon, the wise king of Israel. Certainly, God could have
brought Solomon into the world another way, but perhaps as a message to us, He chose Bathsheba. What a message! Confess your sins,
worship God, and get on with your life. You can experience the
mercy of God no matter what you've been through.

Potential Obstacles to Receiving This Truth

We Only Believe What We See

Our greatest obstacle to experiencing regeneration is that we don't
look different and sometimes we don't act much differently. As we
recognize the results of justification, reconciliation, and propitiation, we will find it much easier to hold to the fact that we have
undergone regeneration. However, it will come down to whether or

not we're willing to accept what God reveals about our true natures. He is not lying to us, and He is not deceived.

Satan wants us to believe the lie *I am what I am. I cannot change. I am hopeless.* How can you begin to experience freedom from the fear of shame? In this important exercise, paraphrase each of the following passages about your new life in Him:

"You are the salt of the earth; but if the salt has become tasteless, how will it be made salty again? It is good for nothing any more, except to be thrown out and trampled under foot by men" (Matt. 5:13).

_____

_____

_____

_____

"You are the light of the world. A city set on a hill cannot be hidden" (Matt. 5:14).

_____

_____

_____

"To all who are beloved of God in Rome, called as saints: Grace to you and peace from God our Father and the Lord Jesus Christ" (Rom. 1:7).

_____

_____

_____

"For if by the transgression of the one, death reigned through the one, much more those who receive the abundance of grace and of the gift of righteousness will reign in life through the One, Jesus Christ. So then as through one transgression there resulted condemnation to all men, even so through one act of righteousness there resulted justification of life to all men" (Rom. 5:17–18).

_____

_____

_____

_____

_____

"There is therefore now no condemnation for those who are in Christ Jesus" (Rom. 8:1).

_____

_____

_____

"And if children, heirs also, heirs of God and fellow-heirs with Christ, if indeed we suffer with Him in order that we may also be glorified with Him" (Rom. 8:17).

_____

_____

_____

"But in all these things we overwhelmingly conquer through Him who loved us" (Rom. 8:37).

_____

_____

_____

"Therefore if any man is in Christ, he is a new creature; the old things passed away; behold, new things have come" (2 Cor. 5:17).

_____

_____

_____

"He made Him who knew no sin to be sin on our behalf, that we might become the righteousness of God in Him" (2 Cor. 5:21).

_____

_____

_____

"I have been crucified with Christ; and it is no longer I who live, but Christ lives in me; and the life which I now live in the flesh I live by faith in the Son of God, who loved me, and delivered Himself up for me" (Gal. 2:20).

_____

_____

_____

_____

_____

"He predestined us to adoption as sons through Jesus Christ to Himself, according to the kind intention of His will" (Eph. 1:5).

_____

_____

_____

"In Him we have redemption through His blood, the forgiveness of our trespasses, according to the riches of His grace" (Eph. 1:7).

_____

_____

_____

"But God, being rich in mercy, because of His great love with which He loved us, even when we were dead in our transgressions, made us alive together with Christ (by grace you have been saved), and raised us up with Him, and seated us with Him in the heavenly places, in Christ Jesus" (Eph. 2:4–6).

_____

_____

_____

_____

_____

"For we are His workmanship, created in Christ Jesus for good works, which God prepared beforehand, that we should walk in them" (Eph. 2:10).

_____

_____

_____

"Finally, be strong in the Lord, and in the strength of His might" (Eph. 6:10).

_____

_____

_____

"And in Him you have been made complete, and He is the head over all rule and authority" (Col. 2:10).

_____

_____

_____

"And so, as those who have been chosen of God, holy and beloved, put on a heart of compassion, kindness, humility, gentleness and patience" (Col. 3:12).

_____

_____

_____

"Because it is written, 'You shall be holy, for I am holy'" (1 Pet. 1:16).

_____

_____

_____

"By this, love is perfected with us, that we may have confidence in the day of judgment; because as He is, so also are we in this world" (1 John 4:17).

_____

_____

_____

These passages describe the stable and secure identity we have in Christ. It is our privilege to be His children; to experience His love, forgiveness, and power; and to express our appreciation of Him to others. Allow me to summarize the four great doctrines we have been pointing to as the solution for the four false beliefs:

1. Because of justification, you are completely forgiven and fully pleasing to God. You no longer have to fear failure.

2. Because of reconciliation, you are totally accepted by God. You no longer have to fear rejection.

3. Because of propitiation, you are deeply loved by God. You no longer have to fear punishment; nor do you have to punish others.

4. Because of regeneration, you have been made brand-new, complete in Christ. You no longer need to experience the pain of shame.

11

Agent of Change

Our redemption was made complete at Calvary. When Jesus lifted up His eyes and cried, "It is finished!" (John 19:30), He told us that the provision for man's reconciliation with God was complete. Nothing more need be done, because the Word of life had been spoken to all mankind. Man needed only to hear the Word, accept it, and place his hope and trust in Christ.

But if the redemption we enjoy is complete, why do we so often fail to see the changes we long for in our lives? Why do we wrestle day after day with the same temptations, the same failings, and the same distractions we have always fought? Why can't we break free and move on toward maturity?

Christ illustrated the reasons for our lack of fruitfulness in the parable of the sower in Mark 4:3–20. In agriculture, productivity depends on the fertility of the soil, the climate, and the presence or absence of weeds. The reasons Christ gave for lack of fruit in the believer's life were: Satan's taking away the Word of God, persecution, and the worries of the world. For most of us, the worries of the world are the primary culprit for our lack of growth. Jesus described it this way:

> And others are the ones on whom seed was sown among the thorns; these are the ones who have heard the word, and the worries of the world, and the deceitfulness of riches, and the desires for other things enter in and choke the word, and it becomes unfruitful. (Mark 4:18–19)

In the context of honesty, affirmation, and patience, we can focus on the forgiveness we have received and reject the deception and worldly desires that choke out the Word of life. We need to base our lives on God's Word and allow His character to be reproduced within us by the power of His Spirit:

> And those are the ones on whom seed was sown on the good ground; and they hear the word and accept it, and bear fruit, thirty, sixty, and a hundredfold. (Mark 4:20)

The moment we trust Christ, we are given everything pertaining to life and godliness (2 Pet. 1:2–4). Immediately, we become His sons and daughters, with all the provisions He has graciously given us. As we allow Him to reign over the affairs of our lives, He transforms our values, attitudes, and behavior so that we are able to glorify Him more and more. Of course we are still chained to a mortal body, but we are reborn in righteousness and holiness of the truth. We have within us the Christ who has authority over Satan. Christ has triumphed over him by the power of His blood to pay for sin and by the power of His resurrection to give new life (Col. 2:15).

Now redeemed, our rightful purpose to rule in life will only be denied if we continue to allow Satan to deceive us. If we fail to recognize our true position of worship and exercise our new power and authority, we will remain trapped in the world's system. Satan's lies and schemes are designed to keep us from recognizing and experiencing these wonderful truths.

In order to overcome Satan's lies and begin to enjoy freedom from false beliefs, we need to have a clear understanding of what Christ has done for us through His death on the cross. The more fully we understand the implications of Christ's sacrifice, the more we will experience the freedom, motivation, and power God intends for us. God's Word is the source of truth: the truth about Christ, the cross, and redemption.

The apostle Peter wrote that the cross is not just the beginning of the Christian life, but it is our constant motivation to grow spiritually and to live for Christ:

> *Now for this very reason also, applying all diligence, in your faith*
> *supply moral excellence, and in your moral excellence, knowledge;*
> *and in your knowledge, self-control, and in your self-control, perse-*
> *verance, and in your perseverance, godliness; and in your godliness,*
> *brotherly kindness, and in your brotherly kindness, Christian love.*
> *For if these qualities are yours and are increasing, they render you*
> *neither useless nor unfruitful in the true knowledge of our Lord Jesus*
> *Christ. For he who lacks these qualities is blind or short-sighted,*
> *having forgotten his purification from his former sins. (2 Pet. 1:5–9)*

This passage clearly teaches that the absence of spiritual growth can be traced to a lack of understanding or a failure to remember the implications of Christ's forgiveness. The cross is central to our motivation and development.

I have given you a beginning exercise for each of the four false beliefs in previous chapters, but this is only a start. In the closing chapters, we'll look at the basics of renewing the heart and mind: experiencing the power of the Holy Spirit and replacing thought patterns that tell us our worth is based on performance plus others' opinions with thought patterns that focus on the truths of God's unconditional love for us.

The principles in this book can be life-changing, but they are applied most readily in an environment where we are encouraged to be honest about our hurt, anger, joys, and hopes. Most of us are not very perceptive about ourselves (though we may be very perceptive about other people), and we need both the objectivity and the affirmation of others as we continue the process of application. It is also important to realize that working through these principles once is not enough. Many whom I have counseled and many who have read this material in its previous edition report that they have experienced dramatic growth only as they have applied these truths at an increasingly deeper level of their lives.

False Beliefs	Consequences of False Beliefs
I must meet certain standards to feel good about myself.	The fear of failure; perfectionism; being driven to succeed; manipulating others to achieve success; withdrawing from healthy risks
I must be approved by certain others to feel good about myself.	The fear of rejection; attempting to please others at any cost; being overly sensitive to criticism; withdrawing from others to avoid disapproval
Those who fail (including myself) are unworthy of love and deserve to be punished.	The fear of punishment; propensity to punish others; blaming self and others for personal failure; withdrawing from God and fellow believers; being driven to avoid punishment
I am what I am. I cannot change. I am hopeless.	Feelings of shame, hopelessness, inferiority; passivity; loss of creativity; isolation; withdrawing from others.

God's Specific Solution	Results of God's Solution
Because of justification, *I am completely forgiven and fully pleasing to God. I no longer have to fear failure.*	Increasing freedom from the fear of failure; desire to pursure the right things: Christ and His kingdom; love for Christ
Because of reconciliation, *I am totally accepted by God. I no longer have to fear rejection.*	Increasing freedom from the fear of rejection; willingness to be open and vulnerable; able to relax around others; willingness to take criticism; desire to please God no matter what others think
Because of propitiation, *I am deeply loved by God. I no longer have to fear punishment or punish others.*	Increasing freedom from the fear of punishment; patience and kindness toward others; being quick to apply forgiveness; deep love for Christ
Because of regeneration, *I have been made brand-new, complete in Christ. I no longer need to experience the pain of shame.*	Christ-centered self-confidence; joy, courage, peace; desire to know Christ

Let's review for a moment. The chart on pages 126–127 depicts the contrast between the rival belief systems. Use the chart to help you when you want to determine if any particular thought is based on a lie or on God's truth. If the thought is based on a lie, learn how to confront it and overcome it with the truth of God's Word.

The Holy Spirit: Our Source of Change

The truths we have examined in this book can have tremendous implications on our every goal and relationship, but now we need to understand how actually to implement them in our lives. How can we begin to experience positive change? Jesus answered this question in His last time of intimate instruction with His disciples (John 13–16). He told them that He would soon be put to death, but that they would not be left alone: "And I will ask the Father, and He will give you another Helper, that He may be with you forever" (John 14:16). That Helper is the Holy Spirit, who came some fifty days later to direct and empower the believers at Pentecost. The same Holy Spirit indwells all believers today and serves as our instructor, counselor, and source of spiritual power as we live for Christ's glory and honor.

Who is the Holy Spirit, and why did He come? The Holy Spirit, the third Person of the Trinity, is God and possesses all the attributes of deity. His primary purpose is to glorify Christ and bring attention to Him. Christ said, "He shall glorify Me; for He shall take of Mine, and shall disclose it to you" (John 16:14). The Holy Spirit is our teacher, and He guides us into the truth of the Scriptures (John 16:13). It is by His power that the love of Christ flows through us and produces spiritual fruit within us (John 7:37–39; 15:1–8). This spiritual fruit is described in many ways in the New Testament, including: intimate friendship with Christ (John 15:14); love for one another (John 15:12); joy and peace in the midst of difficulties (John 14:27; 15:11); steadfastness (Eph. 5:18–21); and evangelism and discipleship (Matt. 28:18–20).

Obviously, this fruit is not always evident in the lives of Christians, but why not? As we all know, the Christian life is not an easy one. It is not simply a self-improvement program. True, we may at times be able to make some changes in our habits through our own discipline and determination, but Christianity is not merely self-effort. The Christian life is a supernatural one in which we draw on Christ as our resource for direction, encouragement, and strength. In one of the most widely known metaphors of the Bible, Christ described the Christian life in John 15, using the illustration of a branch and a vine. He said:

> *I am the true vine, and My Father is the vinedresser. . . . Abide in [live, grow, and gain your sustenance from] Me, and I in you. As the branch cannot bear fruit of itself, unless it abides in the vine, so neither can you, unless you abide in Me. I am the vine, you are the branches; he who abides in Me, and I in him, he bears much fruit; for apart from Me you can do nothing. (John 15:1,4–5)*

Nothing? Yes, nothing in terms of that which honors Christ, is spiritually nourishing to us, and is genuine Christian service. Anything done apart from the love and power of Christ amounts to *nothing*. Although we may expend tremendous effort at a great personal cost, only that which is done for Christ's glory in the power of His Spirit is of eternal value. The very power of God that was evident when Christ was raised from the dead (Eph. 1:19–21) is available to every believer who abides in Him, who desires that He be honored, and who trusts that His Spirit will produce fruit in his or her life.

Just as the cross of Christ is the basis of our relationship with God, it is also the foundation of our spiritual growth. Christ's death is the supreme demonstration of God's love, power, and wisdom. The more we understand and apply the truths of justification, propitiation, reconciliation, and regeneration, the more our lives will reflect His character. Spiritual growth is not magic. It comes as we apply the love and forgiveness of Christ in our daily circumstances.

It comes as we reflect on the unconditional acceptance of Christ and His awesome power and choose to respond to situations and people in light of His sovereign purpose and kindness toward us.

The apostle Peter stated very clearly that our forgiveness, bought by the death of Christ, is the foundation of spiritual growth. Again, the clear implication from this passage is that the absence of spiritual growth signifies one's lack of understanding concerning forgiveness. Seeking an emotional experience, going to seminar after seminar, or looking for a "deeper life" may not be the solution. Emotional experiences, seminars, and studies are only valid if they are founded on the love, forgiveness, and power of the cross and resurrection of Christ. There is nothing more motivating, nothing more comforting, nothing else that compels us more to honor Christ, and nothing else that gives us as much compassion for others as the sacrificial payment of Christ that has rescued us from eternal condemnation.

At least five obstacles stem from a misunderstanding of Christ's love and forgiveness, and often prevent us from experiencing His presence and power:

1. We have wrong motives.

2. Our approach to the Christian life is too mechanical or regimented.

3. We are too mystical.

4. We lack knowledge about the availability of Christ's love and power.

5. We are harboring sin that blocks our fellowship with Christ.

Let's take a closer look at these obstacles.

Wrong Motives
Determining where we err in our motivations is often difficult. We usually have a variety of motives for what we pursue and probably

do nothing with completely pure motives. However, we must examine some of the reasons we may be following Christ before we can consider whether or not our motivations might be hindering our walk with Him.

Many of us tend to approach Christian living as a self-improvement program. We may desire spiritual growth, or we may have one or more fairly serious problems from which we desperately want to be delivered. While there is certainly nothing wrong with spiritual growth or desiring to be rid of a besetting problem, what is our motivation in wanting to achieve goals like these? Perhaps we desire success or the approval of others. Perhaps we fear that God can't really accept us until we have spiritually matured, or until "our problem" is removed. Perhaps we just want to feel better without having to struggle through the process of making major changes in our attitudes and behavior.

Motivations such as these may be mixed with a genuine desire to honor the Lord, but it's also possible that deep within us is a primary desire to glorify ourselves. When self-improvement, rather than Christ, becomes the center of our focus, our focus is displaced.

It is important to understand that fruitfulness and growth are the results of focusing on Christ and desiring to honor Him. When growth and change are our primary goals, we tend to be preoccupied with ourselves instead of with Christ: *Am I growing? Am I getting any better? Am I more like Christ today? What am I learning?*

This inordinate preoccupation with self-improvement parallels our culture's self-help and personal-enhancement movement in many ways. Personal development is certainly not wrong, but it is misleading and can be very disappointing to make it our preeminent goal. If it is our goal at all, it should be secondary. As we grasp the unconditional love, grace, and power of God, then honoring Christ will increasingly be our consuming passion. God wants us to have a healthy self-awareness and to periodically analyze our lives, but He does not want us to be preoccupied with ourselves. The only one worthy of our preoccupation is Christ, our sovereign Lord, who told the apostle Paul, "My grace is sufficient for you, for power is perfected in weakness" (2 Cor. 12:9).

If, through affirming Christian relationships, the power of God's Word, His Spirit, and time, we can begin to realize that our needs for security and approval are fully met in Christ, we will gradually be able to take our attention and affections off of ourselves and place them on Him. Only then can we begin to adopt Paul's intense desire to honor Christ: "Therefore also we have as our ambition . . . to be pleasing to Him" (2 Cor. 5:9).

Too Mechanical

Some of us are too mechanical in our approach to the Christian life. Although we may rigorously schedule and discipline our lives in an effort to conform to what we believe is a biblical lifestyle, our lives may exhibit little of the freshness, joy, and spontaneity of Christ.

One man had organized his life into hourly segments, each designated to accomplish some particular biblical purpose. True, he was organized and accomplished some good things, but he was miserable. This man was trusting in himself, instead of the Holy Spirit, to produce a life that pleased God.

Eventually, this man joined a church Bible study on God's grace. One of the men leading the group began meeting with him regularly. He had a lot of questions, and slowly he began to realize that Christ's foremost commandment is to love Him and others (Matt. 22:36–40) and that joy, peace, and kindness are much more important to God than adhering to strict rules (for which Jesus rebuked the Pharisees). Over the next few months, as he continued in this affirming relationship, he gained a new perspective, which later resulted in a new lifestyle of love and joy. This man is still an organized person, but being organized no longer dominates his life.

Though we may not be as extreme, many of us do have certain Christian activities (church attendance, tithing, Bible studies, and so on) that we feel we must do to be good Christians. These activities themselves are obviously not wrong, but a performance-oriented perspective is wrong. Christ wants us to receive our joy and acceptance from Him instead of merely following rules or schedules. He is the Lord; He alone is our source of security, joy, and meaning.

Too Mystical

A third obstacle to abiding in Christ is becoming too mystical or depending on supernatural feelings to dictate our relationship with God. This dependence on feelings leads to two problems. The first occurs when we wait for feelings to motivate us, and the other occurs when we see virtually every emotion as a "sign" from God. Let's examine these problems.

Some of us won't get up in the morning until the Lord "tells us to." We may not want to share Christ with others until we feel that God is prompting us. What we may be forgetting is that Christianity is primarily faith in action. Our emotions are not the most reliable source of motivation. Yes, the Holy Spirit does sometimes prompt us through impressions, but He has already given us the vast majority of what He wants us to do through the Scriptures. Rather than waiting for a "holy zap" to get us going, we need to believe the truth of God's Word and take action for His glory.

Must we wait until we feel like loving other Christians, praying, studying the Scriptures, sharing our faith, or serving His cause? No. We need to follow the examples recounted in Hebrews 11 of the men and women who acted on their faith in God, often in spite of their feelings. True, these people were often reflective, praying for God's direction, but they always acted on His truth.

The second problem with depending on our feelings occurs when we believe that our emotions are a primary means of God's communication with us and are, therefore, signs from God that indicate His leading. This conclusion may compel us to make authoritative statements about God's will (for both ourselves and others) that are based on little more than how we feel. As in the first extreme, the Scriptures may take a backseat as we sometimes justify foolish and even immoral acts by this false "leading from the Lord."

Though the Scriptures encourage us to be real and honest about our emotions, they never tell us to live by them. Biblical truths are the only reliable guide for our lives. Our feelings may reinforce these truths, but they may also reflect Satan's lies that God doesn't love us, that the fun of a particular sin is more satisfying than following God, or that God will never answer our prayers. The truth of God's Word is our authority, not our feelings.

Does this mean that we should repress our feelings or deny that we have them? No, but we need a safe environment (a friend or small group) with whom we can be honest about how we feel. We also should express our feelings to the Lord, fully and freely, and look at the Scriptures to determine what He would have us do. Then, with the encouragement of mature believers, the power of His Spirit, and in obedience to His Word, we should do what honors Christ. Many times, when we obey Christ in spite of our feelings, the emotions of joy and peace will follow sooner or later.

Again, our emotions are God-given; it is not wrong to have them, but by themselves, our feelings aren't enough to determine God's direction in our lives. Understanding God's leading requires that we blend a proper understanding of the Scriptures with a sensitivity to His Spirit. The Bible is our ultimate authority, and we need to become good students of it so that we will understand both the character and will of God. As Paul told Timothy: "All Scripture is inspired by God and profitable for teaching, for reproof, for correction, for training in righteousness; that the man of God may be adequate, equipped for every good work" (2 Tim. 3:16–17).

We also need to develop a sensitivity to the Holy Spirit's leading that goes beyond emotionalism. This sensitivity takes time to develop and is an awareness of His conviction of sin, what He wants us to say and do in certain situations, His prompting to share the gospel, and so forth. Discerning whether or not an impression is of God comes from three primary sources: the clear teaching of the Scriptures, previous experiences of learning, and the agreement of mature believers. If an impression is from God, it will not violate biblical principles.

Lack of Knowledge

Many of us are hindered in our walk with God because we do not realize the nature and depth of the love and power available to us in Christ. We haven't yet fully comprehended the magnificent truths of the Scriptures—that we are deeply loved, totally forgiven, fully pleasing, totally accepted, and complete in Christ, with all the power of His resurrection available to us. We may be like the West Texas sheep rancher who lived in poverty even though vast resources of oil were under his property. He was fabulously rich but didn't even know it. Since its discovery many years ago, this oil field has proven to be one of the richest and most productive in the world. Similarly, we have incredible resources available to us through the Holy Spirit, who enables us to experience the reality of Christ's love and power in many ways, including:

- expressing Christ-like characteristics to us through other believers over a period of time (John 13:34–35, 1 John 4:7, 12).
- revealing sin in our lives so that we can confess it and prevent our fellowship with God from being hindered (1 John 1:9).
- helping us choose to honor Christ in our circumstances and relationships (2 Cor. 5:9).
- enabling us to endure as we follow Christ (Rom. 5:1–5).
- producing spiritual fruit in our lives (John 15:1–8, Gal. 5:22–23).

Harboring Sin

Willful sin is a fifth obstacle that clouds our fellowship with God. Indeed, sin may be pleasurable for a moment, but inevitably, its destructive nature will reveal itself in many ways: broken relationships, poor self-esteem, and a poor witness for Christ. Whether it is a blatant sin of immorality or the more subtle sin of pride, we must learn to deal with all sin decisively, for our benefit and for Christ's glory.

Christ's death paid for all of our sins; they are completely forgiven. Comprehending His love and forgiveness encourages us to admit that we have sinned and claim forgiveness for any and every sin as soon as we become aware of it. Again, this prevents our fellowship with Christ from being hindered and enables us to continue experiencing His love and power. Paul wrote to the Galatian Christians: "The fruit of the Spirit is love, joy, peace, patience, kindness, goodness, faithfulness, gentleness, self-control" (Gal. 5:22–23).

As we respond to the love of Christ and trust His Spirit to fill us, these characteristics will become increasingly more evident in our lives. The filling of the Holy Spirit includes two major aspects: our purpose (to bring honor to Christ instead of to ourselves) and our resources (trusting in His love and power to accomplish results instead of trusting in our own wisdom and abilities). Although we will continue to mature in our relationship with the Lord over the years, we can begin to experience His love, strength, and purpose from the moment we put Him at the center of our lives.

Spencer, a university student, had been a Christian for several years. He had trusted Christ as his personal Savior when a friend from his dorm shared the gospel with him during his first semester. Although he was growing in his relationship with Christ, intramural athletics and parties with his rowdy friends became the focus of Spencer's life by the middle of his sophomore year. He still went to church frequently, but he was confused and often felt guilty about his relationships with his friends and their activities. He tried talking with them about this, but they only laughed. Despite his occasional feelings of discomfort, Spencer felt like he needed these friends, and he continued spending time with them.

Then, in the fall of his junior year, Spencer went to several Christian meetings on campus. He began hearing about the love and power of Christ and how the Holy Spirit can enable us to live for Him. Another young man, Phil, took an interest in Spencer and began to disciple him. Through Phil's supportive friendship, Spencer began to develop an eternal perspective, slowly recognizing that worldliness and sin are destructive but that following Christ is eternally significant. One night, Spencer spent some time alone, praying and thinking about what he had learned. He realized that his life was confusing, frustrating, and dishonoring to the Lord. Spencer also realized that Christ is worthy of his love and obedience, and he decided to live for Him. As he began to confess the specific sins the Holy Spirit brought to his mind and as he asked Him for the power to live in a way that is pleasing to Christ, Spencer felt a surge of relief and joy. He was doing the right thing.

Phil was excited about the steps Spencer was taking, but Spencer was primarily concerned about his other friends. Realizing that he might be rejected, Spencer made plans to tell them about his decision to follow Christ. When he did, some of them laughed. Others were surprised, and a few were even angry. For the next year, Spencer still spent some time with these friends but now at ball games instead of wild parties. He shared Christ with many of them and had the joy of seeing two trust Christ. Spencer had plenty of struggles and spiritual growing pains, but his life began to reflect a new consistency, a new purpose, and a new attitude of thankfulness to the Lord.

Like Spencer, our own willingness to be filled with the Holy Spirit is a direct response to the magnificent truths centered in the cross and the resurrection of Christ and our participation in relationships in which we sense His love for us. We are deeply loved and completely forgiven by God, fully pleasing to God, totally accepted by God, and complete in Him. Are you depending on God's Spirit to teach you, change you, and use you in the lives of others? If so, continue trusting Him! If not, review the five obstacles to following Christ and see if any of these are obstructing your relationship with Him. Are there specific sins you need to confess? Confession means to agree with God that you have sinned and to accept that Christ has completely forgiven you. It also means to repent, to turn from your sins to a life of love and obedience to God.

As you continue in the process of experiencing more of God's grace, take time to reflect on His love and power. Trust Him to guide you by His Word, fill you with His Spirit, and enable you to live for Him and be used by Him in the lives of others. Abiding in Christ does not mean deliverance from all of your problems, but it will provide a powerful relationship with the One who is the source of wisdom for difficult decisions, love to encourage you, and strength to help you endure.

12

Guilt Versus Conviction

There is no burden that produces pain, fear, and alienation quite like the feeling of guilt. Many of us know it as a constant burden. Some of us respond to it like a whipped puppy, beaten down and ashamed. Some of us avoid it through the numbing effects of denial. Our association with guilt may be prompted by many factors: poor parental modeling of Christ's love and forgiveness, divorce, neglect, a particular past sin, and the emphasis some believers place on the "oughts" and "shoulds" of Christianity. Regardless of these influences, guilt need not be a way of life for us.

In Romans 8:1, Paul tells us, "There is therefore now no condemnation for those who are in Christ Jesus." When I shared this important truth with a troubled Christian brother, his jaw dropped and his eyes filled with tears. He looked at me incredulously and exclaimed, "You mean, all this guilt I have been carrying for so long is unnecessary? I can be free from these tormenting feelings of condemnation? Why hasn't somebody told me this before?"

The apostle Paul has been trying to tell us just that for centuries, but few of us have listened. We feel we deserve condemnation, and we fail to realize that Christ has freed us from the guilt and condemnation our sins deserve.

What exactly is guilt, anyway? Sigmund Freud said that guilt is a result of social restraint. To Freud, guilt was born in the mind of a child whose parents scolded him or her; it was rooted in the child's fear of losing the love of someone significant to him or her. Therefore, according to Freud, we experience guilt when we fear a loss of social esteem, when instinctive drives cause us to act in ways other than the accepted social norm. Alfred Adler wrote that guilt arises from a refusal to accept one's inferiority. Therefore, he concluded, guilt feelings are those pangs of self-incrimination we feel anytime we think or behave inadequately. Both Freud and Adler tried to explain the pain of guilt from a perspective that denies the righteous judgment of God and our personal responsibility for sin. To them, guilt could only be explained on a human, existential basis.

Christian authors Bruce Narramore and Bill Counts represent a more biblical perspective when they differentiate between true guilt and false guilt. True guilt, they explain, is an objective fact, but false guilt is a subjective feeling of pain and rejection. They emphasize that while the Bible discusses the fact of legal or theological guilt, it never tells the Christian to feel psychological guilt. These distinctions are helpful, but they may not clarify the issue for those who equate any guilt with condemnation. For this reason, we will use guilt and conviction to distinguish between the condemnation our sin deserves and the loving motivation prompted by God to live in a way that brings honor to Him. Though many people confuse these two concepts, they are actually worlds apart. The comparisons given later in this chapter clearly illustrate their differences.

Perhaps no emotion is more destructive than guilt. It causes a loss of self-respect. It causes the human spirit to wither, and it eats away at our personal significance. Guilt is a strong motivation, but it plays on our fears of failure and rejection; therefore, it can never ultimately build, encourage, or inspire us in our desire to live for Christ.

Some of us understand guilt as a sense of legal and moral accountability before God. We may try to distinguish it from low self-esteem by reasoning that guilt is the result of a sinful act or moral wrongdoing while low self-esteem is derived from a feeling of social or personal inadequacy. Consequently, a lie makes us feel unacceptable to God and brings guilt, while bad table manners make us feel unacceptable to the people around us and bring low self-esteem. This perspective shows some depth of thought, but it focuses on an emotional response to guilt rather than its root cause. At its root, guilt is the condition of being separated from God and of deserving condemnation for sin. Low self-esteem can be experienced by Christians or non-Christians, anyone who believes Satan's lies and feels like a failure, hopeless and rejected.

As we have determined, guilt has a restricted meaning in the New Testament. It refers only to man's condition prior to his salvation. Only the non-Christian is actually guilty before God. He has transgressed the law of God and must face the consequences. Guilt shakes its fist and says, "You have fallen short and must pay the price. You are personally accountable." Our condemnation is removed only through Christ. He took all of our guilt upon Himself when He accepted the penalty for our sins and suffered the full punishment for all sin. Because of His substitution, we need never face guilt's consequences. We are acquitted and absolved from guilt, free from our sentence of spiritual death.

Many of us have been told that we are still guilty even after we have trusted Christ to pay for our sins. And sadly, we have heard this in places that should be loudly and clearly proclaiming the forgiveness and freedom found in the cross—our churches. Perhaps some people think that if they don't use guilt for motivation, we won't do anything. Guilt may motivate us for a short while until we adjust to being properly motivated. But a short period of waiting is well worth the long-term results of grace-oriented, intrinsic motivation.

Learn to identify incorrect teaching, guilt motivation, and the results of guilt in your own thoughts. Then refuse to believe the lies any longer, and focus instead on the unconditional love and forgiveness of Christ. His love is powerful, and He is worthy of our intense zeal to obey and honor Him. The result of proper motivation is an enduring, deepening commitment to Christ and His cause rather than the prevalent results of guilt motivation: resentment and the desire to escape. Christians are freed from guilt, but we are still subject to conviction.

The Bible frequently speaks of the Holy Spirit's work to convict believers of sin. He directs and encourages our spiritual progress by revealing our sins in contrast to the holiness and purity of Christ. Although the Holy Spirit convicts both believers and unbelievers of sin (John 16:8), His conviction of believers is not intended to produce pangs of guilt. Our status and self-worth are secure by the grace of God, and we are no longer guilty. Conviction deals with our behavior, not our status before God. Conviction is the Holy Spirit's way of showing the error of our performance in light of God's standard and truth. His motivation is love, correction, and protection.

While guilt is applicable to nonbelievers and originates from Satan, conviction is the privilege of those who believe, and it is given by the Holy Spirit. Guilt brings depression and despair, but conviction enables us to realize the beauty of God's forgiveness and to experience His love and power.

Perhaps the following will better illustrate the contrasting purposes and results of guilt and conviction:

- **Basic focus:** *Guilt* focuses on the state of being condemned: "I am unworthy." *Conviction* focuses on behavior: "This act is unworthy of Christ and is destructive."
- **Primary concern:** *Guilt* deals with the sinner's loss of self-esteem and a wounded self-pride: "What will others think of me?" *Conviction* deals with the loss of our moment-by-moment communication with God: "This act is destructive to me and interferes with my walk with God."
- **Primary fear:** *Guilt* produces a fear of punishment: "Now I'm going to get it!" *Conviction* produces a fear of the destructiveness of the act itself: "This behavior is destructive to me and others, and it robs me of what God intends for me."
- **Agent:** The agent of *guilt* is Satan: "The god of this world has blinded the minds of the unbelieving, that they might not see the light of the gospel of the glory of Christ" (2 Cor. 4:4). The agent of *conviction* is the Holy Spirit: "But if by the Spirit

you are putting to death the deeds of the body, you will live"
(Rom. 8:13).

- **Behavioral results:** *Guilt* leads to depression and more sin: "I
  am just a low-down, dirty, rotten sinner"; or to rebellion: "I
  don't care. I'm going to do whatever I want to do."
  Conviction leads to repentance, the turning from sin to
  Christ: "Lord, I agree with You that my sin is wrong and
  destructive. What do You want me to do?"
- **Interpersonal result:** The interpersonal result of *guilt* is
  alienation, a feeling of shame that drives one away from the
  person who has been wronged: "I can't ever face him or her
  again." The interpersonal result of *conviction* is restoration,
  a desire to remedy the harm done to others: "Father, what
  would You have me do to right this wrong and restore the
  relationship with the one I have offended?"
- **Personal results:** *Guilt* ends in depression, bitterness, and
  self-pity: "I'm just no good." *Conviction* ends in comfort, the
  realization of forgiveness: "You have made me complete and
  have given me the righteousness of Christ, even though my
  performance often falls short. Lord, I confess my sins to You.
  [List them. Be specific.] I agree with You that these things are
  wrong. I also agree that they have been destructive to my life.
  Thank You for Your grace and forgiveness. Is there anything
  I need to return, anyone I need to repay, or anyone I need to
  apologize to? Thank You."

It is important to affirm our righteousness in Christ as well as
to confess our sins. God does not need to be reminded of our right
standing in Him, but we do. Therefore we need to make the above
prayer a daily experience and allow it to pervade our thoughts and
hearts. As we yield to the gentle prodding of God-given conviction,
confess our sins, and affirm our true relationship with Him, we will
be gradually shaped and molded in such a way that we will
increasingly honor the one who died and rose again on our behalf
(2 Cor. 5:15).

We may not experience joy and freedom immediately, especially if we have developed the painful habit of prolonged self-condemnation as a way of dealing with sin. Loving friends who listen to us and encourage us can be an example of God's forgiveness to us. As we become more honest about our feelings through these affirming relationships, we will be able to increasingly experience the freedom, forgiveness, and freshness of God's grace.

The following example provides an insight in how we should approach failure and how we should help others. Frank told of a deep, bitter inner struggle he was having. He had found himself thinking about having sex with another man. At first it was just a fleeting thought, but now that thought seemed to rule his mind. I told him his first step was to agree with God about this thought activity. Even though he had never acted on his thoughts, what he was thinking was wrong. I instructed him to ask God to show him what excuse he had been using for thinking like this in the first place and to show him how destructive his receiving all this condemnation had been.

When we met again, he told me all that God had shown him. Frank's freedom was gained as he agreed with God on all that he had been shown. He realized the excuses he used and how destructive this disobedience had been in his life. But equally important, God showed him that his accepting condemnation was coming from the same place as the homosexual thoughts. During this process, God also revealed how bitter Frank was because of having been mistreated by his father. It was this mistreatment and Frank's self-pity that had provided the basis for Frank to feel that he had a right to do what he wanted to do (or to think what he wanted to think).

The final step was for Frank to dwell on how much he was forgiven until thankfulness overwhelmed him and he forgave his father. It was only living in the light of God's forgiveness that set Frank free.

The Legal Trap

There is a relationship between the law and the sin nature that few Christians understand. In fact, when the first part of Romans 5:20

is quoted to many Christians, they will deny it is a part of Scripture: "And the Law came in that the transgression might increase." Examine the following:

> *For while we were in the flesh, the sinful passions, which were aroused by the Law, were at work in the members of our body to bear the fruit for death. But now we have been released from the Law, having died to that by which we were bound, so that we serve in newness of the Spirit and not in oldness of the letter.*
>
> *What shall we say then? Is the Law sin? May it never be! On the contrary, I would not have come to know sin except through the Law; for I would not have known about coveting if the Law had not said, "You shall not covet." But sin, taking opportunity through the commandment, produced in me coveting of every kind; for apart from the Law sin is dead. And I was once alive apart from the Law; but when the commandment came, sin became alive, and I died; and this commandment, which was to result in life, proved to result in death for me; for sin, taking opportunity through the commandment, deceived me, and through it killed me. So then, the Law is holy, and the commandment is holy and righteous and good. (Rom. 7:5–12)*

> *Christ redeemed us from the curse of the law, having become a curse for us—for it is written, "Cursed is every one who hangs on a tree." (Gal. 3:13)*

Law and *sin* (*sin nature*) are technical terms. This means you cannot assign just any meaning to them. You must understand them through the particular definition given them by the text. In other words, the way you use a term in everyday speech may not be the way the term is used in Scripture. For instance, everyone talks about God. The Bible uses the term *God* to refer to the infinite triune God. Thus, two people using the same word could be referring to opposite concepts unless they take time to define the word *God*.

Understanding this, the term *sin* in these passages refers to a *sin nature*. The sin nature mechanism is in operation to motivate man to sin. The sin nature is not just some theoretical concept. It exists as surely as your heart exists. Treat it as some vague idea and you will be at a great disadvantage in combating it.

Law is the other term needing definition. This word generally refers to a relationship between two separate events. The law of gravity means that if something goes up in the earth's gravitational field (event 1), then it will come down (event 2). Laws are generally written in an *if . . . then* format. Let's look at Romans 8:2: "For the law of the Spirit of life in Christ Jesus has set you free from the law of sin and of death." If we were to paraphrase this into the *if . . . then* format, it would read, *"If* you operate in the Spirit of life in Christ Jesus *then* you will be set free from the law of sin." The law of sin is stated as follows: *"If* you operate in sin *then* you will die." Operating in the Spirit of life always brings freedom from the law of sin. Operating in sin always brings death. They are simply undeniable and unchangeable laws.

The definition of the law referred to in Romans 5 and 7 is completed in Galatians 3:13. These verses identify that there is a curse associated with the law. Therefore, *if* we do not fulfill certain standards *then* we are cursed (condemned). The law in Romans 5 and 7 must be understood in these *if . . . then* terms. The law here condemns when failure occurs.

The impact of Romans 8:1 is that the believer is released from the law and its inherent condemnation. This does not mean we are without standards of conduct. Sin is naturally destructive. It does mean that our failing to meet these standards does not bring condemnation or depreciation.

Now that you know how *sin* and *law* are used, look at Romans 5:20 and Romans 7:5–12:

> *And the Law came in that the transgression might increase . . . the sinful passions, which were aroused by the Law. . . . But sin, taking opportunity through the commandment, produced in me coveting of every kind; for apart from the Law sin is dead. . . . for sin, taking opportunity through the commandment, deceived me, and through it killed me.*

The sin nature obviously has a strong reaction when it's in the presence of this type of law. God doesn't indicate why this is so, only that it is. The sin nature will be reactive whether the law comes from God or man. The prerequisite is that a behavior standard be present that carries with it depreciating condemnation.

The first great benefit of our sin nature's reaction to the law is that it is easier for us to recognize the depraved condition of our person. We are already condemned, "for all have sinned," but God, knowing man would not realize his desperate need for Jesus without being exposed to his depravity, introduced the law, and then the sin nature excitedly produced all types of sin.

However, the law was not just to bring us to Jesus. Remember, God is determined that you be unsuccessful in gaining self-worth through your performance. Your success at meeting this self-worth would limit your acceptance of His plan. The law insures you won't win.

You cannot experience your death to the law as long as you are a part of Adam's plan. Adam's plan ensures your openness to condemnation when you fail. Even though you have been set free from the law and its inherent condemnation, you will act, and your sin nature will respond just like you are a lost man. Your sin nature will keep so stirred up by the law that you are assured to fail. Like Pavlov's dogs, when our sin nature encounters the law, it responds. Failure is in your future. Through the law this is assured.

13

The Trip In

At this point, you should wonder, *Well, what do I do now? I realize that I have bought into the satanic formulas. I recognize that my life has been affected by the four false beliefs. But I have believed this way all my life. Is there any hope to break free from thought patterns I have held for so long?* You may even realize by now that you have used the four false beliefs on yourself numerous times. In fact, you may even feel frustration trying to understand how you would function when thinking differently.

For you to correct your thought process is hopeless unless you cooperate with God to release His power in your mind. "And do not be conformed to this world, but be transformed by the renewing of your mind, that you may prove what the will of God is, that which is good and acceptable and perfect" (Rom. 12:2).

"Renew your mind." But how do you do that? It is more than self-talk. It is more than repeating some words over and over. It is actually changing some of the thought patterns by which we have lived our entire lives. If this is going to occur we are going to have to experience the following:

- agreeing with God that we have been deceived
- agreeing with God that we have been believing a lie and we need to repent for doing so
- allowing God to show us how destructive this lie has been in our lives

- choosing to reject the lie we have been believing so long and committing ourselves to believe what God says to be true
- being willing to stand on the truth that God discloses to us about ourselves instead of using our normal responses

God has given us a supernatural deception detector, the Holy Spirit, who wants to bring us to truth. However, He has also given us a natural deception detector, our emotions. Our hurtful, negative emotions are similar to the body's mechanism of creating fever. When you have an infection, your body increases your body temperature. One of the uses of that mechanism is to alert you that you are sick. We would never take medication that would eliminate this process from occurring, as we could become deathly ill without knowing what was happening. However, many of us have a preoccupation with finding ways of avoiding all hurtful emotions through alcohol, drugs, or some form of activity that keeps us active and away from thinking about what is bothering us.

The Feeling Wheel on page 151 is a visual tool designed to help people recognize and identify their own feelings. When a person is asked to express feelings, there is frequently a real vagueness in identifying the way he or she feels, something like:

- "I feel good."
- "I feel bad."
- "I feel better."
- "I feel worse."
- "I'm okay."

I recall a lady who attended a retreat to get help because she had reached the point in her life where she felt there was no hope. She had decided that this retreat was her very last chance to be helped. If this didn't work, she was going to kill herself. Apparently, she grew up in a family that had abused her verbally and physically. She had been taught that it was not permissible to talk about the way she felt. She had to stuff her feelings away

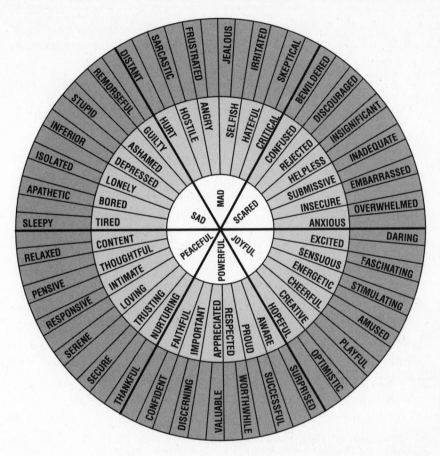

Developed by and available from Dr. Gloria Willcox,
4444 Fifth Avenue North, St. Petersburg, FL 33713

because she was never allowed to express them. The greatest barrier at the retreat was that she couldn't relate how she felt because her problems were of such a hidden and devastating nature. She would make statements such as, "I'm okay." "I'm all right." "Everything's okay." "Everything's all right."

Every exercise was to help people be honest about what had hurt them. She was scared she would begin to feel the pain of the past. She said, "It's just too painful to think about the way I feel inside."

Fortunately, God had His hand on her. By means of the Feeling Wheel she was able to begin to understand how she felt inside. Others in the group shared their feelings, and this encouraged her. She was soon able to think about the situations that had created what she felt. By the end of the retreat she experienced a great amount of freedom and was able to express these feelings.

As a result of the freedom she received, she was able to go on with her life. One of the statements she made was, "This is the first time in my life I have ever been able to talk about the way I feel inside with other people."

She left the retreat knowing that God had really come through for her and that she did have a chance for life. Suicide was no longer an alternative.

The Feeling Wheel will enable us to identify more ways to communicate how we feel inside. The ability to identify our emotions is extremely important. This seems to be the real barrier in relationships. A close relationship with anyone is next to impossible without being able to relate emotions. First, identify emotions, and second, talk about them.

All intimacy in a relationship comes from communicating our feelings to one another. When people see a list of emotions such as those on the Feeling Wheel, they will begin to relate to them very quickly.

The Feeling Wheel is divided into six parts like a pie. Each part has a root, such as sad, mad, scared, peaceful, powerful, or joyful, and the other emotions come out of the root emotions. It is interesting that most of the people we see relate to mad, sad, and scared. They do, however, identify peaceful, powerful, and joyful as what they have desired. Mad, sad, and scared, have dominated the way most have felt during their lives.

When people put words to their feelings, it may surprise them. Identifying their emotions seems to bring some freedom to go on with the exercise called "The Trip In."

Beginning the Trip

If you ask someone why he or she is mad, for instance, that person will tell you about something that has *occurred* in his or her life. It is as though, we believe that *situations* cause emotions.

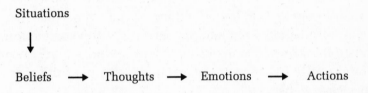

Situations

↓

Beliefs ⟶ Thoughts ⟶ Emotions ⟶ Actions

The fact is that we perceive situations through the grid of our beliefs. Mary goes to a party and finds the people at the party cold and rejecting. Bill goes to the same party and finds the people warm and friendly. Mary has experienced a great deal of rejection in her life and has spent a lot of time thinking about all the rejection she has experienced. She has internalized the rejection to the extent that she feeds herself rejection messages even when there is no one present to reject her. Bill, on the other hand, has not had these life experiences and responds to the accepting messages and behavior that he finds at the party.

The first step to freedom is recognizing that life is distorted by our *expectations* of what we are going to experience. However, let us assume that Mary and Bill meet someone who is a critical, demeaning person who puts down everyone. Mary encounters this person and responds by feeling awful about herself. The meeting triggers all those negative messages she is carrying around inside. Bill meets the same person and walks away with the thought, *What a miserable, angry person. I wonder what's wrong with him.* Mary wonders what is wrong with herself; Bill wonders what is wrong with the other person. What is the difference? It is that the situation (meeting this angry, mean person) has triggered long-held beliefs in Mary's mind that she is not a valuable person, that she should be rejected, and that she only gains value if she can get everyone to value her.

So from where do our destructive emotions come? Answer: Destructive thoughts. What triggers destructive thoughts? Answer: False beliefs. And how are the false beliefs energized? Answer: Our life situations.

Can we control our life situations to the degree that we can keep our false beliefs from being triggered? We try sometimes, but obviously that cannot be done. Therefore we have a great need to destroy the false beliefs and replace them with the truth that God has disclosed to us.

We call this process The Trip In. Often, if we have something medically, internally wrong with us, we undergo some type of imaging examination that can "look" for what is wrong. The Trip In allows us a similar process to look for false beliefs.

Before we look at the mechanics of The Trip In process, you should understand that you can do this on one of two levels. You can try to accomplish this by depending only on your natural mind, or you can seek God's guidance through the process. Doing The Trip In "naturally" can lead to some real bouts with depression, and you will come up with some very interesting information. However, you will not be experiencing God's power in this process. If it is God who opens up an area to you, then you can be sure He is ready to heal that area. If it is just your mind going through rumination and introspection, then God may or may not intervene in a process that He did not start.

Phase One: Bondage

We have already referred to the way situations trigger false beliefs. In those situations there are almost always individuals who we blame for our emotions. We think, *I feel this way because of Harry.* We become upset with Harry both for what he did and for our own response.

The next time you become upset and blame someone for your response, think about your tube of toothpaste. This morning you

The Trip In

	The Situation			
Bondage - phase 1 Use emotions to identify false beliefs, destructive thoughts	False Beliefs →	Destructive Thoughts →	Destructive Emotions →	Destructive Behavior
Obedience - phase 2 Identify false beliefs, acknowledge destructive thoughts and behavior	Confession of False Beliefs, Destructive Thoughts & Behavior →	→	→	Repentance and Obedience
Freedom - phase 3 Replace false beliefs with God's truth	God's Truth →	Healthy Thoughts →	Healthy Emotions →	Healthy Behavior

squeezed your toothpaste tube, and out of it came toothpaste. The reason the toothpaste came out is because that is what was in the tube. Someone may have squeezed you once, and out of you may have come responses that were really ungodly, maybe even embarrassing. You blame another for your responses, but you have to understand what came out of you was what was in you. Often God allows us to undergo troubling circumstances so that we can see what is inside of us.

When Sally began describing her feelings about God, all of a sudden, streams of profanity came out of her mouth. She was shocked to hear this anger and bitterness coming from her. She was now face to face with an issue with which God wanted to deal. God was not upset with what He heard. The hatred and bitterness were destroying her life whether or not she would have expressed her feelings.

Destructive Thoughts

Thoughts can be tricky. A thought that can seem and sound harmless can really stand for other thoughts that, when understood, are obviously the reason for the destructive emotions. Sam's motto was "Don't just work hard, work smart." This is obviously a reasonable motto for living. Sam had heard this all his life. However, the real meaning to him was "You have to be better than the rest or you're worthless." This destructive thought and belief became associated with the harmless motto through the teachings he received from his father. It was not until God revealed to him what was behind this simple saying that he could do anything about the destructive thoughts.

Sometimes destructive thoughts simply make no sense, but we still live by them. Joan came from wealth and felt that she was an absolute failure because she had a job. Forget the fact that she was a young single woman; she still had an overwhelming sense of failure every day when she went to work. Her counselor suggested during one session that they call his wife, who worked with a marketing company. He said, "Joan, why don't we call up my wife and tell her what a valueless failure she is for going to a job today." Of course Joan was appalled at the thought, but the light went on inside her as she recognized how irrational her sense of failure was. This recognition did not change her emotions right away, however. As we shall see soon, recognition must be followed with other action.

Destructive Behavior

Destructive behavior takes the form of either external behavior (what you can see and count) or internal behavior (thought activity). Often we are far more concerned with external behavior even though it is always preceded by internal behavior.

Susan and Jim, both married to different people, thought about having sex with each other for several months before they found themselves at a motel room being unfaithful to their spouses.

George thought for a long time how unfair the company he worked for was before he falsified his expense reports.

Think about your own life. How many times do you think of why you are justified in doing something before you actually do it?

Destructive behavior may be obviously wrong, such as an affair; or it may be something that seems rather innocent. Several years ago, I lived in a city that was crazy about softball. Softball leagues would play past midnight. Some of the men would play in several different leagues. Playing softball is not necessarily destructive, but playing softball to avoid being at home with one's family is. We must be careful how we justify our actions that appear innocent on the surface.

Phase Two: Obedience

If we have the correct perspective on obedience, we will get the most out of the times when we are confronted with the choice of either staying with old beliefs or standing firm on what God has revealed to us.

Sarah worked for a real jerk. He enjoyed giving her a hard time. If there was the smallest mistake, he would make a big deal out of it. She just wanted out. All her life she had had performance anxiety, and he was just making her life miserable. I suggested a different perspective. Her boss could become a real asset to her as she escaped the trap of evaluating herself on the basis of others' opinions.

We set up a plan whereby she would begin to use these outbursts to identify the messages she had believed all her life. These messages were those associated with judging herself on the basis of how well she performed and what others thought of her.

Sarah was resistant at first. But soon she was well into using all phases of The Trip In. She soon lost her fear of him, and he quickly realized that he wasn't getting the desired response out of her. Several months later she was offered a better job, and she moved on. Sarah will always see her former boss as instrumental in her identification of the false beliefs that had ruled her life.

It may seem odd to you that we would talk about confessing and repenting for being deceived. Confession means that we agree with God that what He says is correct. Therefore, God wanted Sarah to agree with Him that she was believing lies about herself. For her confession to really be complete, she would need to recognize how destructive these false beliefs were in her life. She asked the Father to show her this, and He did. Repentance meant that she was to turn from relying on these old false beliefs and begin to live by what God says is true.

Besides agreeing with God about the destructiveness of the false beliefs, the destructive thoughts, and the destructive behavior, it was also necessary for her to forgive her boss (many times). If she had held on to unforgiveness, she would have been unable to live in the light of her own forgiveness and claim her new identity.

Phase Three: Freedom

Trying to reject the false beliefs without replacing them with God's truth is impossible. We have held on to and used these false beliefs for so long that they seem normal to us. If we approach our life situations passively, they will always rule. Therefore, our model is to identify, confess, reject, and then replace.

Using Sarah's example, it would go something like this:

Situation: *Sarah's boss throws a letter she had just typed back at her because he wants some changes made. He tells her that he can't understand why she didn't catch this mistake and wonders aloud about her intelligence.*

Sarah's response: *Sarah recognizes the knot in her stomach and a sense of fear and dread. She immediately begins to talk to God (silently) about what she is experiencing. She asks Him for wisdom* *and to show her what false beliefs and old hurtful messages are being triggered. As she picks up the sheet of paper to see what is concerning her boss, she begins to recall that this is how she felt one time when she had broken one of her mother's favorite dishes. She also recognizes that she uses the sense of that scolding to condemn herself even when no one except herself knows that she has failed at something. She makes a note of these remembrances and then retypes the paper.*

Obedience phase: *On her next break, Sarah asks the Holy Spirit to reveal to her how holding on to these false beliefs and destructive messages has affected her. Although saddened that her life has been so impacted by that which is false, she continues to allow God to show her how much she has missed out on due to her believing a lie. This process goes on for most of the day.*

That evening, Sarah recounts to God all that she believes He has revealed to her. She agrees with Him that she has based her life in this area on a lie. She dwells on how much she has been forgiven and how much Christ had to pay in order for her to live in that forgiveness. Out of a sense of thankfulness for her own forgiveness, Sarah forgives both her boss and her mother.

"And they overcame him because of the blood of the Lamb and because of the word of their testimony, and they did not love their life even to death" (Rev. 12:11). Based on this scripture, Sarah declared (aloud) that she was bought by the blood of Christ, that His salvation provides her a new life, and that she has been made acceptable in Him. She declares that she rejects the false beliefs on which she has been operating her life. Sarah then thanks the Father for being so good and so caring that He has made a way for her to escape these lifelong thought patterns.

Sarah did the above many times. In fact, she began to see her boss as a valuable tool that God was using to free her. It is not that she never gets caught up in performance anxiety anymore, but she is now able to recognize when she gets caught up in it and why.

In Conclusion

The Father is busy in our lives even when we are unaware of His activities. He wants us to find freedom in this life. He is determined that we have a chance for this freedom. Although we will never experience absolute freedom this side of heaven, if we are willing to cooperate with His plan we can experience much more than we could ever imagine.

This will be a process. It will only occur as we are willing to go to a deeper level in our relationship with Him. There will be struggles and many failures along the way. However, the Father does not get tired of being there to bring us to victory. The only question is, Are we willing to go with Him?

THE SEARCH FOR SIGNIFICANCE

Workbook

Specially Designed Bible Studies
and Applications

Introduction

General Douglas MacArthur said that one of the most important rules of war is to know your enemy. If we are unaware of Satan's schemes and lies, we will be ineffective in spiritual warfare. The purpose of this workbook is twofold: to help you uncover Satan's deceptions in your thoughts and beliefs and to replace those lies with the powerful Word of God.

The goal of going through this workbook is not simply to fill in the blanks but to understand and apply God's truth to your life. Don't rush through it. Take time to think. It is very important that you allow the Holy Spirit to show you those specific thoughts, emotions, relationships, or events that you need to deal with. This will take time and concentration.

Although self-analysis is a part of this workbook, the material presented here is designed to focus your attention primarily on Christ, not on yourself. If you tend to be introspective (which comes from trying to find error in ourselves to blame, or good in ourselves to justify our existence), the truth brought out in this workbook will help you begin to experience freedom from that bondage. You will learn how to use scriptural truths, rather than your performance or the opinions of others, as the basis of your value. You will see that you do not have to get angry or disgusted when you or someone else fails. You will realize that you are not in a hopeless rut. You will discover the potential for a far deeper, more intimate relationship with Christ and with others. And you will gain a genuine appreciation for yourself. You will want to serve Christ and live for Him more than ever.

The workbook is divided into three sections:

I. Background: How have Satan's deceptions affected mankind (steps 1–2)?

II. Satan's Lies Versus God's Truth: How does the world system tell us we can obtain significance? What do the Scriptures say about our significance and worth (steps 3–10)?

III. Application: How can we replace destructive beliefs with God's truth so that our thoughts, words, and actions reflect God's love and purpose (steps 11–13)?

Each step includes questions for personal reflection and application, followed by a discussion for additional insight.

Special note: There are many wonderful truths outlined in the workbook, but application is a critical part of the process of seeing the truths become a part of daily life. Steps 12 and 13 are pivotal points! Learn to master the process of tracing painful emotions back to their root false beliefs and replacing them with God's Word. If you don't learn to do this, the workbook may become just a collection of nice material without profoundly affecting your life.

After you begin this workbook, it will be helpful for you to reread certain chapters of *The Search for Significance* as you go along. It is a good idea to do the workbook exercises as a regular part of your devotions. You may want to go through the material with a friend or teach the steps to a group. However you choose to proceed, be persistent. Don't let the enemy of our soul get you off-track. And, again, don't hurry. Reflect. Think. Consider.

It is my heartfelt prayer that God will use this workbook to enlighten the eyes of your heart so that you will "proclaim the excellencies of Him who has called you out of darkness into His marvelous light" (1 Pet. 2:9).

Section I

Background

How have Satan's deceptions affected mankind?

Step 1

The Light Comes On

Read chapter 1 in *The Search for Significance*.

This step is designed to help you understand the compelling need people have for self-worth. Let's examine two systems that we can use to meet this need.

1. How do you define *self-worth*?

Our feelings about our extrinsic value

Being at PEACE with who we are

2. Take several minutes to consider each of the following questions:

a) Are you glad you are you?

b) Do you have a healthy sense of self-worth?

If you answered no to either of these questions, your sense of self-worth is lower than that which God wants you to have.

3. a) Read Ephesians 1:3–14 and list what God has done to you and for you:

Blessed us in the heavenly realms w/every spiritual blessing in Christ. Chose us in him before the creation of the world to be holy & blameless in his sight. In love he predestined us to be adopted as sons has freely given us grace

b) What phrases does Paul use to show you the extent of God's love?

_____

_____

_____

_____

_____

c) How do you feel about these truths?

I have a hard time believing they are true about me.

_____

4. Why do we have a basic desire for personal significance? Why does man wrestle with the basic questions Who am I? and Why am I here?

_____

_____

_____

5. There are two possible options we can choose to determine our self-worth:

- The world's system: Self-Worth = Performance (what you do) + Others' Opinions (what others think or say about you)
- God's system: Self-Worth = God's Truth About You

a) List some activities, relationships, or achievements that make you feel better about yourself;

riding, butchering, doing things other women don't do, Jana, Linda, Cynthia, Alison

_____

_____

168

b) List some activities, poor relationships, or failures that make you feel bad about yourself:

_____

_____

_____

_____

_____

6. What difference would it make in your attitude, relationships, and goals if you grasped the reality that your worth is not conditional (for example, based on performance) but is based on the truth of the unconditional love, forgiveness, and acceptance of God?

_____

_____

_____

7, a) Whose opinion of you do you value most?

_____Jack's_____

b) What is your most common response to that person?

_____nervousness_____

_____

8. Think of the person you know who loves you most. How does that love make you feel?

_____

_____

_____

9. Why does the equation *others' opinions = self-worth* cause us to be concerned about our performance?

_____

_____

_____

10. Is it difficult to view yourself in terms other than your performance or others' opinions of you? If so, why?

_____

_____

_____

11. a) A number of the major problems in our lives originate from how we value ourselves—our self-worth. However, many of the answers to these problems are superficial bumper-sticker solutions. What are some examples of these, like "Just have faith" or "Just trust God"?

_____

_____

_____

b) How are these answers inadequate?

_____

_____

_____

Most of the steps in this workbook include a section called "For Additional Insight." Compare your answers with these observations to get a deeper understanding of the questions presented in each step.

For Additional Insight

1. Self-worth, often called self-esteem or personal significance, is characterized by a quiet sense of self-respect and a feeling of satisfaction with who we are. True self-worth, unlike pride, is not based on an evaluation of our performance.

2. a) Are you glad you are you? If you aren't, you probably think that you would be happier if you could perform like someone else.

b) Do you feel you have a healthy sense of self-worth? This is not a neutral feeling about yourself but a prevailing sense of value that is not related to your performance. A healthy self-concept is the recognition of one's value and worth: the understanding that as a unique human being, one has certain gifts and abilities unlike anyone else and can contribute to the world in a special way. Success is both pleasing and encouraging, but it is the by-product of stability not self-esteem. Someone with a healthy self-concept will experience the pain of failure and defeat but won't be devastated by it. Someone with a positive sense of self-esteem can enjoy personal strengths and tolerate the awareness of weaknesses. This is a wholesome love for oneself. Do you love yourself this way? Do you enjoy being you?

3. a) God has blessed you with every spiritual blessing, chosen you, declared you holy and blameless, adopted you, redeemed you, forgiven you, made known to you the mystery of His will, and sealed you with the Holy Spirit.

b) Some of the phrases Paul used in Ephesians to describe what God has done for us are:

According to the kind intention of His will, to the praise of the glory of His grace, which He freely bestowed on us in the Beloved. . . . according to the riches of His grace, which He lavished upon us. . . . according to His kind intention which He purposed in Him. . . . to the praise of His glory. (1:5–9, 14)

c) You may feel very happy and thankful, you may be overwhelmed with the magnitude of God's love, or you may be thinking, *This can't be true. I don't feel like this at all.* That's okay. It's better to be honest and feel pain than to deny it and try to convince yourself that you are happy. Remember, your feelings are not the basis of truth. God's Word is our authority. What He says is true, whether or not we feel it. The more we understand God's Word and live by it, the more our feelings will reflect His character and love.

4. When God created man, He gave him a sense of purpose. When man rebelled against God, he lost that God-given sense of significance. Since then, he has tried to find purpose and meaning apart from God. But God has made us in such a way that He is the only One who can meet our needs. Money, fame, fine homes, sports cars, and prestige in a given profession are only counterfeits of the true significance we have in Christ. Though these counterfeits promise to meet our need for fulfillment, that which they provide is always short-lived. God and His purposes alone can give us a profound, lasting sense of significance.

5. a) You may feel better about yourself as a result of academic, athletic, or professional achievements, or even Christian activities (devotional time, prayer, witnessing, Bible study, church attendance).

b) Failure to meet our standards (or the standards of others) in any area can cause us to feel poorly about ourselves.

6. Realizing that your worth is not conditional will increasingly free you from the fears of failure and rejection, and it will give you joy, thankfulness, and a desire to honor the one who loves you so much.

7. a) Perhaps you most value the opinions of a parent, girl-friend, boyfriend, spouse, peer group, or boss.

b) Possible responses to that person or group could include loyalty, obedience, fear, hard work, depression, or anger.

8. One of the many ways God communicates His love for us is through the committed and accepting love of another person. Love conveys the message that we are significant, that we have value and worth. This is exactly the way God wants us to feel! Recognizing this truth is a major step toward positive change in

how we perceive ourselves and in how we relate to God and other people.

9. The opinions others have of us are primarily based on our performance. If we are seeking our self-worth from others, peer pressure can cause us to conform to a certain standard. We learn acceptable behavior through a socialization process. Peer pressure conforms the behavior of each individual to fit the acceptable norm of the group—whether or not the behavior is best for that individual.

10. It is usually difficult to evaluate ourselves without considering our performance and the opinions of others. This standard of evaluation is primarily the input we receive from our society: radio, television, friends, clubs, work, school, billboards, magazines. It is no wonder, then, that changing our value system is an uphill but very necessary struggle.

11. a) • "Jesus is the answer."
  • "Give it to God."
  • "Just trust God, and it will work out."
  • "Just pray about it."

b) The reason these answers are inadequate is because our problems are made up of specific elements. Unless we apply God's specific answers to our specific problems, we have nothing but a hollow ritual. Inadequate religious answers to life's problems may be more devastating than secular answers. If we apply what we think is God's answer and fail to find a solution, we are truly without hope. Unfortunately, some religious leaders give inadequate answers, and then they blame those who seek their advice when the answers fail to yield solutions. Those of us who have received inadequate answers most of our lives may have a tendency to accept second-rate experiences and even defend the answers that have led us nowhere.

A Final Word

The central questions man must face in life are Who am I? and Why am I here? These questions relate directly to man's search for self-worth and significance. The world has programmed us with a specific system of evaluating ourselves. This system is contrary to God's system, no matter what our standard of performance is or whose approval we are seeking. The world's system will allow us fleeting moments of success and pride, but it will never let us enjoy lasting personal significance. Success and approval cannot ultimately fulfill our need for self-worth.

Step 2

The Origin of the Search

**Part I: The Fall of Man—How Sin Has Affected
Our Relationship With God**

Read chapter 2 in *The Search for Significance.*

This part of step 2 will help you to understand God's purpose for creating man and how man's rebellion caused him to be separated from God and His purposes.

The Creation of Man

1. Read Genesis 1:25–31 and answer the following questions.

a) What do you think it means for man to bear God's image?

_____

_____

_____

_____

_____

b) What are two responsibilities that God gave to Adam?

_____

_____

_____

_____

c) What was God's evaluation of creation before Adam was created? What was it after he was created?

_____

_____

_____

d) Was the basis of this evaluation based on Adam's performance or God's declaration?

_____

_____

_____

The Fall of Man

2. Read Genesis 3:1–10 and answer the following questions about the Fall of man:

a) How did Satan tempt Eve?

_____

_____

_____

b) Where was Adam when Eve ate of the fruit? (Gen. 3:6)

_____

_____

_____

c) When Adam rebelled, did he know what he was doing? (see 1 Tim. 2:14)

_____

_____

_____

d) How did the Fall affect man's desire for significance?

_____

_____

_____

3. Consider man's relationship with God and the effects of man's rebellion.

a) Read Isaiah 59:2. How has sin, resulting from the Fall, affected man's relationship with God?

_____

_____

_____

b) Read 1 Corinthians 6:9–10, Galatians 5:19–21, and Ephesians 2:1–3. List some characteristics of fallen man:

_____

_____

_____

c) Read John 8:44, Ephesians 2:2, and 1 John 3:8. Fallen man is dominated by whom?

_____

_____

d) Read John 8:34 and Romans 6:12–17. Fallen man is a slave of:

_____

_____

e) Read Matthew 25:46, 2 Thessalonians 1:6–10, Revelation 14:9–11, 20:11–15. What is fallen man's final outcome?

_____

_____

_____

f) What effects of the Fall were evident in this morning's newspaper stories or last night's television news programs? List specific events:

_____

_____

_____

_____

g) On a scale of 0 to 100 percent, how sure are you that you would go to heaven if you died tonight?

0%__ 10%__ 25%__ 35%__ 50%__ 75%__ 85%__ 95%__ 100%__

h) If you died tonight and stood before God and He asked you, "Why should I let you into heaven?" what would you say?

_____

_____

_____

Compare your answers to the following:

For Additional Insight

1. a) Man is to represent God on the earth by demonstrating His love, integrity, compassion, forgiveness, wisdom, joy, patience, goodness, and gentleness, among His other characteristics. This doesn't mean that man has all the capacities of God but that there is a uniqueness about man that separates him from the rest of creation. In the same way that two spheres of different sizes are both similar and different, so man, created in the image of God, is uniquely similar to God and yet vastly different from Him.

b) Man was created to bear God's image and exhibit His glory in that role, and he was given the two responsibilities of dominion over the earth and procreation, filling the earth with people who would also bear the image of God.

c) Genesis 1:31 reveals that God's view of creation changed from "good" to "very good" after man was created.

d) Since Adam's creation was said to be "very good" before he did anything, the basis of God's evaluation could not have been his performance. Adam was acceptable because God said he was.

2. a) Satan tempted Eve to be like God, knowing good and evil (Gen. 3:5). He accomplished this by causing Eve to question God's Word when he said, "You surely shall not die" (Gen. 3:4).

b) Adam was with Eve, well aware of what was happening.

c) Adam knew what he was doing. He was not deceived.

d) The Fall isolated man from his true source of significance: God. Since then, man has sought success, wealth, prestige, and/or the approval of others to meet his need for significance.

3. a) Sin has separated man from God.

b) Fallen man is dead in his trespasses and sins, walks according to the course of the world, is led by the prince of the power of the air (Satan), is disobedient, lives in fleshly lust.

c) Satan.

d) Sin.

e) Fallen man is denied heaven and instead receives eternal punishment in hell.

f) Effects of the Fall may be seen today in personal problems: sickness, loneliness, suicide; interpersonal problems: murder, rape, war; or natural disasters: drought, famine, earthquakes.

g) If your response is less than 100 percent, it may indicate that your assurance of salvation is at least partially dependent on your performance or good deeds to earn God's acceptance.

h) Read Romans 3:19–28 and Titus 3:4–7. We do not gain a right standing before God based on our good works. There is no amount of good deeds, religious or otherwise, we can do that will obligate God to accept us into His eternal kingdom.

Romans 3:24–26 reveals the only certain basis for us to be accepted by God: We are brought into a right relationship with Him based on our trust in what Jesus Christ accomplished for us upon the cross. Christ's death was a substitutionary death for us. Even though we deserve death as punishment for our sins, Christ took our punishment upon Himself and died on the cross to pay for our sins. If you have never trusted in Christ to pay for your sins and to give you new life, you can do so by expressing to Him your desire for a personal relationship with Him. The following is a suggested prayer that might help you communicate your attitude to God.

Lord Jesus, I need you. I want You to be my Savior and Lord. I accept Your death on the cross as the complete payment for my sins. Thank You for forgiving me and giving me new life. Help me to grow in my understanding of Your love and power so that my life will bring honor to You. Amen.

A Final Word

The *Westminster Shorter Catechism* says, "The chief end of man is to glorify God and enjoy Him forever." Man, however, rejected God's purpose and chose to go his own way. Because of that rebellion, he experienced spiritual death, separation from God. Cut off from God, man had to find a new source of worth, so he turned to his performance and the approval of others. Still, God didn't give up on man. The loving Father offered His own Son as a sacrifice to bear the punishment we deserve. "For the wages of sin is death, but the free gift of God is eternal life in Christ Jesus our Lord" (Rom. 6:23).

Part II: Satan's Deceptions

This part of step 2 is designed to explain the implications of attempting to gain our self-worth through the world's system. We will examine the process of healing so that we can increasingly experience hope and health in our lives.

Man has been sadly deceived since the Fall. His mind has been darkened (Eph. 4:17–19), and he has chosen to believe the lies of Satan instead of God's truth.

Satan's lies are a direct result of his character:

> *He [Satan] was a murderer from the beginning, not holding to the truth, for there is no truth in him. When he lies, he speaks his native language, for he is a liar and the father of lies. (John 8:44, NIV)*

1. You may have heard that Satan is the father of lies, but have you ever considered what his lies are? List some of the lies you've been told by Satan:

_____

_____

_____

_____

_____

2. The following are four general beliefs that many of us apply daily in our relationships and circumstances. To what extent are you affected by these? Estimate the percentage to which you live by each of these beliefs, from 0 to 100 percent:

_____% I must meet certain standards to feel good about myself.

_____% I must have the approval of certain people (boss, friends, parents) to approve of myself. Without their approval, I cannot feel good about myself.

_____% Those who fail (including myself) are unworthy of love and, therefore, must be blamed and condemned.

_____% I am what I am. I cannot change. I am hopeless. In other words, I am the sum total of all my past successes and failures, and I'll never be significantly different.

(Note: When we first begin to examine and confront these lies, our percentage scores may fluctuate. This is normal, the beginning of change. In time, the percentage to which we're affected by these lies will decrease.)

3. Proverbs 23:7 says, "As [a man] thinks within himself, so he is." Our lifestyle is usually a reflection of what we think about ourselves. Analyze your lifestyle. Describe:

a) The things you talk about:

_____
_____
_____

b) The places you like to go:

_____
_____
_____

c) The people you spend time with:

_____
_____
_____

d) Your ambitions and dreams:

_____
_____
_____
_____
_____

e) How you spend your time:

_____

_____

_____

_____

_____

f) How you spend your money:

_____

_____

_____

g) The main reasons you do these things (to gain the approval of others, to be a success, to avoid failure, to honor Christ, to fulfill someone's expectations, to help people):

_____

_____

_____

_____

Your attitudes, values, goals, and actions are primarily reflections of what you believe about yourself. Paul wrote that our lives are to be transformed by the renewing of our minds (Rom. 12:2). If you believe you must please people to be acceptable, you will be dominated by others' opinions. If, however, you believe that you are loved and accepted by God, you will grow to be a more secure, loving, and accepting person. This diagram illustrates how our beliefs affect our thoughts, emotions, and actions:

Situations

↓

Beliefs → Thoughts → Emotions → Actions

Each of us has a set of beliefs through which we evaluate life. Any given event may trigger thoughts that evoke certain emotions and lead to actions. Therefore our emotions and actions are usually reflections of our belief systems.

4. Think of the last situation that really angered you or made you feel afraid. What was the situation? What were your feelings? How did you act on those feelings?
a) Situation:

_____

_____

_____

_____

_____

b) Emotion(s):

_____

_____

_____

c) Action(s):

_____

_____

_____

5. a) Which of the four beliefs in question 2 most apply to that situation? (It may be more than one.) How were the emotions you experienced and your subsequent actions a reflection of this belief?

_____

_____

_____

_____

_____

_____

b) Is this belief based on God's truths or Satan's lies?

_____

6. Reflect on the situation you described in question 4. If you had replaced the false belief with God's truth about you—that you are deeply loved, completely forgiven, fully pleasing, totally accepted, and absolutely complete in Christ—how do you think your emotions and actions would have been different?

_____

_____

_____

_____

7. God has provided love, peace, acceptance, and purpose through Christ's payment on the cross for us. He has made us so that He is the only One who can provide these blessings in a lasting and fulfilling way. Yet virtually every television commercial and magazine ad claims that a product or service will provide either love, happiness, comfort, or status. Will it? Think about this. How many people who start using a certain toothpaste are suddenly asked for a date by the person of their dreams? Will using a certain credit card suddenly make people happy, comfortable, and desirable, or will it put them in debt? Few of us are aware of the many deceptions we encounter each day.

a) What commercials or magazine ads promise love, happiness, comfort, or status? (Consider ads for beer, investment firms, computers, credit cards, cars, perfume, and toothpaste.) Be specific.

• Love:

_____

_____

• Happiness:

_____

_____

- Comfort:

_____

_____

- Status:

_____

_____

Satan has enslaved most of mankind by convincing us that: Self-Worth = Performance + Others' Opinions. Many of his lies can be summarized by these four false beliefs, each of which results in a specific fear:

1. False belief: *I must meet certain standards to feel good about myself. If I fail to meet these standards, I cannot really feel good about myself.* This belief results in the fear of failure.

2. False belief: *I must be approved (accepted) by certain people to accept myself. If I do not have the approval of these people, I cannot accept myself.* This belief results in the fear of rejection.

3. False belief: *Those who fail are unworthy of love and deserve to be blamed and condemned.* This belief leads to the fear of punishment and propensity to punish others.

4. False belief: *I am what I am. I cannot change. I am hopeless. This means that I am simply a total of all my past performances, both good and bad. I am what I have done.* This belief leads to a sense of shame.

At this point in our study, many of us will have recognized the influence of these false beliefs in several different areas of our lives. But some of us may still be struggling to see the correlation between these lies and our attitudes and behavior.

You may be one who doesn't seem to be affected by others' opinions or by the fear of failure. If this seems to describe your situation, consider the fact that you live in the same world system as everyone else and have, like everyone else, been taught to evaluate yourself on the basis of what you do and what others think of you. How have you been able to deal with this method of evaluation so well that the opinions of others seem to have no effect on you?

Perhaps you feel that you have already overcome these lies and fears and are living by the truths of God's Word. However, it's also possible that you have deceived yourself and only *think* you've overcome these issues. Deception of this nature may stem from a number of possible factors, two of which are given below:

1. Talent

Recall the rich young man who came to Jesus, wanting to follow Him (Matt. 19:16–24). When Christ told him that being complete in Him would mean giving up what he had been depending upon (in this case, wealth), the young man was tremendously disappointed. He had wanted to meet Christ on his own terms.

You, too, may have a wealth of skills in your work, studies, or relationships. You may be making a number of contributions and high achievements, even within the scope of Christian service. If this is the case, success may be preventing you from seeing the impact of Satan's lies on your attitudes and behavior and hindering you from a more complete life in Christ.

Regardless of our talents or vocation, outward success can deceive us into believing that we have overcome the lies of the world.

2. Fear

There is nothing more personal than our self-worth, and it is frightening to admit that we have been basing our value on the wrong things. Success and the opinions of others are precarious sources of self-esteem. If making achievements and gaining approval are our primary means for obtaining self-worth, we will tenaciously hold to them until we are absolutely convinced that only God's love and acceptance of us can ultimately meet this need. A young woman who came for counseling provides a good example of how we can seek fulfillment our way rather than God's way. Due to a difficult relationship with her father, this woman found herself continually trying to gain the approval of men. She would even enter into obviously terminal relationships (such as with married men), and excuse her behavior by stating that she "just had to have someone to hold and love her." She would not allow herself even to consider that this need for acceptance could be met by the love of God and fellow believers.

If you have difficulty recognizing Satan's lies in your life, ask someone you trust to take the tests in *The Search for Significance* book and record his or her observations of you. This might give you further insight.

For Additional Insight

1. By the very nature of deception, we are often unable to recognize those times when we are being deceived. These are a few of the lies Satan tells us:

- If you obey God, you'll be miserable.
- The abundant life is trouble-free.
- Unbelievers don't want to hear the gospel.
- You couldn't help yourself . . . the temptation was too great.
- If you fail, you're a failure.
- You are what others think of you.
- God can't use you.
- You can't obey God.
- If you do certain things, God will be pleased with you, and you will earn His affection.

It is interesting that Satan lies to unbelievers to convince them that they are *not* guilty while he lies to believers to convince them that they *are* guilty.

2. To the extent (percentage) that you believe these lies, your life will be influenced by the world's system. Each belief stems from the concept that your self-worth = performance + others' opinions. We will continue to discover solutions to these lies in the remainder of this workbook.

3. Your actions and emotions are usually indicative of your belief system. Why do you do what you do, say what you say, and go where you go? How much of what you do is to honor God, and how much is to please people? We may say that we believe one thing, but our lifestyles often reveal that we believe something quite different.

4. Be specific in describing the situation and your feelings.

5. Realize that your emotions are integrally related to your belief system. Note that if you believe something that is false, it will affect your life as powerfully as if it were true. For instance, if you believe you are unwanted and a bother to God, you will probably be lonely and depressed, even though the truth is that you are precious to God and deeply loved by Him (Isa. 43:4 and Zeph. 3:17). Your beliefs, true or false, can dictate your emotions, actions, and ultimately, your life.

6. If you had replaced the false belief with God's truth, you most likely would have had a dramatically different emotional response. Also, your actions would probably have been much different. For example, rather than feeling depressed and unloved, you might have felt more secure and hopeful in light of God's love and acceptance. But remember that such a drastic change in attitude is a process and that it's important to be honest about your emotions. Don't try to feel what you don't feel. Put yourself in an environment of honesty and encouragement so that you can experience the process of growth.

7. Learn to recognize deception. Instead of just sitting through television commercials, try to analyze what they are communicating.

Are the ads deceptive? What does the product or service promise? Being an astute observer of the world around you will enable you to see how many lies are communicated to you each day. If you can't view the world's deceptions objectively, you are much more likely to believe them and be adversely affected by them.

A Final Word

One of the most tragic results of the Fall is that man's mind became darkened. Satan has deceived the world into believing that Self-Worth = Performance + Others' Opinions. Satan continues to lie because he is the "father of lies" (John 8:44). But God has a solution! He has given us His Word so that we don't have to be enslaved by the deceiver's schemes (2 Cor. 2:11). By learning to recognize deception in the world around us and by confronting it with the truth of God's Word, we will increasingly experience the liberation He intends for us in the many aspects of our lives.

Section II

Satan's Lies Versus God's Truth

How does the world system tell us we can obtain significance?

What do the Scriptures say about our significance and worth?

Step 3

The Performance Trap

Read chapter 3 in *The Search for Significance*.

In this step, you will examine the effects of the fear of failure, which stems from the false belief *I must meet certain standards to feel good about myself.*

1. a) List three recent situations in which your performance did not measure up to the standard you had set for yourself. Identify the standard you felt you needed to meet. Then try to remember what thoughts and emotions accompanied each occasion and the actions you took that reflected those thoughts and feelings. (Use a separate sheet of paper if necessary.)

Example:
Situation: I failed a test.
Standards: I must make at least a B in the class to feel good about myself.
Thoughts: I'll never make it through this class. I'll flunk, and my friends will think I'm stupid. My parents will be so ashamed of me.
Emotions: Anger, depression.
Actions: I yelled at my professor and blamed my roommate for making so much noise that I couldn't study for this test. I then withdrew from my friends.

(1) Situation:

_____
_____
_____
_____
_____
_____

Standards:

_____
_____
_____
_____

Thoughts:

_____
_____
_____
_____

Emotions:

_____
_____
_____
_____

Actions:

_____
_____
_____
_____

(2) Situation:

_____

_____

_____

_____

_____

_____

Standards:

_____

_____

_____

_____

Thoughts:

_____

_____

_____

_____

Emotions:

_____

_____

_____

_____

Actions:

_____

_____

_____

_____

(3) Situation:

_____
_____
_____
_____
_____
_____

Standards:

_____
_____
_____
_____

Thoughts:

_____
_____
_____
_____

Emotions:

_____
_____
_____
_____

Actions:

_____
_____
_____
_____

b) Do you see any patterns reflected in your emotions and actions? If so, what are they?

_____

_____

_____

_____

2. Why do people use performance as a measurement of personal worth?

_____

_____

_____

_____

3. a) Do you have to be successful in order to feel good about yourself? What would you have to be or do to feel like you are a success?

_____

_____

_____

b) In what area(s) would you never allow yourself to fail?

_____

_____

_____

_____

_____

4. a) What Christian activities do you use to evaluate yourself spiritually?

_____

_____

_____

_____

b) Does performing these activities make you more pleasing to God?

_____

_____

_____

5. How does your desire to meet your performance standard affect your relationships with others?

_____

_____

_____

6. How do you feel toward those who hinder your ability to meet your standard?

_____

_____

_____

_____

_____

_____

7. What things do you do in order to avoid failure?

_____

_____

_____

_____

_____

_____

8. How do you think your life would be different if you did not experience the fear of failure?

_____

_____

_____

Compare your answers to the following:

For Additional Insight

1. a) Your list may include occasions dealing with academic responsibilities, professional activities, relationships, daily tasks, scheduling, and more.

b) In almost any activity or relationship, we are susceptible to the fear of failure. When we fail, we usually experience anger, resentment, worry, anxiety, fear, depression, and other negative emotions. In turn, these emotions express themselves through actions like withdrawal, hostility, being rude, and blaming others. If we analyze our responses to failures, we can usually see that they have a pattern. How do you tend to respond to failure?

2. When our performance meets our standard, it can give us a sense of pride that we may mistake for self-worth. We feel good; we feel significant. We will then want to meet another standard so that we can feel good about ourselves again.

We use performance to evaluate our self-worth because the system reinforces itself: When we perform well, we feel good. This so-called success makes us feel that the system works, so we continue to use it. (Please note: It is not wrong to be glad about being successful at something. The issue is not primarily how we feel but the basis of our self-worth. Either our performance leads us to pride, or God's truth leads us to true joy and the desire to honor Him.)

If you reject God's provision for self-worth and instead embrace the world's false promises, then your performance is your only alternative for meeting this deep, almost all-encompassing need. You usually act according to your beliefs. If you believe that you are a failure, you will probably either withdraw from activities that involve a risk of failure or drive yourself to succeed to prove that you're not a failure.

Again, your performance often reflects your belief system. If your belief system is based on false beliefs, then your thoughts, emotions, and actions will usually reflect those false beliefs.

3. Be honest! You may be trying to gain a sense of worth from your participation in academics, athletics, your relationships, your job, club memberships, the cleanliness of your house or car, teaching Sunday school, tithing, or some other activity or Christian service.

4. a) Your list may include daily devotions, Bible study, witnessing, fellowship, church involvement, and giving.

b) Any standard of performance, even a Christian standard, used to obtain a more positive sense of self-worth is contrary to God's truth and is, therefore, an ungodly means to fulfill your need for significance. If this is the case, then you are still trapped in the world's system.

Once we realize that our self-worth is secure in Christ, we will begin wanting to do things that bring honor to Him. Our efforts then, coming from that motivation, are pleasing to God.

5. You might enter some relationships with selfish personal goals that could prompt you to manipulate others in an effort to reach those goals. Sometimes we even use kind and encouraging remarks to get others to do what we want them to. Sooner or later, these people usually realize that our kind remarks are actually being used as manipulative devices. This leads to alienation and bitterness in our relationships.

6. If people hinder you from meeting your standards, you might become angry, enraged, or resentful; you might blame them, reject them, or withdraw from them. They have kept you from meeting one of your deepest needs!

7. Some of the coping methods we use are: avoiding situations where failure is likely, working only in areas of strength, offering excuses, explaining away failure, trying harder to perform, lowering our standards, blaming others, and becoming lazy.

8. As you become less influenced by the fear of failure, you will probably be happier, more loving, more spontaneous, and more thankful to God for His love.

A Final Word

The fear of failure is like stacking marbles: a very difficult task but not any more difficult than trying to win the performance game. When we evaluate ourselves by our performance, we're ultimately going to lose, no matter how successful we are at the moment.

If we believe that our self-worth is based on our success, we will try to avoid failure at all costs. Most of us have become experts at avoiding failure. We attempt only those things in which we are confident of success. We avoid those activities in which the risk of failure is too great. We spend time around those who are not a threat to us. We avoid people who, either by their greater success or by their disapproval of us, make us feel like failures. We have trained ourselves very well!

A rat placed in a box and shocked until it huddles in one particular corner soon learns to run to that corner as soon as it is placed in the box. How much of our energy is expended avoiding the disapproving "shocks" of those around us? Even though we are meant to experience the freedom of God's love and eternal purpose, how much time do we spend huddled in a corner like a laboratory rat?

Another consequence of having to meet certain standards in order to feel good about ourselves is a rules-dominated life. Many of us know people who have a set of rules for everything and who always place their attention on their performance. However, the focus of the gospel is on relationships, not regulations. Christ's exercise of His lordship in our lives is dependent on our attending to His moment-by-moment instruction. Focusing only on rules will relegate our lives to the prison of self-examination.

On the other hand, we may feel very good about ourselves because we are winning the performance game. We may be so talented that we are reaching virtually every goal we have set for ourselves. We can't afford to mistake this pride for positive self-worth. We must realize that God is able to bring about whatever circumstances are necessary to cause us to stop trusting in ourselves. God intends to bring us to Himself through prayer and the study of His Word so that we can know, love, and serve Him. Sometimes He will allow us to fail miserably so that we will look to Him instead of to ourselves for our security and significance.

Before becoming upset that God would allow you to experience failure, remember that any life less than God intended is a second-class existence. He loves you too much to let you continue to obtain your self-worth from the empty promise of success.

Step 4

God's Answer: Justification

Read chapter 4 in *The Search for Significance*.

As a result of Christ's death on the cross, our sins are forgiven and God has imputed Christ's righteousness to us. Therefore, we are fully pleasing to God.

1. Read Romans 3:19–28, 4:4–5, and 5:1–11. What does it mean to be *justified*?

_____

_____

_____

2. Read 2 Corinthians 5:21, Colossians 1:22, 3:12, and Hebrews 10:14. Are you as righteous, holy, and blameless as Christ? Why or why not?

_____

_____

_____

3. Read Romans 3:9–23, 5:6–10, and Ephesians 2:1–3. Why did you need to be justified and have Christ's righteousness attributed to you? Describe God's view of you before your justification:

_____

_____

_____

4. How was your justification accomplished?

a) Rom. 3:24, Titus 3:7

_____

_____

_____

_____

b) Rom. 3:28, Gal. 2:16

_____

_____

_____

c) Rom. 5:1, Gal. 3:24

_____

_____

_____

d) Rom. 5:9, Heb. 9:22

_____

_____

_____

5. What are the results of justification?

a) Rom. 4:7–8

_____

_____

_____

b) Rom. 5:1

_____

_____

_____

c) Rom. 5:9

_____

_____

_____

d) Rom. 8:1, 33–34

_____

_____

_____

e) 2 Cor. 5:14–15

_____

_____

_____

f) 2 Cor. 5:21

_____

_____

_____

g) Titus 3:7

_____

_____

_____

6. a) Read Romans 4:6–8 and Hebrews 10:17. Are you remembering sins that God has forgotten? If so, why?

_____

_____

_____

b) Does remembering sin help you in any way? If so, how?

_____

_____

_____

7. How does being justified and having Christ's righteousness lead you to the conclusion: *I am completely forgiven by God, and am fully pleasing to Him?*

_____

_____

_____

8. If your good works won't make you more pleasing to God, why should you be involved in good works? (See Rom. 6:12–13, 1 Cor. 6:18–20, Col. 3:23–24, and Titus 2:11–14.)

9. Read 1 Corinthians 3:11–15. What will determine whether or not a deed will honor God? (See also Rom. 14:23 and 1 Cor. 10:31.)

10. Review question 1 of step 3. Using one of the occasions you listed, chart how your behavior would have been different if you had believed God's truth that you are completely forgiven by God and fully pleasing to Him, rather than the false belief, *I must meet certain standards in order to feel good about myself.*

Situation:

_____

_____

_____

_____

_____

_____

God's truth: *I am completely forgiven and fully pleasing to God.*

Thoughts:

_____

_____

_____

Emotions:

_____

_____

_____

_____

Actions:

_____

_____

_____

_____

11. Memorize Romans 5:1.

Compare your answers to the following:

For Additional Insight

1. To be justified is to be placed in right standing with God. Justification is the judicial act of God by which He declares righteous the one who trusts in Christ. The justified person is acquitted from all guilt of sin and is declared holy, righteous, and blameless.

2. If you have trusted in Christ's death on the cross for the forgiveness of your sins, God has declared you to be perfect in His sight! If you were anything less than that, you would not be pleasing enough to Him to be His companion for eternity.

However, justification is often stated in ways that cause it to lose its impact. We sometimes seem to say to God, "In heaven, I guess this is true, but down here in the real world, we just aren't that way." We may respond like this because we are convinced that our worth is dependent on our performance. But to God, our worth is established and secure because He has sovereignly imputed to us the righteousness of Christ.

Suppose Christ were seated in a chair next to you and someone asked God, "Which person do You love the most? Which person is more acceptable to You? Which person is holy, righteous, and blameless to You? Which person is holy, righteous, and blameless before You?" The Father would respond to each question the same way: "They are equally loved, acceptable, and righteous."

3. Without Christ's righteousness, you would have no basis on which to stand before God. Before your justification, God viewed you as being unrighteous, sinful, and an enemy. You were dead in your sins, separated from God, disobedient in nature, and an object of God's wrath. Romans 3:9–20 is God's description of unjustified man. You may be thinking, *I was never really that bad.* But to God, even your best attempts at righteousness were as filthy rags (Isa. 64:6). Romans 14:23 and Hebrews 11:6 also state that anything not done in faith is sin and displeases God. But take heart! The living God has seen your helplessness and has extended justification to you through Christ's death and resurrection.

4. a) His grace. He gave you what you didn't deserve.

b) Not by works (meeting certain standards)—it is His gift.

c) Faith, a means by which you appropriate what Christ has done for you.

d) Your justification was accomplished by the shedding of His blood.

5. a) Because of justification, your sin is forgiven and forgotten.

b) You have peace with God. You are no longer considered His enemy.

c) You are saved from His wrath.

d) There is no condemnation remaining for you to bear.

e) You can now live to honor Him and reflect His image.

f) You are declared righteous.

g) You are an heir of His eternal kingdom.

6. a) Satan deceives us into thinking that remembering and reliving sin is somehow a part of repentance. But this is not true! Remembering and reliving sins are the flesh's way of trying to pay for sin and control our actions. The thinking goes like this: *By remembering and reliving these sins, I inflict pain upon myself. That pain will become associated with these sins so I will never do them again. Therefore, remembering sin is helpful and good.*

Why does recalling these sins cause pain? Each time you remember them, you judge yourself according to your poor past performance. The evaluation always comes out negative, and the pain of self-hatred follows. If you were not evaluating yourself by your past performance, you would probably not dredge up the painful memory of these sins.

b) Reliving sin is a destructive way of trying to produce a godly life. God's method is to forgive our sins and remember them no more (Heb. 10:17). What sins do you need to stop remembering?

7. Because you have been given the righteousness of Christ, you are just as pleasing to the Father as He is! There is nothing you can do to add to or take away from what Christ did for you on the cross. As a result of your justification, you are completely forgiven and fully pleasing to God. Although you may try to justify yourself by doing good deeds to show God that you deserve your justification, it is a vain attempt to gain what you already have. Your new life is a product of God's workmanship in which He is very pleased. As

your mind is renewed by this truth, you will increasingly reflect this in your attitudes and behavior.

8. You should be involved in good works because they are an opportunity to bring honor to Christ. As you are gripped by what He has done for you, your natural response will be to honor Him in your daily life. Your good works are *not* a means to earn righteousness but a way to bring Him delight and glory.

9. The issue is more than just doing the right things. The question is, Are you doing the right things for the right reasons? Jesus had the most trouble with those religious people who were doing religious works for the wrong reasons. If you are honest, you probably realize that you perform many of your good deeds to make yourself more acceptable to others, to God, and, perhaps, to yourself. But all of these good works will burn someday. Are you motivated to do the right things in response to what Christ has done for you? If not, it will help you to reflect more on the lostness of man, the forgiveness of Christ, and the righteousness He bought for you by His blood.

In motivating others, we need to point people to God—to His grace—and let Him motivate them. Motivating people by guilt is an easy recourse, but it is not honoring to the Lord.

10. Example:
Situation: I failed a test.
God's truth: I am completely forgiven by God and am fully pleasing to Him.
Thoughts: I did my best under the circumstances. God can use the situation. It's not the end of the world.
Emotions: Peace eventually overcame my feelings of anger and depression.
Actions: I got some help in the class and talked to my roommate about the situation; we decided that in the future, we'll both study in the library or in another quiet place.

A Final Word

Justification is the great doctrine that is the bedrock of our self-worth: "Therefore having been justified by faith, we have peace with God through our Lord Jesus Christ" (Rom. 5:1). To be justified means to be placed in right standing before God. But what exactly does this mean? Justification is the judicial act of God by which He declares us free from the guilt of sin. All the sin we will ever commit has already been forgiven. To be justified means that the blight of our sin has been removed and that we have been completely cleansed by the blood of Christ. God sees us this way at this very moment! However, as marvelous as that is, justification means more than being forgiven. God not only forgives our sinfulness, but He also provides our righteousness. Righteousness is the worthiness to stand in God's presence without fear of personal condemnation because He has imputed the very righteousness of Christ to us.

Step 5

Approval Addict

Read chapter 5 in *The Search for Significance.*

This step is designed to help you understand the fear of rejection and the resulting false belief, *I must be approved by certain others in order to feel good about myself.*

1. a) Are you adversely affected by anyone's disrespect or disapproval? If so, list the individual(s) or group(s):

_____

_____

_____

b) How does the fear of being rejected (disapproved of) by these people affect your life? Give examples:

_____

_____

_____

_____

_____

2. To see how others' expectations can affect you, select one of the people you listed in question 1a) and answer the following:

a) _____ would be more pleased with me if I would:

(1)_____

(2)_____

(3)_____

b)_____ is proud of me when I:

(1)_____

(2)_____

(3)_____

c) How does _____ attempt to get me to change by what he (or she) says and does?

(1)_____

(2)_____

(3)_____

d) Things I do or say to get _____ to approve of me include:

(1)_____

(2)_____

(3)_____

(Use a separate sheet of paper and repeat this exercise for each of the other people or groups you listed in question 1a.)

3. List several specific instances when others (friends, boss, parents, children) have withheld approval or have used criticism, silence, sarcasm, or praise to manipulate you into doing what they wanted you to do. What did they say or do? Did they succeed? Why or why not?

a)_____

_____

_____

b)_____

_____

_____

c)_____

_____

_____

d)_____

_____

_____

4. What emotions accompanied the occasions given in question 3?

       Occasion   Emotions

a)_____   _____

b)_____   _____

c)_____   _____

d)_____   _____

5. What belief is at the root of the fear of disapproval?

_____

_____

_____

6. a) How does the fear of rejection influence your moral standards (drinking, substance abuse, theft, lying, physical relationships, lifestyle)? Can you recall specific instances in your life when this fear has greatly influenced your morals? If so, list them.

_____

_____

_____

_____

_____

b) How did the fear of rejection affect your behavior?

_____

_____

_____

_____

7. If you run from rejection, are you really in control of your life? If not, who is?

_____

_____

_____

8. a) How does the fear of rejection affect you when you want to share Christ with a friend? Do unbelievers ever use this fear to motivate you to refrain from sharing Christ with them?

_____

_____

_____

b) How would your zeal for evangelism be affected if you no longer depended on the approval of others for your self-worth?

_____

_____

_____

9. How have you used disapproval, silence, sarcasm, or criticism to get others to do what you wanted them to do?

_____

_____

_____

10. Sometimes, rather than praising others because we genuinely appreciate them, we use praise as a form of manipulation. Our motive is to influence them to do something we want them to do.

a) How do you feel when people praise you only to manipulate you?

_____

_____

_____

b) Have you used praise to manipulate others? If so, why, and how have you used it?

_____

_____

_____

_____

_____

c) How could manipulating others by praising them be considered a form of rejection?

_____

_____

_____

_____

Compare your answers to the following:

For Additional Insight

1. a) These individuals might include your parents, boyfriend, girlfriend, spouse, peer group, or boss. God might also be on your list.

b) The fear of being rejected may cause us to avoid situations in which we are prone to fail or experience disapproval and lead us to do only what we are good at doing, expecting our good performance to earn the approval of others. We also might tend to exaggerate the truth or make sure we wear or own just the right thing— whatever we think we need to do to gain the acceptance of those who are important to us.

2. For example:
a) My father would be more pleased with me if I called him more often, wore my hair the way he wants me to, and got a better job.

b) My father is proud of me when I get a promotion, when I remember important family dates, and when I win in sports.

c) He criticizes me, is sarcastic with me, and sometimes ignores me.

d) To gain my father's approval, I tell him only what he likes to hear; I exaggerate the truth a little; I work really hard to be a success.

3. You probably can list far more than four occasions in which you've experienced rejection. For example: a friend's disgusted look, a professor who joked about your paper, a rejection letter from a company you wanted to work for, a dating relationship gone sour, being left out of a group function, being chosen last on an athletic team, or being ignored by someone to whom you've said hello.

4. Our emotional responses in these situations may vary from slight annoyance to deep hurt, anger, and bitterness.

5. Our fear of rejection is proportional to the degree by which we base our self-worth on the opinions of others. If we believe the lie *I am what others say I am,* the fear of rejection will plague us.

6. Some of us have established our moral standards on the approval or disapproval of others. Rather than referring to God's Word as our authority on matters of life, we have referred to people, doing what they approve of or encourage us to do. This may have led some of us to compromise our sexual purity, our moral and ethical integrity, or our walk with God. God has revealed His good, acceptable, and perfect will for our lives in His Word (Rom. 12:2). We must learn to embrace and apply His truth and refuse to believe the lie *I am what others think of me.*

7. If you run from rejection, whomever you avoid is actually determining your actions and is, therefore, your controller. As you begin to experience freedom from the control of others' opinions,

your life will be increasingly focused on the Lord and controlled by Him, resulting in your growth and His glory.

8. The fear of rejection keeps many of us from sharing our faith. Unbelievers are well aware of the pain of rejection; nothing sends the message *I don't care about you or what you have to say* faster than rejection does. Sometimes unbelievers use rejection to threaten us so that they won't have to deal with the gospel. Some examples:

- "You don't believe that junk, do you?"
- "How could anyone with brains be a Christian?"
- "Christianity is a crutch."
- "I believe religion is a personal issue—don't talk to me about it."
- "Only losers are Christians."

What are they doing? They are rejecting us (inflicting emotional pain) to silence us. Becoming aware of this will give us more freedom to boldly take the initiative with others and lovingly present the gospel to them.

9. If you don't think you use rejection to motivate others, see if any of these sound familiar:

- "If you loved me, you'd . . . "
- "Come on, Joe, everyone else is going."
- "You didn't know that?"
- "Have you heard what Susie did?"
- "If you can't do better, I'll get someone else who's more competent."
- "That's stupid!"
- "Nice shirt. Did that color cost extra?"

10. a) If you perceive that someone is praising you only to manipulate you, then you may very well feel used, like an object instead of a person. You may resent it. You may feel sorry for the

person because you realize that he or she uses people and doesn't know how to love others.

b) Think of a situation and ask yourself, Why did I praise that person? Did I expect to get something out of him (or her)?

c) Manipulating others with praise is using them as tools to accomplish goals and rejecting them as people. Praise and appreciation can be a powerful force to build up a person, but if the goal of praise is to get someone to help us accomplish our goals, then it can be a powerful but subtle and destructive force in his or her life.

A Final Word

For whatever reason and to whatever degree we have experienced rejection, our fear of going through that pain again can affect us profoundly. We learn how to deal with physical injury early in life, but because emotional pain is sometimes perceived as a sign of weakness and because we have not learned how to respond appropriately to this pain, we avoid it. If we are hurt, we may attempt to deny our pain by ignoring it. We may drive ourselves to accomplish tasks we think others will approve of. Some of us can't say no for this reason. Or, we may become passive, withdrawing from others and avoiding those decisions and activities that others might criticize or that can't guarantee success for us. Our goal in these instances is usually to avoid the pain of rejection by not doing anything that might be objectionable, but this also prevents us from enjoying the pleasures of healthy relationships and achievements.

Other behaviors related to the fear of rejection include:

1. being easily manipulated

2. being hypersensitive to criticism

3. being defensive

4. reacting with hostility toward others who disagree with us

5. allowing only superficial relationships

6. exaggerating the truth to impress people

7. exhibiting shyness

8. being passive

9. having a nervous breakdown

How many of these behaviors are apparent in your life?

Evaluating our self-worth by what we and others think of our performance leads us to believe that any time our performance is unacceptable, we are unacceptable as well. To some extent, virtually all of us have internalized the following sentence into our belief system and hold to it with amazing tenacity: *I must have acceptance, respect, and approval to have self-worth.* This is the basic false belief behind all peer pressure.

Rejection can be communicated in a number of ways. We can easily see how criticism, sarcasm, and silence convey this message, but it may not be quite so obvious that praise can also serve as a form of manipulation and is, therefore, a form of rejection. We must ask ourselves what we are trying to accomplish when we praise someone. What is our goal? If we desire to help the person, to build him or her up, and to instill encouragement through appreciation, then praise is a godly form of communication. If, however, our desire is to get someone else to assist in accomplishing our goals, to contribute to our program, or to help us look good in front of others, then praise is a subtle but powerful form of rejection. Unfortunately, many people—including ourselves—fall prey to this manipulative praise because we so desperately want to be appreciated and will often do whatever it takes to get it from others.

If you realize that you manipulate others through praise, confess it as sin and choose to seek their good instead of your goal. Be willing to ask, What am I trying to accomplish? in your interaction with others, and strive to communicate genuine, heartfelt appreciation because Christ has given them worth by sacrificing His life for them.

There are four basic levels of acceptance and rejection. Understanding these levels will help you understand the nature of your relationships with other people concerning both how you are treated and how you treat others. These levels center around the question What does one have to do to be accepted?

1. *Total rejection:* "No matter what you do, it's not good enough." Example: relationships characterized by deep bitterness or hurt.

2. *Highly conditional acceptance:* "You must meet certain requirements to be accepted." Examples: most jobs, relationships with demanding people.

3. *Mildly conditional acceptance:* "I will be more happy with you if you do these things." Examples: most marriages, most parent-child relationships, most friendships.

4. *Unconditional acceptance:* "I love you and accept you no matter what you do. There is nothing you can do that can make me stop loving you." (This does not mean that we can do as we please or that we are to ignore unacceptable behavior in others. Unconditional acceptance may include loving confrontation, correction, and in some cases, discipline. The focus here is on the individual rather than his or her behavior.) Examples: God, godly relationships.

Use a separate piece of paper and make a list of the major relationships in your life: family members, friends, people in your school, office, or church, and so forth. How does each of these people tend to treat you? How do you tend to treat each of them? How should you respond to each of them? How can you put fewer demands and conditions on your acceptance of them?

Step 6

God's Answer: Reconciliation

Read chapter 6 in *The Search for Significance*.

God's answer to the pain of rejection is reconciliation. Christ died for our sins and restored us to a proper relationship with God. We are acceptable to God and are accepted by Him. We are not rejected! We are His.

1. a) Define *reconcile*. (Use a dictionary if necessary.)

_____

_____

b) Who caused the alienation in your relationship with God? (See Isa. 53:6; 59:2; Rom. 3:9–12.)

_____

_____

2. Read Ephesians 2:1–3 and 2 Thessalonians 1:8–9. How severe was the barrier between you and God?

_____

_____

_____

3. Read Colossians 1:21–22. Compare your former state to your present condition.

_____

_____

4. Read Romans 5:8–11.

a) Who initiated restoring your relationship with God?

_____

b) How did God reconcile you to Himself?

_____

c) What is your response to God? (What does it mean to *exult*?)

_____

_____

_____

5. a) What is wrong with the statement, "Thank You, Lord, for accepting me even though I am so unacceptable"?

_____

_____

_____

b) Are you currently acceptable? _____

c) To what degree are you acceptable? _____

d) To whom are you acceptable? _____

e) Why are you acceptable? _____

6. If you are completely and fully accepted by the perfect Creator of the universe, why do you fear the rejection of men?

_____

_____

_____

7. Read John 17:19–26 and 20:17 to see the extent of your reconciliation to God.

a) Whom does the Father love more, Jesus Christ or you?

_____

b) How does Christ refer to you in John 20:17?

_____

c) Whom does Christ desire to be with Him for all eternity?

_____

d) How do these verses make you feel?

_____

_____

8. Can you think of recent situations in which you felt rejected or in which someone disapproved of something you said or did? If so, list and describe your response. How would your response have been different if you had believed the truth of your total acceptance in Christ?

a) Situation:

_____

_____

_____

_____

_____

_____

Your response:

_____

_____

_____

_____

_____

How believing the truth would have changed your response:

_____

_____

_____

_____

b) Situation:

_____
_____
_____
_____
_____
_____

Your response:

_____
_____
_____
_____
_____
_____

How believing the truth would have changed your response:

_____
_____
_____

c) Situation:

_____
_____
_____
_____
_____

Your response:

_____
_____
_____
_____

How believing the truth would have changed your response:

_____

_____

_____

9. Memorize Colossians 1:21–22.

Compare your answers to the following:

For Additional Insight

1. a) *Reconcile* means to restore a friendship.

b) Leon Morris, in his book *The Atonement,* states that reconciliation implies three states: friendship, then a quarrel, then friendship again.[1] Man was responsible for the quarrel (Gen. 3 and Rom. 3). Our rebellion and sin shattered our relationship with God.

2. God hates sin. As a result, you were an object of His wrath, separated and completely alienated from Him.

3. Because of your sin, you were an enemy of God. Your sin made you subject to God's wrath, but if you have trusted in Christ, God has declared you holy, without blemish, and free from accusation.

4. a) It was almighty God who deeply loved you and restored your relationship with Him. You were His enemy; now you are His beloved child.

b) God reconciled you to Himself through the death of His precious Son, Jesus Christ.

c) To *exult* means "to take great delight in." We can greatly delight in God, knowing that He loves us and that He has reconciled us to Himself.

5. You are acceptable to God! He does not just *tolerate* you. You are 100 percent acceptable to the highest judge: the perfect, holy, and righteous God Almighty. You are accepted by God for one reason: Christ has abolished the barrier and made peace with God through His blood on the cross. You have the righteousness of Christ (2 Cor. 5:21). You can't ever be any more acceptable to God than you are now (Rom. 5:8–10; Eph. 2:14–18; Col. 1:21–22).

6. You fear rejection when you believe the lie, *I am what others think of me,* instead of believing God's truth, *I am totally acceptable and accepted because of Christ.* You will never begin to experience freedom from the fear of rejection until you realize that God has completely accepted you. If you refuse to believe God's statement, the only other option is to turn to others to meet your need for acceptance and significance, and you will be painfully disillusioned. The primary issue is this: Whose acceptance do you value more, God's or man's?

7. a) God loves you and His Son, Jesus Christ, equally! You have the same standing and the same righteousness as His Son!

b) Jesus calls you "My brother/sister" and addresses God the Father as "our Father."

c) Christ wants you with Him every day throughout eternity.
Meditate on these incredible truths until they begin to become a part of your daily thinking.

8. You might have listed something like this:

Situation: *Frank laughed at my idea in the committee meeting. (Others laughed too.)*
Your response: *I felt deeply hurt and didn't say another word. I left as soon as the meeting was over.*
How believing the truth would have changed your response: *I probably would have felt hurt, then I might have asked Frank to tell*

me why he thought the idea was funny. (I might have laughed at the idea myself!) But I wouldn't have crawled into my shell. I would have continued to participate and would have forgotten about the incident because my sense of self-worth would not have been threatened.

A Final Word

When God chose to redeem us so that we could relate to Him and rule with Him, He did not make us partially righteous, nor has He allowed for our righteousness to be marred by our poor performance. The blood of Christ is sufficient to pay for all sin. Because of His blood, we are holy and righteous before God, even in the midst of sin. This does not minimize the inherent destructiveness of sin. Instead, it glorifies the indescribable sacrifice of Christ.

There is no biblical tenet more neglected in its practical application than the doctrine of reconciliation. The Colossian reference to this doctrine reveals its application to us:

> And although you were formerly alienated and hostile in mind, engaged in evil deeds, yet He has now reconciled you in His fleshly body through death, in order to present you before Him holy and blameless and beyond reproach. (Col. 1:21–22)

Relish those last words. God declares us as "holy and blameless and beyond reproach" at this very moment. This is not merely a reference to our future standing; it describes our present status as well. It tells us something very significant: We are totally accepted by God.

This line of reasoning from the Scriptures might appear to be new but probably would not seem so if we asked, Is there any sin so filthy that it can prevent a Christian from going to heaven? I believe most Christians would answer with a resounding no! A believer is eternally secure; heaven is a certainty for him or her (1 Pet. 1:3–5). But salvation is more than just a ticket to heaven when we die. It is the basis of a relationship. God received us into a loving, intimate, personal relationship the moment we placed our faith in Christ. We are united with God in an eternal and inseparable bond (Rom. 8:38–39). We are born of God in an indissoluble union as fellow heirs with Christ. Recognizing that there is no sin so filthy that it can make a Christian unacceptable to God is not presumptuous. It is God-honoring faith in a blood-sealed warrant with the Holy Spirit, who is given as a pledge of our inheritance with a view to the redemption of God's own possession (Eph. 1:14).

On the other hand, is there anything a Christian can do to become more acceptable to God? No! If there were, then the cross would be insufficient. If we can do anything to be more acceptable to God, then Christ either lied or was mistaken when He cried out on the cross, "It is finished!" (John 19:30). If that is the case, what He should have said was, "It is almost finished, and if you live a perfect life, you and I together might make you acceptable."

Since our relationship with God was bought entirely by the blood of Christ, it is the height of pride to think that our own good works can make us acceptable to God. The Bible speaks to the contrary: "He saved us, not on the basis of deeds which we have done in righteousness, but according to His mercy" (Titus 3:5). Christ has reconciled us to God, and He allows us to experience the incredible truth, *We are totally accepted by and acceptable to God.*

What should we do when we have failed or when someone disapproves of us? A practical way of summarizing the truth we've examined is: *It would be nice if _____ (my boss liked me, I could fix the refrigerator, my complexion were clear, James had picked me up on time), but I'm still deeply loved, completely forgiven, fully pleasing, totally accepted, and complete in Christ.*

This statement doesn't mean that we won't feel pain or anger. We need to be honest about our feelings. A statement like the one above is simply a way to quickly gain God's perspective on whatever we are experiencing. It is not magic, but it enables us to reflect on the implications of biblical truth. We can apply this truth in every difficult situation, whether it is someone's disapproval, our own failure to accomplish something, or the failure of another person.

Memorize the truth in the above statement and begin to apply it in your situations and relationships.

Step 7

The Blame Game

Read chapter 7 in *The Search for Significance*.

This step is designed to aid you in understanding the fear of punishment and the propensity to punish others.

1. Do you really deserve to feel good about yourself? Why or why not?

_____

_____

_____

2. Describe three recent incidents in your life in which you feared being blamed or punished. Why did you have this fear?

a)_____

_____

_____

_____

b)_____

_____

_____

_____

c)_____

_____

_____

_____

3. a) Do you spend much time thinking about your weaknesses and failures? If so, why? (List as many reasons as you can.)

_____

_____

_____

b) What are the three most negative terms you use to describe yourself? What derogatory names do you call yourself?

_____

_____

_____

4. Does condemning yourself help you become a better person? Why or why not?

_____

_____

_____

5. a) Think of a close friend or family member with whom you've had a conflict. What did you say or do to inflict emotional pain?

_____

_____

_____

b) What are some reasons you said or did those things?

_____

_____

_____

6. After sinning, do you ever believe you have to feel bad about yourself before you can feel good about yourself? If so, list some of the situations in which you've done this:

_____

_____

_____

_____

7. Do you want to go to the Father after you've sinned? If not, why?

_____

_____

_____

8. If something goes wrong, do you assume the Lord is punishing you?

_____

9. Does God punish His children?

_____

Compare your answers to the following:

For Additional Insight

1. Yes, because you are God's precious son or daughter, He accepts you, loves you, and has made you complete. Because of this, no one should feel better about himself than you! You may have said no because you have failed at something very important to you. You may think that anyone who failed that badly has no right to feel good about himself. The fact is, no one deserves to feel good about himself. We all deserve God's wrath and condemnation, but you can feel great about yourself because Christ loves, forgives, and accepts you.

2. Perhaps you feared being blamed or punished because you didn't measure up to someone's standards. Maybe someone has threatened to punish you (either emotionally or physically) if you don't please him or her. You have this fear because the world operates under the false belief that failure must be punished. Therefore, if you've failed, you probably will conclude that you'll be punished in some way.

3. a) If you are preoccupied by your weaknesses and failures, you are probably often discouraged because you believe that when

something goes wrong, someone is to blame. You blame yourself and others to be sure that someone pays for the failure. This is really a system of works. If you perform well, you feel worthy of love, so you reward yourself. If you fail, you feel unworthy of love, so you blame yourself. You probably treat others the same way.

b) We usually give ourselves demeaning names because of recurring failures. These names are distinctive for each individual, but some of these terms might sound familiar: *lazy, ugly, stupid, social klutz, unpopular, incompetent, fearful.* These may be used in comparison to someone else, like, *I'm not as pretty as* _____; *My grades are lower than* _____; *His ideas are a lot better than mine; I'm a stupid fool.*

4. You might think it does, but self-condemnation does not make you a better person. Using a guilt/blame motivation to perfect your performance (and thus feel good about yourself) is unscriptural and harmful to you. For a short time, blame may motivate you to perform better, but your self-concept will suffer from your condemnation. Ultimately, your self-concept is far more important than your short-term performance.

5. a) To punish others, perhaps you withdrew love, affection, and encouragement from them. Perhaps you were sarcastic or laughed at them; or maybe you were abrupt in speaking to them. Maybe you abused them verbally, or even physically.

b) You probably reacted this way because you believed that *those who fail are unworthy of love and that failure must be punished.* You may have even appointed yourself to carry out the sentence of punishment.

6. Before answering no to this question, think about the following:

- How long should John feel bad about himself for lying to the IRS?

- How long should Sam feel bad about himself for committing adultery?
- How long should Christy feel bad about herself for getting drunk while her husband was at work?
- How long should Sherman feel bad about himself because he was insensitive to his wife?
- How long should Rick feel bad about himself for stealing from his employer?

Feeling bad about ourselves is a way of doing penance, trying to pay for our sins by our own deeds or feelings. This is performance, or works-righteousness. If we believe that those who fail are unworthy of love and deserve to be blamed and condemned, then we probably will use feelings of guilt as a form of self-condemnation and penance. We think that if we feel bad enough for long enough (the severity and length depending, of course, on the magnitude of the sin), the sin will be forgiven, and we can go on with life. For people with this perspective, repentance is merely a rededication to prevent failure and avoid being embarrassed again.

Please note: I am not advocating that we should feel good about sin. Dishonoring the Lord and bringing harm to ourselves and others produce a sorrow that is right and proper. But God intends for this sorrow to be a response to the destructiveness of sin and the righteousness of Christ, not an attempt to pay for sin through penitent bad feelings. This godly sorrow is described by Paul in 2 Corinthians 7:10: "For the sorrow that is according to the will of God produces a repentance without regret [without the penance of prolonged bad feelings], leading to salvation; but the sorrow of the world produces death [spiritual deadness, works-righteousness]."

7. If you believe that God is waiting to "lower the boom" on you, then you probably won't want to pray. No one likes to be punished, so if you believe that God's attitude toward you is anger and condemnation, you will try to avoid Him.

8. Most people have been deceived about God's character. As a result, they live in fear of what God will do to them because of their sin. But God has demonstrated His love for us on the cross when our sins were paid in full by Christ. Therefore, God doesn't punish us for our sins. He has already taken His wrath out on Christ at the cross.

9. No, God does not punish His children, but He does discipline them. Discipline is rooted in love. God disciplines us because sin is destructive, and He does not want us to self-destruct. The goal of His discipline is to restore, develop, and perfect. Punishment, on the other hand, is retaliation and is used to impose a penalty. Christ has borne your punishment and blame for sin.

It is crucial that you understand the difference between discipline and punishment. God's discipline can be severe, but it is prompted by grief, not anger. His willingness to discipline you is indicative of His love for you.

A Final Word

The proof of blame's effectiveness is that we use it so often. We often believe that we deserve to be blamed for any significant shortcoming, and we think self-inflicted punishment will clear us of guilt and enable us to feel good about ourselves again.

Both self-inflicted punishment and the compulsion to punish others result from the false beliefs *Those who fail are unworthy of love and deserve to be blamed and condemned.*

Charles's stepfather was a corporate executive who was driven to succeed. Nothing Charles did was good enough for him. He often laughed at Charles and called him an idiot and a wimp. Why do we use such terms to describe ourselves and others? We use them because we believe that condemnation is motivational and will provide favorable change. However, the only way this will really work is if the target will accept the message that he or she is unworthy of love.

After he betrayed Christ for thirty pieces of silver, Judas experienced such unbearable guilt that he flung the money across the temple floor and cried, "I have sinned by betraying innocent blood" (Matt. 27:4). He then went out and hanged himself! It is the common conviction of all men, even atheists, that they must pay for their sins. Indeed, the need for punishment to relieve guilt and restore justice is widespread.

Without even realizing it, you probably have internalized a concept that sounds like this: *When I fail, I am unworthy of love (and when others fail, they are unworthy of love) and deserve to be blamed and condemned.*

We have been conditioned to accept personal blame or condemnation every time our performance is unsatisfactory. After reading this, some people immediately recognize this automatic response in their lives, but others do not. You may think that you are not affected by this false belief at all—but you probably are. Do you generally have an urge to find out who is at fault when something fails? Do you look for excuses when you fail? Rather than work out our problems and objectively evaluate our performance, most of us tend to defend ourselves. Counterattack triggers counterattack. The more we criticize other people, the more defensive they usually get, and the less likely they are to admit their errors (especially to us). Criticism can lead to a counterattack from both sides, and pretty soon, it's like a volleyball game, with each person intensifying the pace while returning blame to the other person's side.

However, it is sometimes even more destructive for people to accept blame without defending themselves. Tom was becoming an emotional zombie under his wife's incessant condemnation, but instead of fighting back, he kept thinking, *Yes, Suzanne's right. I am an incompetent fool.* He was like the workout punching bag of a heavyweight fighter.

One of the most common problems among parents is dealing with the misbehavior of their children. It is tremendously painful for most parents to face up to the wrongdoing of their child. But a primary reason why a child's misbehavior is so painful and embarrassing is that parents tend to blame themselves for it.

Between spells of crying, Joyce said, "Mary wouldn't act like this if I'd been the mother I should have been." Dave, on the other hand, ignored his son's misbehavior with the excuse that his boy was simply "going through a stage." He rationalized his son's wrongdoing because he couldn't face the guilt of being a failure as a parent.

When their children get into trouble, parents usually alternate between blaming themselves and blaming their children. After all, someone has to be blamed. The problem in either case is not that parents are loving their child too much or too little but that their personal significance is wrapped up in their performance as parents. Therefore when the child does well, the parents feel good about themselves. When the child does poorly, however, they often blame each other or the child. Beneath it all is the internalized and unconscious belief: *Someone has to take the blame.*

Our worth is totally secure in Christ, so our children's success or failure doesn't affect our value in the least. We need to see our children the way our heavenly Father sees us: *deeply loved, completely forgiven, fully pleasing, and totally accepted.* Then, when they disobey, our discipline will be like the Father's discipline of us: in love, not anger. If we approach our children with an attitude of grief rather than anger when they disobey, it will make a tremendous difference! What a difference it will make if we go to our children with the attitude and words, "It's sad that you disobeyed. It was harmful to you, and I love you so much that I don't want you to harm yourself. I need to discipline you to help you remember not to do it again. Remember, the reason I am disciplining you is that I love you so much!" instead of, "You've done it again, and I'll make sure you regret it! I wonder if you'll ever amount to anything!"

Responding to our children in grief instead of anger will have monumental implications on both them and us. Our children won't be afraid of us, our relationship with them won't be marred by anger, and they will be more likely to view God as a loving Father rather than as a tyrant. As parents, we will have a more accurate perception of God's love and gracious discipline, and we will be more in control of our emotions. We won't try to deny that we are getting angry at our children's misbehavior, letting our anger build and build until we explode. Instead, we will be able to express our displeasure more quickly and acceptably because it will be wholesome grief instead of unholy anger. These are powerful and welcome implications, indeed!

Step 8

God's Answer: Propitiation

Part I

Read chapter 8 from *The Search for Significance.*

At the cross, God poured out His wrath against sin. Part I of this step will help you see that God's wrath has been satisfied; therefore, there is no need to fear punishment.

1. Define *propitiation:*

_____

_____

_____

2. We each have had an incalculable number of sinful (disobedient, self-centered) thoughts and actions. How many sins can a holy God overlook?

_____

_____

3. Read Ezekiel 7:8–9, Romans 2:4–5, and Ephesians 2:1–3. Does God's wrath have a specific object? If so, what is it?

_____

_____

_____

4. Read Genesis 19:1–26, Jeremiah 4:4, Ezekiel 5:11–17, 23:22–30, and 2 Thessalonians 1:6–10. List some characteristics of God's wrath from these passages:

_____

_____

_____

_____

_____

_____

5. Read 1 John 4:9–10.
a) Are you loved by the Father?

_____

b) How do you know you are loved?

_____

c) Do you feel loved?

_____

6. a) Consider what it would be like to experience the wrath of Almighty God. Then read Isaiah 53:4–10. Place your name in the place of appropriate pronouns ("Surely He took up _____ 's infirmities.") The wrath that you deserved has been poured out on Christ.

b) In what ways can you express your gratitude to Christ for what He has done for you?

_____

_____

7. The more we understand God's love and forgiveness, the more we will be willing and able to forgive others. If we think about it, the things that others do to us (ranging from acts of genuine

hatred or taking out a hard day's frustration on us to not liking us because of the clothes we wear or the way we keep our homes) are all trivial in comparison to our sin of abject rebellion against God, which He has graciously forgiven. This is why Paul encouraged the Christians in Ephesus to forgive each other "just as God in Christ also has forgiven you" (Eph. 4:32), completely and willingly.

a) Are there any sins (or even personality differences) in others that you have difficulty forgiving? If so, list them, and confess your lack of forgiveness to God:

_____

_____

_____

_____

_____

_____

b) How do these things compare to your sins that deserved God's wrath but instead received the payment of Christ's substitutionary death?

_____

_____

_____

8. Memorize 1 John 4:9–10.

Compare your answers to the following:

For Additional Insight

1. *Propitiation* means "satisfaction." Theologically, propitiation refers to Christ's payment on the cross, which satisfied the penalty for our sins. Christ's death propitiates, or averts, the wrath of God. God's righteous anger is directed against all sin and, therefore, against all of sinful mankind. Christ's death removed God's anger from repentant sinners.

2. God cannot overlook sin, not even a "little one." Even our "righteous" deeds—those deeds we do to look good in the eyes of people or to try to earn God's acceptance—are like filthy rags to God (Isa. 64:6).

3. Yes. God's wrath is personal and is directed toward the sinner and his or her sin. In fact, in Ephesians 2:3, Paul describes unbelievers as simply *children of wrath.* All of us deserve God's righteous condemnation because all of us are sinners (Rom. 3:23).

4. God's wrath is swift, complete, all-consuming, terrifying, and justly deserved, and is His response to sin and rebellion against Him.

5. a) The fact that God poured out His wrath on His Son for you is proof beyond question that He loves you.

b) Propitiation demonstrates God's love for you.

c) God loves you more than you know, although you may not feel loved until you take the time to meditate on this truth.

Reflecting on God's Word will help you to replace the false belief—that God wants to punish you—with the truth—that He loves you dearly. Spend some time thinking about the truth of Romans 8:28–39.

6. a) This exercise will help you to personalize what Christ Jesus has done for you.

b) We can express our gratitude to God directly in prayer, by studying His Word and obeying His commands, by serving Him, and by forgiving others as He has forgiven us.

7. a) It may be difficult for you to forgive those who've hurt your feelings, gossiped about you, didn't take time to answer your questions, laughed at your mistakes, or blamed you for an error. Your list may also include people who don't dress the way you'd

like them to, who don't clean up the way you'd like them to, who are more shy or more gregarious than you, or who don't spend their money as you do.

b) For the comparison, look at Matthew 18:21–35. When anyone sins against you or offends you in any way, reflect on this: *There is nothing that anyone can do to me that can compare with what Christ has forgiven me for!* This will help you to gain a proper perspective on how you can truly forgive other people.

A Final Word

God's plan for us is centered in the cross. To understand His plan, we must first understand the meaning of propitiation.

Prior to our spiritual birth, even our good deeds were despicable to God (Isa. 64:6). If we are honest about our performance, we must admit that we have sinned thousands of times, even after having accepted Christ.

The problem with our sinfulness is that God is absolutely holy, pure, and perfect. There is absolutely nothing unholy in Him. God is light, and in Him there is no darkness at all (1 John 1:5). Therefore, since God is holy, He cannot overlook or compromise with sin. It took one sin to separate Adam from God. For God to condone even one sin would instantly defile His holiness, which He indicates by His righteous condemnation of sin (Rom. 6:23).

The Father did not escape witnessing His Son's mistreatment: the mocking, the scourging, and the cross. He could have spoken and ended the whole ordeal, yet He kept silent. Confronted with the suffering of His Son, He chose to let it continue so that we could be saved. What an expression of love! Its depth is unsearchable.

Try to recall an experience in which you were loved by someone special. That person adored you and wanted to be with you. You didn't have to perform; just being you was enough. The thought of that person selecting you to love was intoxicating. All other facets of life seemed to diminish. He or she loved you, and that love was soothing to you and satisfied many of your inner longings.

If the love of a person can make us feel this way, consider how much greater joy the heavenly Father's love can bring. We can't truly experience the love of the Father unless we realize that it supersedes any experience of being loved by another man or woman.

Frederick Faber was consumed with love for the Father. A song he wrote reveals his single-minded devotion:

Only to sit and think of God,
Oh what a joy it is!
To think the thought, to breathe the Name;
Earth has no higher bliss.
Father of Jesus, love's reward!
What rapture it will be,
Prostrate before Thy throne to be,
And gaze and gaze on Thee!

One of Faber's sermons says of Christ:

Wherever we turn in the church of God, there is Jesus. He is the beginning, middle and end of everything to us . . . There is nothing good, nothing holy, nothing beautiful, nothing joyous which He is not to His servants. No one need be poor, because, if he chooses, he can have Jesus for his own property and possession. No one need be downcast, for Jesus is the joy of heaven, and it is His joy to enter into sorrowful hearts. We can exaggerate about many things: but we can never exaggerate our obligation to Jesus, or the compassionate abundance of the love of Jesus to us. All our lives long we might talk of Jesus, and yet we should never come to an end of the sweet things that might be said of Him. Eternity will not be long enough to learn all He is, or to praise Him for all He has done, but then, that matters not, for we shall be always with Him, and we desire nothing more.[1]

God loves you, and He enjoys revealing His love to you. He enjoys being loved by you, but He knows you can love Him only if you are experiencing His love for you. Propitiation means that His wrath has been removed and that you are deeply loved!

Many of us have a distorted concept of the heavenly Father. We believe that God is thrilled when we accept Christ and are born into His family. But many of us also believe that He is proud of us for only as long as we perform well and that the better our performance, the happier He is with us. We may perceive God as being like the management in a factory. If we produce, the managers love us; if we don't produce, they fire us. We may believe that if we really foul up, God is going to put us on the shelf somewhere. He will take care of our most basic needs because He has obligated Himself to do that, but only the beautiful, producing Christians will enjoy His love and acceptance. This is a distorted view of our heavenly Father!

In reality, God loves us, and not a moment goes by that He isn't thinking loving thoughts about us (Ps. 40:5). We are His children, and we are individually special to Him because of Christ! Propitiation, then, means that Jesus Christ has satisfied the Father's righteous condemnation of sin by His death. The Scriptures give only one reason to explain this incredible fact: God loves us!

Part II: Forgiving Others

One way we inflict punishment on those around us is by refusing to forgive them. We tend to keep score, tallying up all those times we've been wronged and all the things we don't like about another individual. We become critical. Punishing others for their failure is our way of "evening the score."

Unforgiveness is a sure way of cutting the flow of God's power in our lives. In fact, there are a number of negative consequences that often result from an unwillingness to forgive others. Before we examine these consequences, let's look at some of the reasons why we may refuse to forgive:

Reasons for Unforgiveness

We often fail to forgive others (and ourselves) because we don't think it's possible. We forget how God has graciously forgiven all of our sins through Christ's death and rationalize why we can't forgive. The following are among the countless excuses we make for our unwillingness to forgive ourselves and others:

• **The offense was too great.** Grant's wife had left him for another man, and he was bitter toward her. Her infidelity was too great a sin for him to forgive. But almost two years after the incident, God began to impress Grant with the idea that he should forgive his wife, just as God in Christ also had forgiven (him), completely and willfully. When Grant finally did forgive her, he felt as though one hundred pounds had been lifted from his back.

Roger sat shaking with anger as he recalled his wife's rape. His anger was destroying his health and his relationship with his wife. *How can any man forgive such an act?* he wondered. The transient who had raped his wife had moved on and, in his perversion, had probably forgotten the incident. He was never caught. Continuing to allow the offense to produce bitterness might ultimately do more harm to Roger and his family than the destructive act of the rape.

• **He (she) won't accept responsibility for the offense.** How many people have offended us but won't agree that they were at fault? The offense might be something slight, such as being overlooked at a social event, or something major, such as being emotionally neglected as a child. Having others agree that they've offended us isn't necessary for us to respond properly to their offense.

• **He (she) isn't truly sorry.** John pulled a practical joke on you that caused you to be late for class, and your professor refused to accept your paper because you didn't have it in on time. John doesn't see anything wrong with a little joke—he's slightly sorry, but he still thinks it was hilarious. Even if John doesn't recognize the trouble he's caused you, you can still extend forgiveness to him through Christ and refuse to hold the offense against him.

• **He (she) never asked to be forgiven.** For whatever reason, the offender never got around to asking you for forgiveness. Are you going to withhold forgiveness until it's requested? Who is suffering, you or the offender? What would God have you do? (Read 1 Cor. 13:5 and Eph. 4:32.)

• **He (she) will do it again.** Candy's husband had been out late playing cards every Friday night for three years. On some nights, he didn't come home. "Me? Forgive that jerk?" Candy asked. The Lord said that the number of times we're to forgive is seventy times seven . . . in other words, regardless of the number of offenses. If Candy doesn't forgive, she will be the bitter loser.

• **He (she) did it again.** David had been a horrible husband to Mandy. However, after much effort, Mandy had forgiven him for his insensitivity, his greater concern for the guys on his softball team, his lack of affection for the children, and his callous, domineering attitude. Then David saw how poor his behavior had become. He began to change. His relationship with Mandy started to improve—until he stayed out late again with the guys. He had done it again! One mistake set the whole conflict in motion again.

• **I don't like him (her).** Generally, we don't have a great deal of appreciation for those who have wronged us. In fact, every emotion within us may call for retaliation against the creep! Only when we realize that forgiveness is an act of the will and not of the emotions, will we choose to forgive those who have hurt us.

• **He (she) did it deliberately.** "He knew what he was doing, and he did it anyway." George had been swindled out of ten thousand dollars by his so-called best friend, Hal. It had been a complex scheme that had required precise timing over a period of several months. As George sat stunned, his mind raced through those times he had been generous to Hal. He thought of how much he had loved Hal and had repeatedly trusted him. The swindle had been completely deliberate, and Hal had used him. George had been played for a sucker. Hal must be laughing at him now. Whether the offense was deliberate or not, God still wants George to forgive Hal.

• **If I forgive the offense, I'll have to treat the offender well.** Ben excused his slander of Steve by pointing out how Steve had offended him. He felt justified in destroying Steve's reputation even though most of the things he had said about Steve were lies.

Shirley was cold to Greg and had been for two weeks. It was her plan to punish him for two weeks because he had offended her. She would forgive him all right—as soon as she was through punishing him.

• **Someone has to punish him (her).** How often do we want God to be merciful to us and yet want Him to skin other people alive? When we don't see them suffer, we sometimes take it upon ourselves to be God's hand of vengeance.

Charles was their pastor, but according to Gloria, he had wasted the church's money. Gloria was in charge of the church women's group. She waited patiently for God to nail Charles, but when God didn't do what she thought He should, she just knew that she was to be the divining rod for Charlie's back. Soon the church had taken sides—pro-Charles or anti-Charles. The result was that the church disgraced itself by splitting in hatred.

Discipline is God's job. "Vengeance is Mine, I will repay," says the Lord (Heb. 10:30) . . . and He hasn't delegated that responsibility to us!

• **Something keeps me from forgiving.** Satan actively promotes unforgiveness. When you attempt to deal with this problem honestly, you may be in for a tremendous spiritual battle, with both confusing and conflicting thoughts and emotions. Don't be surprised if you have to resist Satan at every turn in order to accomplish the task of forgiving the offender. Forgiveness is primarily an act of the will, not a warm feeling.

• **I'll be a hypocrite if I forgive because I don't feel like forgiving.** It's amazing how we confuse hypocrisy with obedience. We are hypocritical only if we do something for selfish gain. For instance, a hypocrite might be a politician who comes to church in order to get its members to vote for him in the next election but who despises the church and its people. To forgive as an act of the will in obedience to the Lord's command is true spirituality, not hypocrisy.

• **I'll forgive, but I won't ever forget.** If we continue to harbor the memory of an offense, we are only fooling ourselves in thinking that we have forgiven the offender, and we will not experience any freedom. In true forgiveness, we give up the right to remember an offense or to bring it up again during arguments. (Note: This doesn't mean that when we forgive a wrong we'll never think of it again. But it does mean that we won't relish the memory. Choose to think about things that are true, honorable, right, pure, and lovely [Phil. 4:8].)

• **I'll forgive because I have found an excuse for the offense.** Hank had been very irresponsible during the early years of his marriage. His wife, Sally, had always been able to forgive him by placing the blame on his mother, who had babied Hank even after he was grown. And yet Sally was continually angered by Hank and his mother. In fact, her volatile temper was destroying her marriage.

Sally thought that she had forgiven Hank when she had really just excused him. By blaming Hank's mother for his immaturity, she had rationalized his behavior and had reduced her perception of his offensive actions. After reducing each offense, Sally then forgave it. The problem was that she did not deal with the real offense but with a distortion of it. Therefore the real offense remained intact in spite of her efforts at forgiveness.

When you offend someone or when someone offends you, do you immediately look for a reason? If you do, you may only be rationalizing. If you come up with an excuse to the question Why did I forgive him (or her)? then you have not truly forgiven the offense. You have excused it.

Results of Unforgiveness

• **Stress:** Sarah announced to the group that her husband did not deserve to be forgiven and that she wasn't going to forgive him if it meant her life. It did. Sarah died of kidney failure. She wanted to kill her husband, but in reality she killed herself. Countless people live under extreme stress due to the bitterness and anger that result from unforgiveness.

• **Self-inflicted reinjury:** Robert recalled this incident: "As I drove home, flashing into my memory was a guy I played basketball with in college. He was a great antagonist of mine. He was one of the few people I have ever met whom I truly wanted to punch out. I began to remember the unkind things he did to me. Soon, anger started creeping up inside of me. I had not remembered this fellow for years, and I'm sure that he doesn't remember me at all. Yet my reliving this event caused me a lot of pain. I had not properly dealt with it in the beginning."

How many times are you reinjuring yourself because past offenses haunt you?

• **No more love:** "I don't know if I can ever love someone again" is a frequent complaint from those offended by a lover. Our deepest hurts come from those we love. One way we deal with the pain of being offended is to simply withdraw, refusing to love anymore. We often make this unconscious decision when we have not adequately dealt with an offense. We may desperately want to love again but feel that we are incapable of it. Refusing to experience love and feeling unable to love are both devastating conditions.

• **Bitterness:** Emotions trace their lines on our faces. We think others don't notice what's going on inside, but our anger can usually be detected by even the casual observer. One person recalled seeing a neighbor go through difficulties in her marriage. Hate created such an impression on her that her face became permanently snarled. She still has that ugly look on her face. Unforgiveness produces ugliness of all sorts.

• **Perpetual conflict:** A couple, both of whom had been previously married, received counseling several years ago. Having been hurt in their first marriages, they each anticipated hurt from their present spouse. At the smallest offense, each would react as if the spouse were about to deliver the final blow. They were constantly on the defensive, protecting themselves from the attacks they imagined the mate would deliver. Having been offended in the past, they anticipated more hurt in the present and future, and they reacted in a way that perpetuated the conflict.

• **Walls that keep others out:** Strangely, many of us refuse to experience love from those who love us. We may often become anxious and threatened when personal intimacy becomes possible.

Jane hoped and prayed that her husband, Frank, would come to know the Lord. This, she thought, would enable him to be more loving toward her and their children. One day, Frank accepted

Christ, and over time, his life began to change. He became interested in Jane and started spending time with her and the children. He was sensitive and loving. Was it a dream come true? Instead of rejoicing, Jane deeply resented Frank for not changing sooner! *If Frank is able to love us like this now, then he's always had the ability,* she thought. She felt confused and guilty about her anger.

Jane's anger was a defense mechanism to keep distance between Frank and herself. The closer they might get, the more pain she might experience if he reverted to his old ways. She had never truly forgiven Frank, so the bricks of unforgiveness were stacked to form a wall that kept him from getting too close. Hiding behind a wall of unforgiveness is a lonely experience.

Forgiveness Is Not Erasure

The modern idea of forgiveness is to approach an offense with a large eraser and wipe it off the books. God has never forgiven like this. For each offense, He demanded full payment. This is the reason for the cross. Beside every offense on our ledger is the blood of Christ, which has paid for our sins in full.

The Christian stands with a unique capacity for forgiveness because he or she can appropriate the forgiveness of the cross. God has forgiven us fully and completely. We, of all people, know what it is like to experience unconditional forgiveness. As a result, we can in turn forgive those around us. Think of it this way: *There is nothing that anyone can do to me (insult me, lie about me, annoy me) that can compare with what Christ has forgiven me for doing.* We gain a better perspective of others' offenses when we compare them to our sin of rebellion that Christ has completely forgiven. In Ephesians 4:32, Paul wrote, "And be kind to one another, tenderhearted, forgiving each other, just as God in Christ also has forgiven you."

List ten things for which you are glad God in Christ has forgiven you. This will prime you to be willing to forgive all other offenders.

1. _____   3. _____

2. _____   4. _____

5. _____   8. _____
6. _____   9. _____
7. _____   10. _____

Summary of Reasons for Unforgiveness

1. The offense was too great.

2. He (she) won't accept responsibility for the offense.

3. He (she) isn't truly sorry.

4. He (she) never asked to be forgiven.

5. He (she) will do it again.

6. He (she) did it again.

7. I don't like him (her).

8. He (she) did it deliberately.

9. If I forgive the offense, I'll have to treat the offender well.

10. Someone has to punish him (her).

11. Something keeps me from forgiving.

12. I'll be a hypocrite if I forgive because I don't feel like forgiving.

13. I'll forgive, but I won't ever forget.

14. I'll forgive because I have found an excuse for the offense.

The following exercise will help you to understand biblical principles of forgiveness and apply them to your relationships with others:

1. Read Matthew 18:21–35.

a) How great was the debt of the king's servant?

_____

b) Was it possible for him ever to repay it?

_____

2. a) Likewise, before you trusted Christ, how great was your debt to God?

_____

b) Was it possible for you ever to repay it?

_____

3. a) What did the servant ask for?

_____

b) What did the king grant him?

_____

4. Why was the king's servant so harsh with his fellow servant over such a small debt?

_____

_____

_____

5. Read Luke 7:36–50 (especially verse 47) and compare it with the parable in Matthew 18:21–35. What is the foundation for being able to love and forgive others?

_____

6. Read Ephesians 4:32 and Colossians 3:12–13.
a) To what degree are we to forgive others?

_____

b) Describe how God has forgiven you:

_____

_____

_____

7. Name some of the effects people experience when they harbor unforgiveness (attitudes toward others, their opinion of themselves, quality of relationships, and so on):

_____

_____

_____

8. Do you see any of the answers to question 7 in your life? In your attitude toward others? Toward yourself? If so, describe them:

_____

_____

_____

9. Is there any particular sin for which you haven't experienced God's forgiveness?

_____

_____

_____

Compare your answers to the following:

For Additional Insight

1. The debt of the king's servant was the equivalent of about ten million dollars. To put this in perspective, in his book *Healing for Damaged Emotions,* David Seamands states that the entire annual taxes of Judea, Samaria, Galilee, Perea, and Idumea was eight hundred thousand dollars. So, the debt of the king's servant was impossible to repay—which is exactly the point.

2. Your debt to God was more impossible to repay than the servant's debt to the king. Apart from Christ, you were destined to carry this impossible debt all your life, knowing that at death you would have to give your eternal destiny to pay for it.

3. Did the servant ask for forgiveness of the debt? No. He asked for time to repay it. The king, though, had compassion and forgave him the entire debt.

4. The king's servant apparently did not believe he had been forgiven and was trying to collect enough money to pay back the debt. He took the king's words to mean, "I'll give you a little more time. Work hard and pay me back." But the king offered total forgiveness by canceling the debt. The debt was *gone*. He did not owe one penny of the ten million dollars. (Note that forgiveness is not experienced until it's fully accepted.)

5. Our ability to extend grace and forgiveness to others is directly related to the degree by which we have personally experienced the same.

6. We are to forgive others "just as God in Christ also has forgiven [us]" (Eph. 4:32). Our every thought and deed, regardless of their motives or results, have been forgiven. That forgiveness is totally unearned.

7. A lack of forgiveness may result in being harsh toward others, self-critical, demanding, guilt-ridden, resentful, finding fault, being motivated by *ought tos* (I ought to do this; I ought not to do that), holding grudges, and working hard to atone for shortcomings. This is merely a partial list. See "A Final Word" for other results.

8. Many of us harbor ill feelings toward one or more people, but we have suppressed them. We often are not consciously aware of these feelings until the Holy Spirit reveals them to us so that we can deal with them. Are there people you don't like to be around? Or whom you can't look in the eye? Or with whom you get angry every time you even think of them?

9. Is there something you can't forgive yourself for having done? God the Father has forgiven you because Christ has paid for your sin. Are you refusing to forgive something God has forgiven?

Think this through carefully. Remember, the extent to which you will be able to love and forgive others is dependent on your acceptance of God's love for you and His forgiveness for your sins.

Use the exercise on the following pages to help you recognize any lack of forgiveness in your life and to enable you to freely forgive as God in Christ has forgiven you.

1. Offense: List in some detail several events that caused you pain.

_____

_____

_____

2. Persons to be forgiven: List all who participated in the offenses.

_____

_____

_____

3. Reasons for unforgiveness: Go through the list of reasons for unforgiveness, noting the ones that apply.

_____

_____

_____

4. Act of forgiveness: Choose to forgive, remembering the complete forgiveness you have in Christ.

Use this prayer (or your own) as an exercise of faith for each offense:

Dear Lord,
I forgive _____ for _____ [offense] on the basis that God has freely forgiven me and commanded me to

forgive others. I have the capacity to do this because Christ has completely forgiven me. I do not excuse this person's offense in any way, nor do I use any excuse for not extending forgiveness. Thank You, Lord Jesus, for enabling me to forgive.

I also confess that I have sinned by using the following excuses for not forgiving:

_____

_____

_____

_____

_____

_____

_____

_____

_____

_____

_____

_____

_____

A Final Word

Being offended by others is a frequent experience in life. We go through periods when it seems that almost everybody is letting us down. We want freedom from being offended, but the beat goes on. We are hurt by both our experience of the offense and our reliving of it. In fact, the initial pain of the wrong usually amounts to only a small fraction of the total hurt. After a while, it should become obvious to us that it is impossible to avoid being offended. However, the majority of our pain can be avoided if we will learn to deal with offenses rather than relive them countless times.

Step 9

Shame

Read chapter 9 in *The Search for Significance*.

This step examines the shame that can arise from a negative evaluation of our past performance or our physical appearance. Shame is a prevailing sense of worthlessness that leads to the false belief *I am what I am. I cannot change. I am hopeless.*

1. Define *shame*.

_____

_____

_____

2. When does shame occur?

_____

_____

_____

3. Why does shame make an impact on our sense of self-worth? How does shame lock us into a low opinion of ourselves?

_____

_____

_____

_____

4. Is there anything you can't keep from doing? When you've tried to stop, but then do it again, how do you feel about yourself?

_____
_____
_____

5. List the things about your appearance or your past performance that prevent you from viewing yourself as a fully pleasing and totally accepted person:

a) Appearance:

_____
_____
_____

b) Past performance:

_____
_____
_____

6. When people with a poor self-concept succeed at something, one would think they would be encouraged and have a more positive outlook. But often, pessimistic people explain or minimize their success and continue in their hopelessness.

a) Do you do this when you succeed? If so, what do you tell yourself and others?

_____
_____
_____
_____

b) Why do you say those things?

_____
_____
_____
_____

7. What sources of input reinforce a low view of yourself?

_____
_____
_____

8. a) Read Psalm 139:13–16. What was God's involvement in the formation of your physical appearance and personality?

_____
_____

b) Are you a Creator critic?

_____

9. If you have a poor self-concept, what do you think it will take for you to overcome it and experience the joy and power of your new life in Christ?

_____
_____
_____

10. a) How do you think other people would describe you?

_____
_____
_____

b) What are their expectations of you?

_____
_____
_____

c) How have their expectations affected your self-esteem?

_____
_____
_____

Compare your answers to the following:

For Additional Insight

1. *Webster's Ninth New Collegiate Dictionary* defines *shame* as "a painful emotion caused by consciousness of guilt, shortcoming, or impropriety; a condition of humiliating disgrace or disrepute."

2. Shame often occurs when a failure in our performance or a flaw in our appearance is considered so important that it creates a permanently negative opinion in our minds about our self-worth. Even when others don't know of our failure or flaw, we may assume that their opinion of us is both poor and accurate.

3. Shame can have a tremendous impact on us if we believe that we can never be different from what we have been. We may view ourselves as a composite of all of our past actions and believe that we will never be able to change. Left in this hopeless state, we are likely to feel trapped in helplessness about ourselves and our future. Because much of what we do is based on our self-concept, our every action reinforces this negative perception of ourselves.

4. Your list may include things like adultery, premarital sex, masturbation, homosexuality, alcohol or drug abuse, an eating disorder, gambling, smoking, being a junk-food junkie, blatant lying, exaggerating the truth, cheating, stealing, or other destructive personal habits. When you attempt to change but fail, it causes you to view yourself as a failure with no hope. You feel guilty and helpless.

5. a) Name the "faults" you find in your appearance, anything from head to toe: height, weight, bone structure, acne, wrinkles, facial features, hair, chest, legs, feet, or teeth.

b) "Faults" in your past performance might include: failure in your marriage or friendships; disappointing your parents; not making good grades; sloppiness; an addiction; being uncoordinated, deceitful, obnoxious, lustful, gay, adulterous, unforgiving, and so forth.

6. a) People with a poor self-concept may tell themselves:
   - It was just luck.
   - I couldn't do it again.
   - I'm still a failure.
   - I should stop while I'm ahead because it will never happen again.

b) If you tell yourself things like this, it may be because you expect failure and rejection so much that you simply can't handle success and appreciation.

7. Sources of input contributing to low self-worth may be what parents or peers actually say or what you assume they are thinking. Your input may also come from comparing yourself with the handsome men and gorgeous women on television, in magazines, or in other forms of advertising.

8. a) God formed you, and He was involved in this process at conception. He has made you carefully and wonderfully. He shaped your frame. Before one day passed in your life, He knew all that would happen, including your family background, personality type, mental capacities, and emotional makeup.

b) If you minimize your self-worth because of your appearance or your personality, you are criticizing God's unique workmanship. He is the all-wise and all-powerful Creator, and He fashioned you according to His wisdom and power. The thing molded will not say to the molder, "Why did you make me like this?" will it? (Rom. 9:20.)

9. You must first recognize that if you are evaluating yourself by your past performance or appearance, you are viewing yourself incorrectly. Your past will affect you to the degree that you evaluate yourself on the basis of previous successes or failures. Second, you must recognize that God has made you into a new creature through Christ's death on the cross. God says you are righteous, deeply loved, fully pleasing, and totally accepted by Him.

10. Others' opinions of us, either good or bad, cannot be the basis of a godly self-esteem. If their opinions of us are good, we are often led to either pride or the fear of failing and losing that good opinion. If their opinions of us are negative, we may believe them and think that we can't change. A good, proper, and godly evaluation of ourselves comes from God's Word, not from other people.

A Final Word

Shame occurs when a failure in our performance or a flaw in our appearance is considered so important that it solidifies a negative self-concept. Even when others don't know of our failure, we assume their opinion of us is poor, and we adopt what we think their opinion might be.

If we base our self-worth on our performance long enough, our past behavior will eventually become the sole basis of our worth. We will see ourselves with certain character qualities and flaws because that's the way we've always been. We then have unconsciously incorporated Satan's lie into our belief system: I *must always be what I have been and live with whatever self-worth I have because that's just me.* Interestingly, we claim only our poor behavior as, "That's just me." We never hear anyone say, "That's just me; I'm so wonderful, honest, and bright."

We may think that humility is self-depreciation, but true humility is an accurate appraisal of our worth in Christ. We deserved God's righteous condemnation, yet we are recipients of His unconditional love, grace, and righteousness through Christ. We are deeply loved, completely forgiven, fully pleasing, totally accepted, and complete in Him. Thankfulness, generosity, kindness, and self-confidence constitute true humility!

Another aspect of a poor self-concept relates to personal appearance. Most of us have some aspect of our appearance that we wish we could change, but much about our appearance can't really be altered. We not only may base our self-worth on our appearance but also may tend to base our acceptance of others on their appearance, even the color of their skin. We may never be any more cruel than when we accept or reject others based on their appearance.

Are you angry with God for the way He made you? Do you compare and rank your appearance with others? If you do, you will suffer at some point in your life because there will always be someone prettier, stronger, cuter, or more handsome. Even if you are spectacularly beautiful or strikingly handsome, you will suffer because you will be afraid of losing your good looks, which you consider the basis of your self-worth.

If we insist on valuing our self-worth by our appearance and performance, sooner or later God will graciously allow us to see the futility of that struggle. The Lord never meant for us to find the fulfillment of our self-worth and significance in the opinions of others. This undeniable, unavoidable need for a sense of value was created in man by God. However, He knows we will never come to Him until we find the importance of people's opinions to be empty and hopeless. At that point, we can turn to Him and find comfort and encouragement in the truths of His Word!

What is the basis of your self-worth? Are you living by these scriptural truths or by these false beliefs?

Scriptural Truths	**False Beliefs**
I am completely forgiven and am fully pleasing to God.	I must meet certain standards to feel good about myself.
I am totally accepted by God.	I must be approved by certain people to feel good about myself.
I am deeply loved by God.	Those who fail (including myself) are unworthy of love and deserve to be punished.
I am absolutely complete in Christ.	I am what I am. I cannot change. I am hopeless.

False beliefs are all a part of the enemy's insidious plan. But God has a different plan. By now, you should see that deception is a part of Satan's scheme to steal, kill, and destroy mankind. God has His own plan for you, and it alone will bring you a stable sense of self-worth. With a godly self-worth comes a new direction and purpose: to honor the One who laid down His life to give you security and significance.

Step 10

God's Answer: Regeneration

Read chapter 10 in *The Search for Significance.*

This step will help you see yourself as a new creature in Christ with new potential and new capacities. The truth that you have been made new in Him will enable you to begin developing a strong, positive self-esteem in spite of "flaws" in your appearance or past failures.

1. Do you really think you can view yourself any differently than you always have? If not, why?

_____

_____

_____

2. Read 2 Corinthians 5:17.
a) Define *regeneration:*

_____

_____

b) What does your having been made a new creature mean?

_____

_____

_____

_____

_____

3. How was your regeneration accomplished?
a) John 1:12–13

_____

_____

_____

b) John 3:16

_____

_____

_____

c) Titus 3:5

_____

_____

_____

d) 1 Pet. 1:3

_____

_____

_____

e) 1 Pet. 1:23

_____

_____

_____

4. Read Ephesians 4:22–24 and Colossians 3:9–10. What process do you need to go through in order to experience your new self?

_____

_____

_____

_____

_____

_____

5. From the passages listed on the following pages, list the characteristics of your old self and your new self:

Characteristics of My Old Self

a) Rom. 6:6

_____

_____

_____

b) Gal. 5:19–21

_____

_____

_____

c) Eph. 2:1–3

_____

_____

_____

d) Eph. 4:17–22

_____

_____

_____

e) Col. 3:5–9

_____

_____

_____

f) Titus 3:3

_____

_____

_____

_____

Characteristics of My New Self

a) Rom. 8:16–17

_____

_____

_____

b) 2 Cor. 5:21

_____

_____

_____

c) Gal. 5:22–24

_____

_____

_____

d) Eph. 4:23–32

_____

_____

_____

e) Col. 2:10

_____

_____

_____

f) Col. 3:10–15

_____

_____

_____

g) Titus 3:1–2

_____

_____

_____

h) 1 Pet. 1:16

_____

_____

_____

6. Read Romans 6:12–23 and 1 Corinthians 6:9–11. How does the truth of regeneration free you from evaluating yourself by your past performance?

_____

_____

_____

7. Read 1 Samuel 16:6–7 and Psalm 139:13–16. How does the truth of regeneration free you from the shame prompted by flaws in your physical appearance?

_____

_____

_____

8. How could an understanding that you are a new creature in Christ affect your personal fitness or grooming habits?

_____

_____

_____

9. How can the fact that you have a new life in Christ affect the way you think, feel, and act?

_____

_____

_____

10. Do you use past failures, your appearance, or some other "flaw" as an excuse for not living for Christ? If so, what is your excuse? How valid is it?

_____

_____

11. Memorize 2 Corinthians 5:17

Compare your answers to the following:

For Additional Insight

1. Much of your self-worth has probably been based on your performance and others' opinions. False beliefs have thus become the primary basis you use to evaluate yourself and the situations you face.

| Belief system based on false beliefs | → | Ungodly thoughts | → | Painful emotions | → | Ungodly actions |

Your beliefs usually influence your thoughts, emotions, and actions. False beliefs are Satan's lies, and they generate ungodly thoughts, painful emotions, and sinful actions. An ungodly performance serves to reinforce these false beliefs, which supports the conviction *I am what I am*. You may feel trapped and hopeless to be anything different from who you are right now. Take heart! There is hope! God has made you a new creature.

2. a) *Webster's New World Dictionary* defines *regeneration* as "renewed or restored; to cause to be spiritually reborn; to cause to be completely reformed; to bring into existence again."

b) You have been made into a new person. At the instant of your conversion to Christ, you were born again as a new spiritual being. God creates by *fiat,* that is, He makes something from nothing. Your new birth brought about more than a change of direction. It gave you a completely new nature with new capacities to reflect God's image in your daily life. This new creature resides in your body, but it is as different from your old self as a horse is from a man.

3. Your regeneration was accomplished:

a) By the will of God.

b) Through believing faith in Jesus Christ's death for you.

c) By the renewing of the Holy Spirit.

d) Through the death and resurrection of Jesus Christ.

e) By the Word of God.

4. The process of experiencing your new self involves three steps:

a) Laying aside the old self—rejecting the old self's hold on you, which dictates how you think, feel, and act, and choosing to stop living in worldliness.

b) Renewing your mind with God's truth—understanding the truth of what Christ has accomplished for you and how that gives you a new capacity to live for Him.

c) Putting on the new self—in your thoughts, words, actions, values, and relationships.

Express the truth of your new character. Your new self can now influence how you think, feel, and act.

5. This exercise will help you see that regeneration has already been completed in your life. You have been transformed into a new creature. You can declare those characteristics that describe your new nature to be true of you: *I am deeply loved by God. I am completely forgiven by God. I am fully pleasing to God. I am totally acceptable and accepted by God. I am a new creation—complete in Christ.*

6. Regeneration gives you a new beginning. No matter what you have done in the past, God has washed the guilt away and set you apart for His own use in the present. First Corinthians 6:9–11 provides a glimpse of the type of individual God can radically transform. You no longer have to think, feel, and act as false beliefs

dictate. You are now free to present yourself to God as an instrument of righteousness.

7. God was not idle during our physical formation in the womb. He was intimately involved with our creation. God fashioned each of us to be physically distinct from one another. Through regeneration, He gives each of us the capacity to reflect His image through our unique personality and appearance.

8. Our view of our self-worth is often expressed through our physical fitness and grooming habits. If we have a low self- image, our grooming habits will reflect that view. As God gives us a new sense of self-worth, it may change the way we care for ourselves. Our eating, exercise, grooming, and dressing habits are all areas in which we can glorify God. Are there any habits you need to improve in order to reflect your new nature? (Ask your spouse or a good friend.)

9. Regeneration provides you with a new system by which you can evaluate yourself and your life:

Belief system based on God's truth about you → Godly thoughts → Emotions → Godly actions

As your mind is renewed by the Spirit of God, and as you apply the Word of God in relationships with the people of God, your life will progressively change.

10. Moses used the excuses "Who am I? No one will listen to me! And I don't speak very well, anyway!" (see Ex. 3:11, 4:1, 10) to try to keep from serving the Lord. Some of us excuse our unavailability to God by blaming our poor background or our lack of education, training, available opportunities, fears, and so on. God has dealt with your excuses by making you a new person with

new potential and new capacities. Write across your excuses, *I am a new creation—complete in Christ.*

A Final Word

Regeneration is the renewing work of the Holy Spirit by which a person literally becomes a new creation. Our regeneration took place at the instant of our conversion to Christ. At that moment, we were given more than a change of direction; we received the impartation of new life.

The part of us that the Holy Spirit regenerated is our spirit. The Holy Spirit has energized our inner spirit with new life. Jesus called it a new birth in John 3:3, 5–6, and said "That which is born of the flesh is flesh, and that which is born of the Spirit is spirit" (3:6). Regeneration is the Spirit-wrought renewal of our human spirit, a transforming resuscitation so that the spirit is alive within us (Rom. 8:10).

The Holy Spirit has been joined to our human spirit, forming a new spiritual entity. A new birth has produced a new being. "Therefore if any man is in Christ, he is a new creature; the old things passed away; behold, new things have come" (2 Cor. 5:17).

Study these words carefully. Ephesians 4:24 says that our new self has (already) been created in righteousness and holiness of the truth, but we must yet put on this new self in order to progressively produce godly thoughts and actions—as the acorn produces an oak tree!

Section III

Application

How can we replace destructive beliefs with God's truth so that our thoughts, words, and actions reflect God's love and purpose?

Step 11

Agent of Change

Part I

Read chapter 11 in *The Search for Significance.*

This step will help you understand the Holy Spirit's ministry of convicting us of sin and guiding us into truth. You also will gain insights about confession of sin.

1. Read John 14:16–17. Why do you need a Helper?

_____

_____

_____

2. What do the following passages say about the role of the Holy Spirit in teaching truth to you?

    a) John 14:26

_____

_____

_____

    b) John 16:13

_____

_____

_____

c) 1 Cor. 2:11–13

_____

_____

_____

3. Read 2 Tim. 3:16–17. How does the Holy Spirit use Scripture in our lives?

_____

_____

_____

4. Another role of the Holy Spirit is to convict the world concerning sin, righteousness, and judgment (John 16:8–11).
a) What does it mean to be convicted?

_____

_____

_____

_____

b) What is the purpose of the Holy Spirit's conviction?

_____

_____

_____

_____

5. Read 1 John 1:9.
a) What is confession?

_____

_____

_____

b) Does confession make you forgiven?

_____

_____

_____

6. Take a moment to allow the Holy Spirit to convict you of any ungodly thoughts or actions in the past week or so. List the sins that come to mind and confess them.

Compare your answers to the following:

For Additional Insight

1. Christ realized that you could never live the Christian life in your own effort. Your bondage to your old nature and your unrenewed mind hinder you from understanding and applying God's truth. You may be overwhelmed with all you have studied so far in this workbook. However, it is the Holy Spirit's role, as your Helper, to enable you to understand and apply biblical truth. Depend on Him, not on your own abilities, to do this.

2. a) John 14:26: He will teach you all things and help you to remember what Christ has said.

b) John 16:13: He will guide you into all truth.

c) 1 Corinthians 2:11–13: He will show you what things are from God, teaching you by combining spiritual thoughts with Scripture.

3. The Holy Spirit uses Scripture for four purposes in the believer's life:
a) Teaching: imparting knowledge of the truth.

b) Reproof: revealing areas in your life where you fall short of the truth.

c) Correction: getting you back on track.

d) Training in righteousness: helping you apply truth in the "nitty-gritty" of your life: your finances, your schedule, your relationships.

4. a) *Convict* means to convince of error or sinfulness. The convicting work of the Holy Spirit is God's way of showing you that your thoughts and/or actions are contrary to your new nature in Christ.

b) As we have seen, our ungodly thoughts, painful emotions, and disobedient actions usually originate in our false belief system. The Holy Spirit convicts us of ungodliness in order to 1) expose the wrongdoing; 2) expose its basis in false beliefs; 3) re-establish God's truth as the root of our thoughts and actions; 4) draw us back into a life of love and service for Christ.

The following are some common mistakes we make when the Holy Spirit convicts us of sin:

1) *Leaning on our own understanding.* The Lord has given the Holy Spirit to convict us of sin. The Holy Spirit needs no help in discovering what sins He wants to reveal to us.

A mature believer knows that the Father does not deal with every sin His children commit. We might go for a long period of time before the Holy Spirit puts His finger on something we should or should not be doing. Our heavenly Father knows how discouraging it would be for us to realize how far our performance is from the mark, so He begins to shape that performance by revealing to us a few sins at a time. The important issue is not that we realize all the sins we commit but that we respond to those He wishes to show us.

The Holy Spirit's work of conviction begins as He reveals our obviously sinful acts to us—stealing or lying, for instance. Then, as we mature, His conviction is more often focused on sins of omission than commission—more on what we do not do than what we do.

Some of the older saints spoke of their hearts breaking when they discovered that their motives for prayer or evangelism weren't totally pure. It wasn't that they weren't sharing their faith or praying but that their motive wasn't totally right. Won't it be wonderful when we mature to the place where this is an issue?

Avoid leaning on your own or any other person's understanding about what is sin in your life. Study the Scriptures to see what God wants for you, and listen to the conviction of the Holy Spirit.

2) *Confusing guilt with conviction.* You commit enough sins without having to worry about those thoughts and actions that aren't sins at all. Take your thoughts and deeds before the Lord to see what He thinks of them. Ask Him to show you which ones are guilt feelings and which ones are actually sins.

3) *Turning conviction into condemnation.* God has declared you to be righteous, holy, and blameless. At the cross Christ bore all the condemnation you deserved. Therefore, the Holy Spirit's conviction of sin in your life is not a condemnation of you.

4) *Not recognizing the root of sins.* Ungodly thoughts and actions are usually a reflection of the false beliefs you use to evaluate yourself. One of the Holy Spirit's goals in pointing out your sin is for you to see that you are basing your self-worth on false beliefs.

Use these points of conviction to identify false beliefs, reject them, and replace them with God's truth.

5. a) *Confession* means "to agree with." Confession is not dragging from our memory all the sins we've ever committed and telling them to God. Confession is agreeing with God concerning the specific sin we are convicted of. We agree with God in three ways:

1) Agreement: I sinned when I

_____

_____

The lie I was believing was

_____

2) Claiming forgiveness: I am forgiven through Christ's death on the cross.

3) Repentance: I am deeply loved, completely forgiven, fully pleasing, totally accepted, and complete in Christ. I now choose to act in a way that honors Him, which means I will

_____

_____

_____

b) Our confession does not make us forgiven. We have forgiveness because Christ died to pay for our sins. Confession is a means for us to experience our forgiveness, not a means for us to obtain it. Confession should be done with an attitude of repentance, which involves turning away from sin and turning to God. Repentance is not a matter of feeling sorry just because we got caught. True confession causes us to reject sin because it grieves the Lord. Confession enables us to experience our forgiveness and enjoy our fellowship with God.

An example of proper confession of sin is:

Dear Father,
The Holy Spirit has pointed out to me that I sinned when I [name specific thoughts and actions]. I was believing the lie (name specific false belief) when I sinned. Thank You that I am completely forgiven and that You choose not to remember my sin. I reaffirm that You have declared me to be deeply loved, completely forgiven, fully pleasing, totally accepted, and a new creature—complete in Christ. Amen.

6. The following points will give you some additional insights about confession:

a) *All sin is against God.* Notice how David recognized this in Psalm 51:4. He had committed adultery with Bathsheba and then murdered her husband to cover up his sin. Although others had been affected by his sin, David recognized that its commission was primarily against God. In confronting David, Nathan the prophet asked, "Why have you despised the word of Lord by doing evil in His sight?" (2 Sam. 12:9). Notice that the focus is on God, not on David or others.

When we have the truth of God's Word to guide us and still choose to sin, God says we are despising Him. Few of us would openly tell God that we have no use for His Word, or worse, that we despise Him. Yet that is actually what we are doing when we sin against Him. Perhaps if, before choosing to sin, we would say to God, "I despise You and Your Word," we would be more enlightened about how sin grieves our heavenly Father.

b) *Confession recognizes the full scope of sin.* Correct confession requires not only that we recognize a specific act as sinful but that we also understand that the ungodly thoughts and false beliefs that generated the ungodliness are sinful as well. The excuses we might use to justify our sin are part of the ungodly thoughts that cause us to act in an ungodly manner. Narrowly defining sin as *only* a wrong action is misleading. We need to deal with the root of the action: the false belief.

c) *Confession involves accepting our forgiveness in Christ.* All too often, Christians construct a penance cycle that they believe they must put themselves through before they can feel forgiven. Once convicted of a sin, they might plead with God for forgiveness and then feel depressed for a couple of days to show that they are really sorry and deserve to be forgiven.

This cycle is typical of works-righteousness. The Lord Jesus died on the cross for our sins and has declared us justified. God not only forgives, but He also forgets. Hebrews 10:17 says, "Their sins and their lawless deeds I will remember no more." We cannot earn our forgiveness by punishing ourselves. Confession is simply an application of the forgiveness we already have. Accepting our forgiveness allows us to move on in our fellowship with the Lord and to serve Him joyfully. God does not put us on the shelf and declare us permanently unusable because of our sin. Even after Peter's denials of Christ, he experienced forgiveness and was used powerfully by God as a leader of the church.

d) *True confession involves repentance.* Repentance means turning away from sin and turning instead to God. When we truly repent, we have a change of attitude about sin. In fact, because repentance involves recognizing the gravity of our sin, it should grieve us as much as it does God.

e) *True confession may involve restitution.* In confession, it may be necessary to make right a wrong. You may need to confess your sin to a fellow believer to ask for his or her forgiveness. You may need to pay back something you stole or replace something you broke. Christ taught us that we should be reconciled to one another before we can move on (Matt. 5:23–24).

A Final Word

The Lord Jesus realized that once He left the world, His followers would need help. The Holy Spirit, our Helper and Teacher, was sent to dwell within believers and to be our source of wisdom and strength. The Holy Spirit helps us to live in a way that honors Christ by convicting us of our ungodliness. Conviction allows us to deal with sin in our lives so that we can continue to experience God's love, power, and wisdom.

Part II: Living by Faith

This part of step 11 is designed to help you understand how God can empower you to live according to His truth. It might be tempting to set new biblical goals for your life and work harder to achieve them in your own efforts, but this would simply be implementing a biblical standard with the false belief *I must meet certain standards to feel good about myself.* Failure would soon follow. We are to depend upon God's Spirit to complete the work He has started within us (Phil. 1:6).

The Holy Spirit: Source of Abundant Life

1. Read John 7:37–39 and answer the following questions:

a) "If any man is thirsty" is a metaphor for our desire and need for Christ. What does it mean to *drink* of Christ?

_____

_____

_____

b) In what ways are you thirsty for Him?

_____

_____

_____

c) What are some aspects of the Christian life that *rivers of living water* might symbolize?

_____

_____

_____

d) Jesus said that these rivers flow from our *innermost* being. What does this mean to you?

_____

_____

2. Read John 15:1–8. This passage contains another metaphor that illustrates how the Holy Spirit is the source of a life that honors Christ. Answer the following:

a) Describe how a branch produces fruit (vv. 4–5):

_____

_____

_____

b) What are some evidences of spiritual fruit within the believer's life?

_____

_____

_____

_____

c) John 15:2 says that God prunes every fruitful branch so that it may bear more fruit. What are some ways that God prunes us?

_____

_____

_____

_____

_____

d) What are some things that prevent a branch from producing fruit?

_____

_____

_____

_____

_____

e) What could prevent you from living a more fruitful, Christ-honoring life?

_____

_____

_____

_____

_____

f) In your own words summarize Christ's teaching in John 7:37–39 and John 15:1–8.

_____

_____

_____

_____

_____

_____

_____

The Scriptures: Basis of a Life of Faith

The Scriptures are filled with facts and promises from God. Facts are statements that are *already* true of us. Promises are statements that we know *will be* fulfilled because of the trustworthiness of God. The following is a very short list of each:

Facts from God's Word

You are completely forgiven by God (Rom. 3:19–25, Col. 2:13–14).

You are righteous and pleasing to God (2 Cor. 5:21).

You are totally accepted by God (Col. 1:19–22).

You are deeply loved by God (1 John 4:9–10).

You are absolutely complete in Christ (2 Cor. 5:17, Col. 2:10).

The Holy Spirit dwells in you (Rom. 8:9–11).

You are God's child (Rom. 8:15–16).

You are a fellow heir with Christ (Rom. 8:17).

God works all things together for good for those who love Him (Rom. 8:28).

Promises from God's Word

Christ will never leave us (Matt. 28:20, Heb. 13:5).

He will abundantly provide for our needs (Phil. 4:19).

We will be in heaven with Him (John 14:1–3).

We will reign with Him (2. Tim. 2:12).

He will strengthen us (Isa. 40:29).
He will give us His peace (John 14:27).
He will accomplish His purposes (1 Thess. 5:24).
He will enable us to give generously (2 Cor. 9:6–11).
We will be persecuted (John 15:18–21).

3. Which three of these facts and promises stand out to you? Why? How would trusting either that God has accomplished these facts, or that He will fulfill these promises affect your life?
a) Fact or promise:

_____

_____

_____

(1) Why it stands out:

_____

_____

(2) How your trust in God would affect you:

_____

_____

b) Fact or promise:

_____

_____

_____

(1) Why it stands out:

_____

_____

(2) How your trust in God would affect you:

_____

_____

_____

c) Fact or promise:

_____

_____

_____

(1) Why it stands out:

_____

_____

(2) How your trust in God would affect you:

_____

_____

4. Romans 4:16–22 is an account of Abraham's faith. What things do you notice about his faith in this passage? In what promise from God was Abraham trusting? (See Gen. 15:5 and 17:5.)

_____

_____

It is very instructive to go through a book of the Bible and identify the facts, promises, and commands listed there. In the next few days, do this exercise with Paul's letter to the Ephesians.

Obstacles to Living a Life of Faith

Obstacles that can keep us from living a life of faith include:

• **Having the wrong purposes.** That is, living a self-centered, self-gratifying life instead of desiring to please Christ. In 2 Corinthians 5:9, Paul wrote, "Therefore also we have as our ambition . . . to be pleasing to Him."

• **Being too mechanical.** The Christian life is first and foremost a relationship with Christ, not a list of rules. Discipline certainly has its place, but the source of living water is our Lord (John 7:38).

• **Being too mystical.** Some of us wait until God has "spoken" to us before doing anything, seemingly oblivious to the clear teaching of the Scriptures to live a life of faith in Christ and His Word. There is definitely a mystical aspect to Christianity, but we must be careful not to fall into passivity. Some of us mistake our emotions as signs from God. We tend to make decisions based on emotions instead of God's Word. We need to choose to read His Word, pray, and actively obey Him whether we sense His presence or not. God is honored by our faith in action despite our feelings.

• **Lack of knowledge about the love and power of Christ.** Sadly, many Christians are uninformed about the wealth of love and power available to them through Christ.

• **Sin clouds our fellowship with Christ.** Sin is destructive to us and dishonoring to the Lord. At its root, all sin is like Eve's rebellion in the Garden. It is the desire to be like God and to run our own lives. It is turning our backs on Christ, our Savior and source of light and life.

• **Spiritual conflict.** The world (the inordinate desire for success, comfort, prestige, and so on [1 John 2:1–17]); the flesh (the inordinate desire to gratify our sensuality, for example, sex, overeating, alcohol, and drugs [Gal. 5:16–21]); and Satan (Eph. 6:10–12) all war against us with the aim of causing us to forsake the Lord and His purposes for the wanton pleasures of this life.

5. Read over these obstacles carefully. Which of these obstacles hinder you in your relationship with Christ? What can you do to begin overcoming them?

_____

_____

_____

_____

_____

_____

_____

Your Response

You can claim God's promises and live a life of faith that honors Him if you desire, confess, present, and obey. Do you honestly *desire* to honor Christ and minister to others? If so, *confess* any sin (or sins). Remember, confession is agreeing with God that a specific sin is, indeed, sin; agreeing with Him that you are forgiven by the death of Christ; and repentance—turning to God in obedience to His Word. Then *present* all areas of your life to Christ as "instruments of righteousness." Paul wrote to the believers in Rome:

> *Therefore do not let sin reign in your mortal body that you should obey its lusts, and do not go on presenting the members of your body to sin as instruments of unrighteousness; but present yourselves to God as those alive from the dead, and your members as instruments of righteousness to God. (Rom. 6:12–13)*

> *I urge you therefore, brethren, by the mercies of God, to present your bodies a living and holy sacrifice, acceptable to God, which is your spiritual service of worship. And do not be conformed to this world, but be transformed by the renewing of your mind, that you may prove what the will of God is, that which is good and acceptable and perfect. (Rom. 12:1–2)*

Obey and give thanks to the Lord for His grace and power, and continue to trust Him moment by moment. Depend on His Word. Let the Holy Spirit use you in the lives of others, and deal with any sin as soon as you become aware of it so that your fellowship with Him won't be hindered.

6. As you reflect on these principles of faith, where are you in this process? What will your next step be?

_____

_____

_____

_____

Use the following to compare your answers and to gain additional insight from this study:

For Additional Insight

1. a) To *drink* of Christ can mean to believe in His love and power, to enjoy Him, and to be satisfied by Him.

b) You may be experiencing a sense of thirst for Christ because you feel distant from Him; you may be grieved because some aspect of your life doesn't honor Him or because you have committed specific sins of immorality, jealousy, worry, criticism, or anger; you may feel very dry and rigid because you live a rules-dominated life.

c) *Rivers of living water* may symbolize the love, joy, and intimacy of knowing Christ; the power to be effective in evangelism and discipleship; love for the unlovely; any expression of the life of Christ flowing through the believer.

d) This means that the rivers are not externally contrived. They are from the heart—a spontaneous overflow of the very nature of Christ produced in us by the Holy Spirit. The sheer strength of the human will *can* produce changes in a life, but because the source isn't the Holy Spirit, pride is the result instead of thankfulness and humility.

2. a) A branch produces fruit by allowing the water and nutrients from the vine to flow through it. The fruit is the natural, spontaneous expression of a healthy branch.

b) Hebrews 13:15 says that a sacrifice of praise to God is "the fruit of lips that give thanks to His name." Galatians 5:22–23 says that "the fruit of the Spirit is love, joy, peace, patience, kindness, goodness, faithfulness, gentleness, self-control"—elements of Christian character. Throughout the New Testament and the history of the church, we see another fruit of those who allow the Holy

Spirit to produce the love and power of Christ in their lives: the salvation of many people.

c) God may prune us by allowing us to experience troubles and difficulties, sickness, failure, or reproof from either Christians or non-Christians.

d) A branch can't bear fruit if it's cut off, contracts a disease, is eaten by insects, is placed in poor environmental conditions, and so forth.

e) Your Christian life could be hindered if your love for Christ grew cold, if you developed an inordinate desire for worldly pleasures, if you sought to gain the approval of others, if you tried to gain your significance from success, if you couldn't experience the wealth of God's love and power, or if you pursued a life of abject disobedience.

f) In your summary, consider the Holy Spirit's purpose to glorify Christ (John 16:14), what the Holy Spirit can produce in one's life; and what could hinder the branch from producing fruit and the thirsty person from experiencing the rivers of living water (John 7:38).

3. These facts and promises may appeal to you because they relate to your security, your physical needs, or your desire to minister to others.
In your future study of God's Word, you might want to put an F, a P, and a C in the margin of your Bible to designate a fact, a promise, and a command. This will make you more aware of Scripture's personal applications.

4. Abraham's faith existed in spite of his circumstances. He did not waiver in unbelief but was fully assured. The specific promise was that he would be the father of many nations.

5. It may be that only one obstacle hinders you or that several of them are problems for you. Write down a clear, biblical remedy

for each obstacle. Ask the Lord to help you. Make yourself account-able by coming back to it periodically to see how you are doing. Don't give up if you fail! Keep trusting Him to strengthen you as you follow Him.

6. We have a choice. The Lord will not force us to follow Him, but He is willing and able to fully meet our needs if we are willing to give Him the glory for the results. A life of joy, fruitfulness, strength, and influence in a needy world awaits any believer who will trust Him. D. L. Moody was an unknown cobbler when he heard someone say, "The world has yet to see what God can do through one man whose heart is completely His." D. L. Moody responded, "Lord, I want to be that man!" Moody became one of the world's leading evangelists because of his intense desire to honor Christ and to be used by Him. Will you respond like D. L. Moody and say to God, "Lord, I want to be that man (or that woman)!"?

A Final Word

The truth that you are *deeply loved, completely forgiven, fully pleasing, totally accepted, and a new creature in Christ* will never work its way into your thoughts, emotions, and actions through a self-improvement program. Thank the Lord for your forgiveness in Christ and ask the Holy Spirit to empower you to experience this great truth. If you have been depending on your own effort to live the Christian life, stop for a moment and confess that as sin.

When we depend on God, will we feel His love and strength? Maybe, maybe not. Our culture would make us think that our feelings are the most important way of determining if our actions are valid. But as Christians, we have a much higher authority than our feel-ings. We have the truth of God's Word, and as an act of our will, we can choose to obey Him. Our will is paramount, not our feelings. The French philosopher Fenelon said, "The essence of Christianity resides in the will." Our feelings may reflect the love of Christ as we forgive others, share our faith, give generously, and demonstrate other spiritual characteristics in our lives. But on many occasions, our emotions are inconsistent, unpredictable, and diametrically opposed to God's Word. Often we refuse to obey Him because we don't feel like it. For example, we may be afraid to share our faith because someone might reject us, or we may continue to indulge in sin because we don't feel like stopping. But what about the times when we earnestly want to obey God and our emotions say *no*? Here are some possible reasons our feelings may oppose the ways of God:

1. Our sinful nature may be prompting us to disobey God. Galatians 5:17 says, "For the flesh sets its desire against the Spirit, and the Spirit against the flesh; for these are in opposition to one another."

2. We may be experiencing spiritual conflict. Satan, our enemy, is a thief who comes only to steal, kill, and destroy (John 10:10). If he can get us to live by our feelings instead of by God's Word, then he will effectively steal our joy, kill our motivation to live for Christ, and destroy the consistency of our Christian testimony.

3. It may be that our negative emotions are simply the residual feelings of the fear of failure or the fear of rejection that we are in the process of overcoming by claiming God's truth.

When you choose to believe God's Word, your emotions may not follow immediately. Does that mean you aren't trusting God? No. Faith is often exercised in the context of a struggle, in the midst of conflicting thoughts and emotions. A look at the people of God in the Scriptures shows that their faith was not in the absence of doubts and struggles but in the face of doubts and struggles. The idea that faith is only found apart from conflicting thoughts and emotions is one of Satan's schemes to confuse and discourage us. When we trust in God, we will experience many obstacles to faith, but placing our trust in His Word—not our feelings—will see us through.

Step 12

Guilt Versus Conviction

Read chapter 12 in *The Search for Significance*.

While guilt is applicable to nonbelievers, and originates from Satan, conviction is the privilege of those who believe, and it is given by the Holy Spirit. Guilt brings depression and despair, but conviction enables us to realize the beauty of God's forgiveness and to experience His love and power. Complete the following exercise to illustrate the contrasting purposes and results of guilt and conviction:

For each facet, ask God to show you what messages are connected to each one. Write your answers in the blanks.

1. Basic focus:
Guilt focuses on the state of being condemned:

_____

_____

_____

_____

Conviction focuses on the behavior:

_____

_____

_____

_____

2. Primary concern:

Guilt deals with the sinner's loss of self-esteem and a wounded self-pride:

_____
_____
_____
_____
_____
_____

Conviction deals with the loss of our moment-by-moment communication with God:

_____
_____
_____
_____
_____
_____

3. Primary fear:

Guilt produces a fear of punishment:

_____
_____
_____
_____
_____
_____

Conviction produces a fear of the destructiveness of the act itself:

_____
_____
_____
_____
_____

4. Agent:

The agent of *guilt* is Satan:

_____

_____

_____

_____

_____

_____

The agent of *conviction* is the Holy Spirit.

_____

_____

_____

_____

_____

5. Behavioral results:

Guilt leads to depression and more sin:

_____

_____

_____

_____

_____

_____

_____

Conviction leads to repentance, the turning from sin to Christ:

_____

_____

_____

_____

_____

6. Interpersonal results:

The interpersonal result of *guilt* is alienation, a feeling of shame that drives one away from the person who has been wronged:

_____

_____

_____

_____

_____

_____

The interpersonal result of *conviction* is restoration, a desire to remedy the harm done to others:

_____

_____

_____

_____

_____

7. Personal Results:

Guilt ends in depression, bitterness, and self-pity:

_____

_____

_____

_____

_____

_____

Conviction ends in comfort, the realization of forgiveness:

_____

_____

_____

_____

_____

Step 13

The Trip In

Part I

Read chapter 13 in *The Search for Significance*.

This step explains the process of laying aside the old self and putting on the new self so that our thoughts, emotions, and actions increasingly reflect the character of Christ.

This exercise is based on 2 Corinthians 10:3–5:

> *For though we walk in the flesh, we do not war according to the flesh, for the weapons of our warfare are not of the flesh, but divinely powerful for the destruction of fortresses. We are destroying speculations and every lofty thing raised up against the knowledge of God, and we are taking every thought captive to the obedience of Christ.*

Believe it or not, desire it or not, understand it or not, we are at war. Most of us don't like to think about spiritual warfare, hoping, like the proverbial ostrich with his head in the sand, that it will pass us by. The battlefield is the mind. Paul instructed: "Be transformed by the renewing of your mind, that you may prove what the will of God is, that which is good and acceptable and perfect" (Rom. 12:2).

Satan's goal is to keep our minds unrenewed so that we won't be transformed. He does this by establishing fortresses of deception which produce thoughts that are against the knowledge or understanding of God. Fortresses of deception are belief systems that are reinforced over the years by the thoughts, emotions, and actions they produce. It is a self-feeding system. For instance, if a person believes that he is a failure, when he succeeds, his belief system (his fortress) will produce such thoughts as: *What luck! It's about time. Look at all the failure you had to go through just to get one success. How unusual for a loser like you to do something right.* If the person fails, his belief system will produce such thoughts as: *I told you I'd fail. What a loser you are. You can't help it, you just can't do any better.*

Whether he succeeds or fails, the result is the same. His belief that he is a failure is reinforced. The following exercise will teach you how to begin establishing a stronghold of truth in your mind through memorization and meditation. This mind-renewal is essential to the application of step 13. You will be ejecting Satan's lies and replacing them with God's truth.

Establishing a Stronghold of Truth

The Truth Card

A simple three-by-five inch index card can be a key factor in helping you base your self-worth on the liberating truths of the Scriptures. Make your own, as described below, or order preprinted cards (see "Resources of Interest" in the back of the book).

1. To make the Truth Card, write out both the following truths and their corresponding verses from Scripture on the front of a three-by-five inch index card:

I am deeply loved by God (1 John 4:9–10).

I am completely forgiven and am fully pleasing to God (Rom. 5:1).

I am totally accepted by God (Col. 1:21–22).

I am a new creation, complete in Christ (2 Cor. 5:17).

On the back of the card, write out the false beliefs listed below.

Belief Systems	
Satan's Lie:	**God's Truth:**
Your Worth = Your Performance + Others' Opinions	Your Worth = What God Says About You.
Those who fail are unworthy of love and deserve to be blamed and condemned (fear of punishment; propensity to punish others).	Propitiation (1 John 4:9–10): I am deeply loved by God.
I must meet certain standards to feel good about myself. If I don't . . . (fear of failure).	Justification (Rom. 3:19–25 and 2 Cor. 5:21): I am completely forgiven and fully pleasing to God.
I must be approved (accepted) by certain others to feel good about myself. If I'm not approved . . . (fear of rejection).	Reconciliation (Col. 1:29–22): I am totally accepted by God.
I am what I am. I cannot change. I am hopeless (shame).	Regeneration (2 Cor. 5:17): I am absolutely complete in Christ.

We can renew our minds by using our emotions to analyze our belief system.

2. Carry your Truth Card with you continuously. Each time you are about to do a routine activity, like have something to drink, look at the front side and slowly meditate on each phrase. Thank the Lord for making you into a person who has these qualities. By

doing this for the next twenty-eight days, you will develop a habit of remembering that you are deeply loved, completely forgiven, fully pleasing, totally accepted, and complete in Christ.

If you have not already done so, memorize the supporting verses listed on the card over the next four days. Look in your Bible for other verses that support these truths and commit them to memory. Doing this will establish God's Word as the basis for your beliefs (Col. 3:16).

Also memorize the false beliefs. The more familiar you are with these lies, the more you will be able to recognize them in your thoughts. Then, as you recognize them, you can more readily replace them with the truths of God's Word.

Properly Evaluating Yourself and Others

"For in the way you judge, you will be judged; and by your standard of measure, it will be measured to you" (Matt. 7:2). From this passage of Scripture and from what we know about ourselves, we can draw the following conclusions and applications:

1. We use the same methods for judging others that we use to judge ourselves.

2. Though some of us are more reflective than others, all of us spend a great deal of time evaluating our performance.

3. We have a choice. We can use the same method we have always used to evaluate ourselves and others (Self-Worth = Performance + Others' Opinions), or we can adopt God's judgment (Self-Worth = God's Truth About Us).

4. If we want our lives to be what God has designed them to be, then we must use His truth (rather than our own opinions) as our standard of evaluation.

5. To accomplish this change in our minds, we need to apply the following action points:

a) When we see another person (especially if this person has offended us in some way), we should think and, if possible, state verbally, "This person has great worth apart from his performance because Christ gave His life for him and, therefore, imparted great value to him. If this person has accepted Christ, he is deeply loved, fully pleasing, completely forgiven, totally accepted, and complete in Christ."

b) We can tell those in our families who are Christians, "You are deeply loved, completely forgiven, fully pleasing, totally accepted, and complete in Christ."

6. As you do this, you will automatically begin to use the same system of evaluation on yourself and thereby reinforce these truths as the basis of your own self-worth.

7. You can apply this exercise in both your own life and your family members' lives after failures. Affirmation of love and acceptance can be powerful in shaping a healthy self-concept.

Exposing Ungodly Thoughts

Our thoughts reveal what we really believe, yet it is difficult for most of us to be objective in our thinking simply because we haven't trained ourselves to be. We usually let any and every thought run its course in our minds without analyzing its worth. Is it a God-honoring thought, or is it a speculation or a "lofty thing raised up against the knowledge of God" (2 Cor. 10:5)?

It is very helpful to be able to identify thoughts that are not honoring to God. Then we can reject them and replace them with truth. One way of identifying such thoughts is to state what is true and see what thoughts come to mind. Hopefully, our thoughts will increasingly reflect our thankfulness to God for who He is and what He has done for us, but sometimes we will respond by contradicting the truth.

For example, you might respond to the truth that you are fully pleasing to God by thinking, *No, I'm not! I mess up all the time; to be fully pleasing, I'd have to be perfect!* When we see it written out, we easily recognize that response as a lie. However, we seldom write down our thoughts and analyze their validity.

As a first step in this analysis, write down your thoughts in response to the four truths we've examined. (Again, they will probably be mixed: some positive, thankful, and godly, and some contradictory to the truth.)

• I am deeply loved by God:

_____

_____

_____

• I am completely forgiven and am fully pleasing to God:

_____

_____

_____

• I am totally accepted by God:

_____

_____

_____

• I am complete in Christ:

_____

_____

_____

Thoughts that contradict these truths are lies. Reject them and replace them with passages of Scripture to reinforce the truth in your mind. Here are some passages to reflect on:

• Justification: Rom. 3:19–24, 4:4–5, 5:1–11, Titus 2:11–14.

• Propitiation: Matt. 18:21–35, Luke 7:36–50, Rom. 3:25, 8:1–8; Col. 3:12–14, Heb. 2:17, 3:4–7.

• Reconciliation: John 15:14–16, Rom. 5:8–10, 8:15, Eph. 2:11–18.

• Regeneration: 2 Cor. 5:17, Gal. 5:16–24, Eph. 2:4–5, 4:22–24, Col. 3:5–17.

A Final Word

Our thoughts are seldom neutral. They reflect either beliefs based on the Word of God or beliefs based on the world's values. The Lord can give us the perception we need to identify the source of our thoughts and determine if they are of Him or not. The more our thoughts are in line with God's Word, the more our actions will be honoring to Him. In fact, the purity of our thoughts ultimately determines how much our lives will honor Christ. Paul told Titus that Christ "gave Himself for us, that He might redeem us from every lawless deed and purify for Himself a people for His own possession, zealous for good deeds" (Titus 2:14).

Part II: Identifying False Beliefs

This is a pivotal point in the process of understanding and applying all that has come before! So take your time. Be honest about your emotions. Reflect on the principles brought out here and apply them to specific instances in your life. As you do, you will probably realize that Satan's lies have controlled your life far more than you previously realized. You will probably also realize that God's love and power can progressively free you from introspection, anger, and fear and give you a heart of thankfulness and a greater desire to live for Him.

First, you need to realize where your emotions and actions come from. Jesus said, "For out of the overflow of the heart the mouth speaks" (Matt. 12:34, NIV). In other words, our communication (which reveals our thoughts, emotions, and the intent of our actions) comes from our hearts (our belief system). Because every situation in our lives is interpreted by what we believe, our belief system—not the situation—is the key to our response! The following diagram illustrates this process:

In addition to comprising our reactions to immediate events, our emotions are products of our family backgrounds, past experiences and relationships, and patterns of responses. Many of us come from homes where we were not loved and affirmed as children. We may have learned to repress painful emotions because we didn't want to believe that something was wrong with our families, our source of stability and security. Some of us have become numb, unable to feel either anger or joy, hurt or love. Some of us have developed a habit of forgetting difficult instances and their accompanying pain as a defense mechanism. There are many different ways to block pain and try to gain a sense of worth, but we need to begin reversing this trend by finding someone who will encourage us to be honest about our feelings. We can use our feelings as a gauge to determine if our response to a situation is based on the truth or a lie.

Painful or distressing emotions, chiefly anger or fear, are often an indication that we are basing our self-worth on our performance or others' opinions of us. These negative emotions surface when that falsely based self-worth has been shattered or is even threatened. There are many variations of anger and fear, including bitterness, rage, disgust, hurt, tension, withdrawal, and anxiety, but not all anger and fear are negative. Feelings are neither right nor wrong. They are signals that tell us something about our environment. We need to be honest about our emotions so that they can tell us what we need to know about our perceptions. Refer to the Feeling Wheel in chapter 13 in order to recognize the real emotions.

When our emotions are painful or distressing, we need to ask, *Why am I responding this way? Am I believing a lie? If so, which one?*

Tracing Emotions to Root Beliefs

Let's suppose that someone (Bill) picked you up late, making you late for work (or school or church or to a committee meeting). Your response is anger. You can trace that anger back to its root false belief in order to replace it with corresponding truths from the Scriptures. The following is an illustration:

How do you determine the false belief responsible for your anger? Ask yourself, Why am I angry? Am I angry because:

• I hate to be late ("certain standard"), and my lateness makes me feel bad about myself. (I must meet certain standards . . .)

• My boss will be displeased with me because I'm late, and her opinion of me means so much. (I must be approved by certain others . . .)

• Bill failed by being late to pick me up. It was his fault, that creep! (Those who fail are unworthy of love and deserve to be punished.)

• No matter what I do, something always goes wrong. (I am hopeless. I can't change. I will always be this way.)

Note that the proper response is not *I'm not angry* when in fact you are. Denial only compounds our problems; it is not a solution.

We need to be honest with the Lord and with ourselves about our feelings.

If the situation in the above example had happened to you, what would your emotion(s) probably have been? Which false belief(s) can you trace your emotion(s) back to?

Recent Situations

Think over the past two weeks and list five recent situations in which you have had distressing or painful emotions. Take time to reflect on the following questions about each occasion. What emotion(s) were you experiencing? What were your actions? What false belief(s) were you believing?

1. Situation:

_____

_____

_____

_____

_____

a) Emotion(s):

_____

_____

_____

_____

b) Ungodly action(s):

_____

_____

_____

c) False belief(s):

_____

_____

_____

2. Situation:

_____

_____

_____

_____

_____

_____

a) Emotion(s):

_____

_____

_____

_____

_____

b) Ungodly action(s):

_____

_____

_____

_____

c) False belief(s):

_____

_____

_____

_____

_____

3. Situation:

_____

_____

_____

_____

_____

a) Emotion(s):

_____
_____
_____
_____
_____

b) Ungodly action(s):

_____
_____
_____
_____
_____

c) False belief(s):

_____
_____
_____
_____
_____

4. Situation:

_____
_____
_____
_____
_____

a) Emotion(s):

_____
_____
_____
_____
_____

b) Ungodly action(s):

_____

_____

_____

c) False belief(s):

_____

_____

_____

_____

5. Situation:

_____

_____

_____

_____

_____

a) Emotion(s):

_____

_____

_____

_____

b) Ungodly action(s):

_____

_____

_____

c) False belief(s):

_____

_____

_____

_____

Recurring Situations

What are some recurring situations in which you frequently have painful or distressing emotions? Some of these may have shown up in the list above and may include things like: meeting new people, seeing someone whose clothes or mannerisms are different than yours, preparing for a big exam, being late, mingling at parties, being alone, spending extended periods of time with your parents, entertaining people at your home, having to clean up when your spouse or roommate leaves the dishes dirty, despairing when someone disagrees with you or is disappointed in you, or being frustrated over a flaw in your appearance.

What recurring situation(s) trigger anxiety, anger, fear, sarcasm, withdrawal, or nagging for you? List some of those situations in the spaces below. How do you usually respond? Which false beliefs are at the root of this response?

1. Situation:

_____

_____

_____

_____

a) Emotion(s):

_____

_____

_____

_____

b) Ungodly action(s):

_____

_____

_____

_____

c) False belief(s):

_____

_____

_____

_____

2. Situation:

_____

_____

_____

_____

_____

a) Emotion(s):

_____

_____

_____

_____

b) Ungodly action(s):

_____

_____

_____

_____

c) False belief(s):

_____

_____

_____

3. Situation:

_____

_____

_____

_____

_____

a) Emotion(s):

_____

_____

_____

_____

_____

b) Ungodly action(s):

_____

_____

_____

_____

c) False belief(s):

_____

_____

_____

_____

_____

4. Situation:

_____

_____

_____

_____

_____

a) Emotion(s):

_____

_____

_____

_____

_____

b) Ungodly action(s):

_____

_____

_____

_____

_____

c) False belief(s):

_____

_____

_____

_____

5. Situation:

_____

_____

_____

_____

_____

a) Emotion(s):

_____

_____

_____

_____

b) Ungodly action(s):

_____

_____

_____

_____

c) False belief(s):

_____

_____

_____

_____

_____

A Final Word

This week, every time you realize that you are responding to a situation with a negative, painful emotion, stop to ask yourself why. And trace it back to its root false belief. Keep a sheet of paper with you and write down those situations, your emotions, your ungodly actions, and the root false beliefs.

Part III: Reject/Replace

Earlier in this step, we saw how we can use our emotions to help us analyze why we respond the way we do. Painful emotions such as anger, fear, resentment, and anxiety can show us that we are believing Satan's lies. Being honest about these and other emotions is crucial in our application of God's Word! Once we become aware of the specific lie that is affecting us, we can then apply God's specific solution from His Word to that lie—a process that often occurs best in the context of affirming relationships.

If we are not aware of the specific lie we are believing, we usually attempt to meet our need with any and every biblical truth—knowing that it is true and hoping that it will help. However, if Scripture doesn't speak powerfully to our specific need, we can become frustrated and disillusioned instead of freed and encouraged.

In this step we will go beyond tracing our emotions to their false beliefs. We will learn how to replace insidious lies with the powerful Word of God so that our thoughts and actions will increasingly glorify God.

Our diagram, then, looks like this:

The Trip In

	The Situation			
Bondage - phase 1 Use emotions to identify false beliefs, destructive thoughts	False Beliefs →	Destructive Thoughts →	Destructive Emotions →	Destructive Behavior
Obedience - phase 2 Identify false beliefs, acknowledge destructive thoughts and behavior	Confession of False Beliefs, Destructive Thoughts & Behavior →	→	→	Repentance and Obedience
Freedom - phase 3 Replace false beliefs with God's truth	God's Truth →	Healthy Thoughts →	Healthy Emotions →	Healthy Behavior

Recent Situations

First let's look at the assignment from Part II of this step. List several of the situations with the corresponding emotions, ungodly actions, and false beliefs you identified in that step. Then write out the specific solution to the situation from the Scriptures with a passage or two. Describe how your initial response would have been different if you had believed God's truth instead of Satan's lie, and finally, complete the statement that summarizes the proper response to that situation. If you don't want to use the situations you described earlier, use any others that come to mind. The example we will use is the same as in Part II.

Situation:
a) Bill picked me up late.
b) I was late for work.

Emotions:
a) I was angry at Bill.
b) I feared that my boss would be upset with me.

Ungodly actions:
a) I hardly spoke to Bill all day.
b) I avoided looking at my boss's eyes. I withdrew from her.

False beliefs:
a) Those who fail are unworthy of love and deserve to be blamed and condemned.
b) I must be approved by certain others to feel good about myself.

God's truth (passages):
a) Propitiation: I am deeply loved by God; therefore, I can love others with God's love (1 John 4:9–11).
b) Reconciliation: I am totally accepted by God (Col. 1:19–22).

Supposed godly response:
a) Forgive Bill; help him any way I can; offer to take my car if his isn't running well; be cheerful.
b) Apologize to my boss; relax and realize there was nothing I could do about being late this morning. Hopefully, she will understand, but if not, I need to do my work with peace and joy.

Summary statement:

a) It would be nice if Bill had picked me up on time, but he didn't. Even so, Bill is deeply loved by God.

b) It would be nice if my boss really liked me and accepted me, but if she doesn't I'm still deeply loved, completely forgiven, fully pleasing, and totally accepted by God.

1. Situation:

_____

_____

_____

_____

a) Emotion(s):

_____

_____

_____

b) Ungodly action(s):

_____

_____

_____

_____

c) False belief(s):

_____

_____

_____

_____

d) God's truth (passages):

_____

_____

_____

e) Supposed godly response:

_____
_____
_____
_____

f) Summary statement: *It would be nice if . . .*

_____
_____
_____
_____

2. Situation:

_____
_____
_____
_____

a) Emotion(s):

_____
_____
_____

b) Ungodly action(s):

_____
_____
_____

c) False belief(s):

_____
_____
_____

d) God's truth (passages):

_____
_____
_____
_____

e) Supposed godly response:

_____
_____
_____
_____

f) Summary statement: *It would be nice if . . .*

_____
_____
_____
_____

3. Situation:

_____
_____
_____
_____

a) Emotion(s):

_____
_____
_____
_____

b) Ungodly action(s):

_____
_____
_____

c) False belief(s):

_____

_____

_____

_____

d) God's truth (passages):

_____

_____

_____

_____

e) Supposed godly response:

_____

_____

_____

_____

f) Summary statement: *It would be nice if* . . .

_____

_____

_____

_____

4. Situation:

_____

_____

_____

_____

a) Emotion(s):

_____

_____

_____

b) Ungodly action(s):

_____

_____

_____

_____

c) False belief(s):

_____

_____

_____

_____

d) God's truth (passages):

_____

_____

_____

_____

e) Supposed godly response:

_____

_____

_____

_____

f) Summary statement: *It would be nice if . . .*

_____

_____

_____

_____

5. Situation:

_____

_____

_____

_____

a) Emotion(s):

_____
_____
_____
_____

b) Ungodly action(s):

_____
_____
_____
_____

c) False belief(s):

_____
_____
_____
_____

d) God's truth (passages):

_____
_____
_____
_____

e) Supposed godly response:

_____
_____
_____
_____

f) Summary statement: *It would be nice if . . .*

_____
_____
_____
_____

Recurring Situations

All of us have developed patterns of responding based on our family backgrounds, our past experiences, and our personalities. These patterns can be very healthy and productive provided loving parents and a consistent life of honesty and courage are present. But the number of dysfunctional families is increasing, and the corresponding response patterns in the lives of family members are becoming more painful and destructive. The response patterns we have developed show up in situations that tend to recur fairly often.

Use the situations you listed earlier in Part II, or add others that have come to mind. Describe your response and write out the corresponding truth with Scripture passages, citing how believing God's truth can affect you if you choose to apply it in these situations.

1. Situation:

_____

_____

_____

_____

_____

a) Emotion(s):

_____

_____

_____

_____

b) Ungodly action(s):

_____

_____

_____

_____

c) False belief(s):

_____

_____

_____

_____

d) God's truth (passages):

_____

_____

_____

_____

e) Supposed godly response:

_____

_____

_____

_____

f) Summary statement: *It would be nice if . . .*

_____

_____

_____

_____

2. Situation:

_____

_____

_____

_____

a) Emotion(s):

_____

_____

_____

b) Ungodly action(s):

_____

_____

_____

_____

c) False belief(s):

_____

_____

_____

_____

d) God's truth (passages):

_____

_____

_____

_____

e) Supposed godly response:

_____

_____

_____

_____

f) Summary statement: *It would be nice if . . .*

_____

_____

_____

_____

3. Situation:

_____

_____

_____

_____

a) Emotion(s):

_____

_____

_____

_____

b) Ungodly action(s):

_____

_____

_____

_____

c) False belief(s):

_____

_____

_____

_____

d) God's truth (passages):

_____

_____

_____

_____

e) Supposed godly response:

_____

_____

_____

_____

f) Summary statement: *It would be nice if . . .*

_____

_____

_____

_____

4. Situation:

_____

_____

_____

_____

_____

a) Emotion(s):

_____

_____

_____

_____

b) Ungodly action(s):

_____

_____

_____

_____

c) False belief(s):

_____

_____

_____

_____

d) God's truth (passages):

_____

_____

_____

_____

e) Supposed godly response:

_____

_____

_____

f) Summary statement: *It would be nice if . . .*

_____

_____

_____

_____

5. Situation:

_____

_____

_____

_____

_____

a) Emotion(s):

_____

_____

_____

_____

b) Ungodly action(s):

_____

_____

_____

_____

c) False belief(s):

_____

_____

_____

_____

d) God's truth (passages):

_____

_____

_____

e) Supposed godly response:

_____

_____

_____

_____

f) Summary statement: *It would be nice if . . .*

_____

_____

_____

_____

A Final Word

Hopefully, you are now gaining a better understanding of how to use your emotions to identify your beliefs so that you can reject Satan's lies and replace them with God's truths. But do not expect perfection! You have built your existing belief system over a period of many years. You may have experienced the deep pain of a dysfunctional family background, neglect, abuse, or chronic condemnation. Belief systems do not change easily or quickly. Sometimes replacing lies with the truth will seem easy while at other times, it will be very frustrating.

The enemy of our souls does not want us to be freed from his lies. Expect spiritual battle, uneasy feelings, and some discouragement. But be patient and persistent! As you apply these principles, the time interval between your painful emotions and your ability to replace lies with the truth will generally become shorter and shorter. As you claim the truth of God's Word, memorizing it and meditating on it, you may even find yourself responding with godly thoughts, emotions, and actions at the outset of difficult situations!

Hang in there. Be alert and aware of Satan's lies (Eph. 6:10–12 and 1 Pet. 5:8–9). The enemy will want to confuse you and muddle your thinking. The simple act of writing out your situations, emotions, and responses can be an amazingly helpful weapon in enabling you to be specific and effective in your battle. You may want to do this at a certain time every day until it becomes second nature to recognize your negative emotions, trace them back to their root false beliefs, and replace them with God's truth.

The Lord is for you! He will give you wisdom, strength, and encouragement—so keep at it!

Notes

Chapter 6: Reconciliation

1. Lori Thorkelson Rentzel, *Emotional Dependency* (San Rafael, Calif.: Exodus International-North America, 1990). Contact Exodus International at Box 2121, San Rafael, California 94912.

2. C. S. Lewis, *The Four Loves* (New York: Harcourt Brace Jovanovich, 1960), 91–92.

3. Rentzel, *Emotional Dependency,* 3–4. Reprinted by permission.

Chapter 10: God's Answer: Regeneration

1. Louis Berkhof, *Systematic Theology* (Grand Rapids, Mich.: Eerdmans, 1941), 468.

Step 6: God's Answer: Reconciliation

1. Leon Morris, *The Atonement* (Downers Grove, Ill.: Inter-Varsity Press, 1984).

Step 8: God's Answer: Propitiation

1. Frederick Faber, as cited by A. W. Tozer, *The Pursuit of God* (Camp Hill, Penna.: Christian Publications, 1982), 40–41.

Services Provided by Search Resources

Telephone Counseling by Experienced Christian Counselors

Intensive Group Intervention
(more interactive than seminars)

Small Groups or Large Groups
Weekend or Full Week*

Small Group Training

Support Group Training

Topical Seminars

Referral Help

*Held in various locations in the United States,
Europe, Asia, New Zealand, and Australia

For Information call
800/880-7222 toll free

Resources of Interest

Truth Cards

Front: Declaration of identity in Christ
Back: The Trip In chart, as shown on page 323
Inside fold: False beliefs and God's truth, in chart form

Truth cards are explained more fully in step 13 of the Workbook.
(For an example of a truth card, see page 306.)

Father Cards

Set of ten cards describing the characteristics of the heavenly Father. On the back of each is a meditation on the characteristic. Space is provided for writing praise and thanks regarding each one.

The Characteristics are:

Comforter	Forgiving
Protector	Holy
Understanding	Faithful
Loving	Gracious
Sustainer	Merciful

Truth T-shirts

Cross Design T-shirt

I have great worth because   Christ gave His life for me.
I am deeply loved, fully pleasing, totally forgiven, accepted, and complete in Christ.

Puzzle Design T-shirt

Because of redemption . . .
. . . deeply loved . . . fully pleasing . . . totally accepted
. . . a new creation in Christ . . . the pieces of my life make sense

Available from:

Deanland Enterprises
2323 Clear Lake Blvd., Suite 180-300
Houston, Texas 77062
888/880-7333 toll-free